A NEW SOCIAL CONTRACT

A NEW
SOCIAL
CONTRACT

The Economy and Government After Reagan

MARTIN CARNOY, DEREK SHEARER,
AND RUSSELL RUMBERGER

HARPER & ROW, PUBLISHERS, New York
Cambridge, Philadelphia, San Francisco,
London, Mexico City, São Paulo, Sydney

1817

FIRST EDITION

Designer: Sidney Feinberg

Library of Congress Cataloging in Publication Data

Carnoy, Martin.
    A new social contract.
    1. United States—Economic policy—1981-
I. Shearer, Derek. II. Rumberger, Russell W. III. Title.
HC106.8.C37 1983   338.973   82-48656
ISBN 0-06-015150-1

83 84 85 86 87 10 9 8 7 6 5 4 3 2 1

Contents

Preface

This book is our contribution to the debate on how to reform the American economy after Reagan leaves the White House.

The supply side nostrums of Reaganomics have not produced the economic revival promised by the President and his devoted followers. Instead, the policies of the administration have contributed to misery and hard times for millions of Americans and significantly worsened the worldwide recession. Compassion for the human victims of these misguided policies, as well as concern for the long-run health of American society, motivates our advocacy of a new approach to running the economy.

In a previous book, two of us analyzed proposals for structural reform in the American economy that might lead to a more equitable and democratic society.[1] We assumed certain social values on the part of our readers and consequently did not devote much attention to an analysis of the country's immediate economic difficulties. The implementation of Reaganomics—supply side theory mixed with monetarism—and especially its initial enthusiastic reception by the press and by many politicians, brought home to us the importance of explaining how the economy has functioned in the post-WW II era, as well as offering prescriptions for improving its performance.

The reform proposals that we advocate in this book follow from

1. Martin Carnoy and Derek Shearer, *Economic Democracy: The Challenge of the 1980s* (Armonk, N.Y.: M.E. Sharpe, 1980).

our analysis of the way the economy has operated. They are relatively short range and can be taken as an agenda for the next
Democratic administration when it comes to power in 1984 or
1988. But immediate as they are, it is the direction and overall
spirit of our policies that are essential. Our reforms are designed
to move away from concentrated economic and political power
towards greater democratic participation—away from policies designed to serve corporate interests towards policies based on the
public interest.

It is important for those who are committed to democratic values to enter into the debate over what will come after Reagan. The
failure of Reaganomics is apparent, but the political strength of
Reagan's anti-government, pro-business rhetoric is still strong and
supported by powerful forces in American society. Even among
opponents of Reaganomics, not all those who celebrate its demise
understand why these policies have failed, nor how previous policies contributed to the current economic state of affairs.

In the past year, the editors of *Business Week*, civic-minded
businessmen like New York investment banker Felix Rohatyn, and
neoliberal politicians like Senator Gary Hart have come forward
with alternative economic plans. While they are all critics of Reagan, they also all underestimate or ignore a vital factor: democracy. Democracy in America has involved not only a drive for
individual freedom, but also action by individuals—workers,
women, blacks, students, the elderly and others—working *together* to have government extend and protect their economic
and social rights. Policies that simply give more economic and
political power to corporations run contrary to this historical dynamic. The expansion of democratic rights is part of the American
heritage and part of the solution to our economic troubles.

We wish to thank Robbin Reynolds, our original editor at
Harper & Row, for understanding the need for our book and for
assisting in the editing of the manuscript, even as she was moving
on to another publisher. Aaron Asher, executive editor, and his
assistant Ellen Sargent took on the manuscript from Robbin and
carried through with the project. We also wish to thank Bill Rey-

nolds, for his careful copy editing.

In recent years, we have had discussions about the economy with a number of friends and colleagues. These include Steve Babson, Ann Beaudry, Barry Bluestone, Samuel Bowles, Manuel Castells, Jeff Faux, Dick Flacks, Sheldon Friedman, Jamie Galbraith, Nathan Gardels, Herbert Gintis, David Gordon, Mark Green, Ben Harrison, Richard Kaufman, Michael Kieschnick, Bob Kuttner, Henry Levin, Ira Magaziner, Ralph Nader, Richard Parker, Robert Reich, Stanley Sheinbaum, David Smith, Marc Weiss and others. All have contributed to sharpening the analysis and arguments in this book. While each of them might differ with us on specifics, it is important to note that there now exists a number of economists in the United States who are committed to a democratic economy. We are proud to be a part of this collective intellectual and political effort.

Of course, our friends have their own books coming out. The views in this work are finally our responsibility.

We dedicate this book to our children, in hopes that as they grow older they too will be part of the movement for economic democracy.

Palo Alto and Santa Monica, Calif.
March, 1983

A NEW SOCIAL CONTRACT

A New Social Contract

There is a crisis in America. To move forward we must have a new social arrangement between all of us living here—employees and employers, women and men, white and nonwhite, those with high and low incomes, young and old, working and retired. The eighteenth-century philosopher Jean Jacques Rousseau called this arrangement a "social contract." We never sign it, but we believe in it. When that belief degenerates, society does not work anymore. It becomes time for a new contract.

We believe that a New Social Contract in America must reaffirm and energize the fundamental dynamic of our history: democracy —a democracy where individuals working together politically make government extend their economic and social rights. In the new contract, government does not restrict liberty, it expands it and makes it a reality. Most people support democracy because under such a system the people who decide are those who must live with the results of their decisions. Neoliberals in the Democratic Party and many conservative Republicans think that the way out of the current crisis is to leave decisions to a few—the "experts" in our complex industrial economy. But increased expertise and corporate bureaucratization for the sake of higher private profits is precisely what has made post–World War II America head down the road to crisis. We think that America must now find ways to reach full employment, more effective and equitable investment policies, higher productivity, lower inflation, a better environment, and income security through *greater*, not less, democratic participation.

Greater democracy means that those with jobs will have much more to say about the way those jobs are organized; those who live in communities will have more to say about what happens to those communities—even whether a plant can simply up and leave after thirty years; consumers will have more to say about the products they buy and the kinds of long-run investments the economy should make; senior citizens will have more to say about their activities and health care; students will participate more in their education; and all citizens can decide together whether the human race should be destroyed by nuclear war or survive in a saner world.

How does that participation work? How do we institutionalize it and make it effective? How does the public make decisions that expand democratic control over the economic and social development process?

These are issues of self-governance. They are crucial to our proposed economic alternative. Eighteenth-century political economist Adam Smith and his present-day conservative followers can separate economics and government by assuming that the economic system is self-governing. We contend not only that this assumption is palpably false but that an alternative must integrate economics and politics on a new basis—a democratic, participative governance of polity and economy. This means asking our fellow Americans to be responsible not only for their individual and family activities but for the collective good.

Our alternative under this new contract is a blueprint for stimulating jobs and investment while preserving the best and most effective elements of the present system. This blueprint includes a necessarily active economic role for government. We also recognize the limits placed on the American economy by huge corporations that dominate productive investment and make their investment decisions increasingly on short-term profit criteria. Our economic reforms put greater investment decision-making in the hands of the workers and communities affected by those decisions.

Where there are winners and losers, we recommend institutional arrangements in which conflicts can be resolved democratically rather than by "experts" whose biases favor the old solutions and already powerful groups in our society.

The cornerstones of democratic economics are direct and indirect public accountability for investment policy and increased worker and consumer control of production—what and how things are produced. Obviously, this means more than financier Felix Rohatyn's suggested Reconstruction Finance Corporation funneling public money into private corporations. It means public and public/private corporations producing for profit but channeling those profits into increased employment opportunities. The production of social goods requires long-horizon investment programs, programs such as light rail transport and high-speed trains. And it can mean public intervention in the automobile, steel, insurance, banking, and especially the oil and gas industries. In these industries there must be greater public planning and public accountability. The main goals of a democratic planning system are to develop innovative solutions to unemployment, set norms for corporate behavior, and develop new kinds of products and more democratic work organization. More local community-based corporations will produce health services, housing, and local transportation.

Democratic planning does not mean that private enterprise and the market system will no longer provide goods and services or ideas. On the contrary, in a host of competitive industries, from high technology to clothing to private services to wholesale and retail trade, the market does and should function to provide these goods and service efficiently. But democratic planning does mean that investment policy at the local and national level will no longer be dominated by a few concentrated industries that control vast sums of capital, nor solely by private banks and insurance companies. There will also be more emphasis on democratic participation—at the community level, at the plant level, at the level of national economic policy.

Our alternative is not utopian. We are not calling for a drastic change in human nature. Furthermore, this alternative will work because it is democratic; it is rooted in the basic American ideals of participation, fairness, and efficiency. We call it economic democracy. Its only drawback is political: it confronts directly the power of large corporations and those elements in the government bureaucracy allied with them. Populism has not always been successful in American politics. But it has been a while since we have had an economic and social crisis of these proportions. And the last time structural changes in our social arrangements *did* take place—in the 1930s—it came from grass-roots populist movements and from a government that responded to those movements. Those changes extended democracy through legitimizing labor organizations and through income guarantees. The only way to emerge from this crisis is to take the next step—to further democratize the economy.

Reagan's conservative appeal is based largely on the ideology of government's alleged inefficiency and corruptive influence in an otherwise perfect free-enterprise system. The majority of Americans, however, believe that government intervention in the economy not only works to raise their standard of living but that it protects them against the worst injustices of the uncaring market. Government grew in the last fifty years because most people wanted it to grow. The nostalgia for an unregulated market has conveniently clouded what the economy was like in the good old 1920s and how that decade ended. In fact, almost no one, including the most conservative representatives of the business community, really desires—or can afford—to eliminate government economic involvement.

There are two aspects of government intervention which are in constant tension. The first contributes to the orderly (*not* regulated) growth of corporate profits through macroeconomic policies and subsidies. The second contributes to social stability—and therefore long-term profit growth—by making it possible for groups who are not being included in the private economy to meet minimum material and human needs with public help. Although both of them work to improve the business climate, programs like investment tax credits, the Export-Import Bank, and space and military contracts are obviously designed to help business. Social welfare spending, however, is not an obvious boon to business. For example, public education, by training future skilled labor, and universities, by undertaking basic research, subsidize business. But some school spending encourages better citizenship or may just be interesting or fun—like spending for art, music, and languages. Social security and Medicare cost business money. Welfare spending probably helps keep social peace, but it also weakens business' ability to depress wages by means of economic insecurity, and therefore unemployment loses some of its bite. Besides, these social welfare measures are largely a response to citizens' demands on government, and so create an indirect assault on profits.

The current debate among conservatives, liberals, and neoliberals focuses on how much government should promote profits rather than social benefits. All three groups assume that for the continued growth of the economy, government should intervene in the business cycle, spend on police and military, and provide at least some public education. Yet, all three also assume that no matter how and for whom government intervenes, the business community should control economic investment policy and be its primary beneficiary. It is business, with its monopoly on capital accumulation, that is allowed to decide where, when, and how to invest capital. The question is what role government should play in stimulating business investment, especially how much *direct* stimulation American business will need to compete in world markets and provide jobs. The answer to that question has implications for social welfare spending, because greater subsidies for business without higher taxes means cutting into other kinds of government programs. And, if social welfare spending is thought to enlarge the bargaining power of workers with employers, cutting that spending also increases business "subsidies," since it reduces limits to profits by giving firms access to cheaper and more docile labor.

We propose a very different approach. We, too, accept that

government economic involvement is here to stay. Like Jack Kemp (Conservative Congressman from New York) and Gary Hart (neo-liberal Senator from Colorado), we also see problems with that involvement, but for another reason. Unlike them, we see social spending as a *positive* force, positive not for its economic efficiency but for the democratic vision that it embodies. Spending on social security, unemployment benefits, government employment, public employment, health care, and education represents the efforts of working Americans to get government to serve their needs. It represents the demands of various social movements, through the political process, to be protected against the injustices of a boom-and-bust enterprise system and to share in postwar economic growth. A democratically elected Congress and President have had to respond to these demands. Government has acted to provide Americans with jobs, more equal income distribution, economic security, and—for women and minorities—the job and income mobility that they never would have achieved in the private sector.

And unlike conservatives, liberals, and neoliberals, we think that much of the business community is failing to fulfill its social mandate. In the real world, the competitive market no longer exists. Dominated by giant corporations, the private sector often operates *against* the public interest by dumping waste, building unreliable products, despoiling the wilderness, and providing unsafe jobs. More than that, the social contract struck during the New Deal and forming the basis of postwar economic growth has been broken—principally by big business. When the share of gross national product earned by private capital fell in the late 1960s— a fall accompanied by worldwide social upheavals—business stopped going along with government and labor under the New Deal accords. Labor began gaining progressively less purchasing power from wages, and government got relatively less and less from corporate taxes. Private investment per employee decreased drastically in the 1970s. Rather than using its profits for increasing productivity as it had in the 1950s and 1960s, business intensified moves, in the United States and abroad, to less unionized regions with a better "business climate," speculated in real estate, and sought growth through mergers. The New Deal accords unraveled because big business wanted a better deal for itself.

Business was trying to end run government economic policy that had unintentionally helped produce higher wages and employee benefits at the expense of profits. But an investment strategy that concentrates on lowering labor costs to increase profits cannot be sustained indefinitely. It means lowering consumer demand, and unless the United States intends to become increasingly an export economy, lower demand at home means slower growth. Whereas neoliberals would like to make the United States over into a Japanese-style export economy, successful only if wages can be kept low, we believe that our future economic development should be built on the expansion of *domestic* demand and production for more productive, better-paid American workers. The world economy is important for the United States, but increasing world markets for U.S. goods or increasing U.S. private investment so that it "runs away" to low-wage labor countries cannot be the main solution to our economic and social problems.

America's powerful corporate sector is as responsible for the present economic crisis as government or labor—if not more so. But government did make a serious mistake in the 1970s. Even as the Carter Administration realized what the corporations were doing, government continued to frame its policies in terms of what was good for profits rather than what was good for the public. Profits accruing to powerful, transnational oil companies, banks, and insurance firms are not necessarily synonymous either with a rational long-term investment policy or full employment.

The current crisis cannot be separated from New Deal policies, including government economic management and the growing role of government in the economy and society. Yet it would be a mistake to conclude that turning the economy over entirely to private corporations is the solution to America's economic and social problems.

First, American business operates under less stringent government controls than their counterparts in many other Western

capitalist economies. Any foreign company exporting to the
United States also has to meet our product requirements: Japanese
cars, for example, must meet all the emission controls put on
U.S.-made vehicles. Furthermore, European countries like the
Federal Republic of Germany, Sweden, Norway, and Holland
have had a much higher percentage of gross national product
going to government and also have had higher growth rates and
more equal income distribution than the United States. And while
Japan has low military spending and lower social welfare spending
per capita than the United States, the Japanese government is
much more actively interventionist in its economy than any U.S.
government would dream of being. University of California political scientist Chalmers Johnson and other experts attribute high
Japanese growth rates directly to this interventionism.

Second, the private sector has never been able to provide the
social services and equality of economic benefits demanded by the
American citizenry. Poverty is far from being eliminated in this
wealthy country; private enterprise discriminates against women
and minorities in the wages it pays and in hiring practices; and
there is a serious question whether the poor would even get necessary health care and education if these services were left to private
concerns.

But we are going to make an even stronger argument. We
contend that the conservative view of the relationship between
government and individual is fundamentally incorrect, and that
the Keynesian view of government as a pro-business arbiter between business and laborers/consumers is unworkable. Government must be the representative of the public as a whole. As a
society, we cannot follow Reagan's prescription of dismantling
government's role as the citizenry's protector against profit- and
property-oriented business, nor continue the New Deal strategy
of making government the "fair" mediator between big-business
interests and social movements, only giving in to those movements in periods of social crisis. A solution based on either one of
these models will not work now. Both models are unstable, because they make the public sector subservient to private profits

and make private profit into the goal of economic development. They ignore the aspirations and hopes of citizens for both economic rights and economic security.

We are not progovernment or antibusiness per se. Rather, we argue that of the two in our democratic society, government has been traditionally much more responsive to citizens' needs and tends to be more publicly accountable. Now government itself must act as an agent of democratization for the public, and in order to do that it must change its approach to private profit-stimulation. This does not mean an end to the market or an end to the importance of private investment and innovation. Yet it does mean that large, private corporations will no longer be the only planning units of the American economy.

Only the national government—with a grass-roots movement behind it—has the power to make such reforms as requiring worker representatives on the boards of corporations and legislating in-plant health and safety committees. These reforms do not centralize bureaucratic control; rather they give new democratic rights to citizens as workers and consumers. But national-level reforms are not enough to revitalize the American economy; to do that we need local and state government institutions that plan and invest in the public interest.

Our democratic alternative stresses increased democratic control of productive investment. It will enhance and streamline the present public programs for guaranteeing social fairness. The only way this can happen is through the greater democratization of economic and political power. The undemocratic power of large corporations has to be curtailed. This does not mean abolishing or nationalizing all of them. Either option is unrealistic. But they can be democratically controlled and guided by new rules of behavior and with democratically determined planning agreements.

We recommend the creation of public corporations that operate under rules whereby public needs dictate investment policy. Such public corporations and more democratically run enterprises of all kinds are the cornerstones of our New Social Contract. Financing through state banks and a national public bank (or banks) which use pension funds and tax monies is essential to such projects. The market will still exist but public or mixed corporations will operate in the important oligopolized sectors and set the public interest norm. Furthermore, our emphasis will be on regional and local democratic planning—planning guidelines with which private corporations will have to comply (much as zoning requirements now guide local economic development)—and on institutions that allow and encourage greater citizen and worker participation in economic decision-making.

Rather than let large, unaccountable private corporations do the planning for society, democratic institutions should plan priorities in finance, transit, land use, and energy. The planning framework should be carried out democratically, and then market relationships would continue within a set of rules that protects consumers, workers, and communities.

The political building blocks for achieving a New Social Contract exist in American society. They await only the leadership and vision necessary to weld them into a governing majority. Pieces of this movement also already exist: the more liberal trade unions, women's organizations, nuclear-freeze groups, tenants' organizations, environmentalists, minority organizations in the neighborhoods, and community organizations such as Massachusetts Fair Share and the Ohio Public Interest Campaign. To carry out this strategy effectively we need a national coalition for economic democracy, an alliance of state and locally based groups with genuine mass memberships willing to engage in electoral politics.

A New Social Contract, when it comes about, will be written by the democratic actions of millions of Americans. Ultimately it will not be any economist's program, but a new economic reality in which people live. However, to get there—and to understand where "there" may be—we must begin by understanding how we arrived at the present impasse.

2 The Rise and Fall of Reaganomics

When voters elected Ronald Reagan, they bought a package of anti-inflationary austerity, cuts in government spending and taxes, Moral Majority family policy, and increased militarization of the economy. If nothing else, the President and his administration have been consistent: they have tried to make good on all his campaign promises.

The heart of the neoconservative appeal, aside from the media power of a senescent father-figure, is its position against government spending and in support of individualistic initiative. There are deep roots for such an appeal. Deepest of all is the belief that democracy and laissez-faire capitalism are inexorably linked—so deeply linked, in fact, that we can measure the health of democratic ideals by how little government "interferes" in the economy. The word *freedom* in America, more than in almost any other country, is associated with individual economic autonomy. The free person is the one who is economically unfettered and unprotected, at liberty to work or not work, succeed or not succeed in the cold, cruel, but potentially rewarding world of free enterprise.

Yet there are contradictions in the neoconservative position. At the ideological level, many Americans may believe in the inseparability of democracy and unfettered capitalism, but in practice, they have generally voted for increased, not decreased, government economic involvement. Democracy in America has therefore frequently conflicted directly with free-market economics. More important, Reagan's strain of conservatism is anything but populist. This divorces the present administration from the more individualistic of the free-market ideologies. We—and the populist conservatives—could conceivably imagine a small-business, competitive economy in America, where most people were self-employed and government's functions were limited and controlled by an active, Jacksonian electorate (with women and minorities included but subordinate). President Reagan, however, never identified with the anticorporatism of populist conservatism. Rather, his administration is an amalgam of supply-siders, monetarists, and neoconservative intellectuals—front men for the present concentration of corporate economic power. Reaganomics never suggested that it would give power back to the people; it only promised to reduce government interference in private production *as it presently exists* and to cut federal spending. According to Reaganomics, such reductions are necessary to halt inflation and stimulate economic growth. Nothing was ever said about reducing the concentration of capital.

The contradictions between what the public *imagined* the neoconservative program to be and what it *is* could well spell its doom forever. But the program's worst political sin was to hold up rapid economic growth as the measure of political legitimacy and then not deliver that growth.

It should have been obvious from the start that Reaganomics was only going to achieve its primary goals: slowing inflation, increasing military spending, redistributing income from poor to rich, and increasing the potential profit rate by cutting corporate taxes and union-busting. It should also have been obvious that this was going to be a costly achievement, much more costly than the middle class could have ever dreamed. Instead of national honor, middle-class Americans got the specter of nuclear holocaust; instead of decreased taxes on higher incomes, they got unemployment and lower consumption; instead of confidence in America's future, they got fear of economic disaster; instead of improving their position relative to the welfare poor, they joined the welfare poor in losing to the rich.

By now, so much has been written on Reaganomics that it seems almost masochistic to review the record once more. But it is important to analyze the corporatist solution to America's economic and social problems and to understand just how inconsistent that solution is with the pubiic's needs. Whatever Reaganomics seemed to promise for jobs, growth, lower taxes, less inflation, political security, and national pride, it delivered a different package. It also put American corporations on trial, bringing out into the open unfettered, pro-business policies.

What Does Reaganomics Profess to Be?

Reaganomics is a two-headed beast. One head is "supply-side" economics; the other is "monetarism." Both heads in this case have the same ideology: reduction of government activity in private markets is essential to economic efficiency and to economic growth with price stability. But the heads are also different, especially in their application.

Monetarism states that although individual prices rise and fall in response to changes in demand and supply of particular goods, price *levels* can shift up or down only if the money supply—defined in some way (there is no agreement on exactly what constitutes money supply)—moves in the same direction. Monetarists come to this conclusion from the simple formula that the quantity of goods and services produced in an economy times the price level equals the supply of money times the rapidity with which money changes hands—the velocity of its circulation. By assuming that the velocity of money is relatively stable, it follows that the rising consumer price index is the direct result of Federal Reserve action to enlarge the capacity of commercial banks to lend more to consumers and corporations (increased money supply). To halt inflation, the growth of money supply must be decreased. Through higher interest rates charged to commercial banks (the Fed's discount rate), by selling government securities, and by printing less money, the Fed achieves such a decrease.

It may take a while, but eventually the economy is cooled off and —according to monetarists—the price level will stop rising. Once it stops rising, long-term interest rates will fall because the demand for speculative investments will fall. The Fed will be able to allow the money supply to increase at the growth rate of gross national product. Indeed, Milton Friedman—the monetarists' crown prince—argues against "fine tuning" and for an unflinching, automatic increase of the money supply at a historic rate of GNP growth. That way, when the economy slumps, the money-supply increase will be stimulatory, and when the economy grows at more than the historic rate, money-supply growth will be expansion-inhibiting. Friedman also argues that the money supply used in this way should be the *only* countercyclical government instrument. While fiscal policy can be used for income redistribution, deficit spending as a means of economic stimulation is verboten and a balanced budget is de rigueur.

The Reagan economic policy, as the President formulated it in his Message to the Congress in February 1981, is a combination of monetarism and supply-side economics. On the one hand, the Federal Reserve was initially to keep the money supply growing more slowly than "normal," resulting in high short-term interest rates and restricted demand. This part of the policy was supposed to reduce inflation. On the other hand, the Reagan budget would cut government spending, especially on consumption subsidies, *and cut taxes,* especially the high rates on nonsalary income. The cut in spending would, along with the Fed's policies, also cut consumer demand. The cuts in taxes would stimulate savings; harder work by wage earners, who would give up a lower percentage of their additional income to government; increased investment by high-income taxpayers, whose marginal rates would be reduced from 70 to 50 percent; and investment by firms getting tax breaks through more rapid depreciation allowances. To further stimulate growth, Reagan pushed for price deregulation of natural gas, deregulation of business in general—particularly in the area of health and safety, pollution controls, and environmental safeguards—and increases in military spending, which were to promote defense-industry and related high-technology production.

Overall, then, Reaganomics hoped to combine an anti-inflation monetary policy—which, once completed, would remove the inflationary distortion from investment markets—with an investment-promoting fiscal policy designed to reduce taxes for everyone, but especially for those with high incomes. The Reagan tax cuts were never supposed to be a stimulus to consumption. As head of the Office of Management and Budget, David Stockman, in his famous 1981 interview, made this clear:

> The original argument was that the top bracket was too high, and that's having the most devastating effect on the economy. Then, the general argument was that, in order to make this palatable as a political matter, you had to bring down all the brackets. But, I mean, Kemp-Roth [the 1981 Kemp-Roth tax bill] was always a Trojan horse to bring down the top rate. (*Atlantic Monthly*, December 1981, p. 46.)

Supply-side economics seems to be inconsistent with Friedman's monetarist recommendations, but it can be consistent over the longer haul. It is in the short run that the two heads of Reaganomics bite each other, and therein lies a tale of frustration and failure. "Supply-side" seems to mean that the old Keynesian solution of stimulating demand has to be replaced in the present inflationary situation with policies that stimulate supply. Supply-side economists suggest that removing government regulations and reducing taxes make it more profitable to save and invest, and this, in turn, increases investment, productivity, and growth. Indeed, the spur to growth from cuts in tax *rates* are so great that absolute tax revenues will quickly catch up to government spending, balancing the budget and allowing the automatic increases in the money supply to become the government's sole macroeconomic policy instrument. The celebrated Laffer curve, brainchild of University of Southern California economist Arthur Laffer, made precisely this argument: Government intervention (taxes) for demand management had become so great that it was killing work and investment incentives in the private sector. This slowed economic growth, and, excepting the inflationary tax, actually lowered potential tax revenues.

But if the Fed keeps interest rates high, this squeezes credit and slows the expansion of investment. David Stockman, as head of the government's most important planning office, recognized early that Laffer-Kemp's tax cuts alone would leave huge, potentially inflationary short-run budget deficits. These would not only be politically unacceptable but would put real pressure on capital markets, keeping interest rates high. Stockman was additionally constrained by Reagan's commitment to an extraordinary expansion of the military budget. The "only choice" was to go for a large budget reduction in many basic programs, including those serving both "weak clients" and "weak claimants." Thus, budget cutting was intended to reduce consumption, thereby reducing inflationary pressure and pressure on interest rates, to allow the Fed to reach its goals early so the economy could begin expanding on the crest of an investment boom stimulated by supply-side tax cuts.

> The nature of the gamble boils down to this: Both the Administration and the Fed are betting that by sticking to tight monetary and fiscal policies, inflation will be beaten down in a convincing way for the first time in decades. And once inflation and the expectations of inflation are curbed, capital investment and economic growth will revive robustly. (*Business Week*, December 28, 1981, p. 76.)

This is the "economics" side of Reaganomics. But investment stimulation also means reducing government interference at other levels. The Reagan Administration made clear its intentions by appointing James Watt, supporter of oil-, coal-, and mineral-exploiting corporations, as Secretary of the Interior and Ann Gorsuch as head of the Environmental Protection Agency. Almost immediately, Watt called for bids on government-owned oil reserves off the California coast from oil companies and began the process of making mineral reserves on government land available for private exploitation. Clean Air Act revisions came before Congress in 1982, but the enforcement of its provisions by the EPA had been severely reduced the year before. All in all, Reaganomics includes a concerted attack on legislation designed to protect consumers against the harmful "spillovers" of private-enterprise production. The rationale for this attack is that such protections increase the cost of production more than the benefit provided to consumers.

Another, not much subtler, piece of Reaganomics is its antilabor policy. If investment is to be stimulated, profit rates must increase. Average corporate profit rates are lower than they were in the 1950s and mid-1960s and—allegedly—this has deterred productive investment. American industry has also suffered at the hands of foreign competition because of relatively high wages in the United States. Finally, according to the argument, one of the most important components of inflation has been labor's demands for higher wages in a period of only slowly rising productivity. To the Reagan Administration, the solution to all these problems lies in a two-pronged attack on labor. The first is to reduce income-maintenance programs. Although the main intention of these reductions may be to save the government money, they also force increased numbers of people into the labor market, creating additional unemployment and—especially among minimum-wage occupations—forcing wages down or at least keeping them from rising. The second—and more direct—attack on labor is to reduce the power of labor unions. Nonunionized labor means less upward pressure on wages and less interference in the profit-making capability of private enterprise.

The air-traffic controllers' (PATCO) strike was a perfect opportunity for the President to project his antilabor message. In crushing the strike, Reagan told organized labor that he would not support union claims to higher than "reasonable" wages or better working conditions. Labor can participate in economic growth under Reaganomics, but the President's economic plan of February 1981 forecast only a 5 percent growth in real wages by 1985. Furthermore, the PATCO experience telegraphed a simple message to public employees' unions, until recently the fastest-growing in the labor movement: strike and you will be subject to permanent job loss. These unions are particularly vulnerable because of proposed major cuts in federal employment and federal aid to the states.

There are two "anomalies" in Reaganomics, with which many of the economists connected with the Administration do not agree: militarism couched in virulent anticommunism, and Moral Majority family legislation. Nevertheless, these anomalies cannot be separated from Reagan's overall political economy—they are the *sine qua non* of postwar neoconservatism. And rightly so. If a Republican administration is going to play hardball with inflation and also redistribute income to corporations and the rich, it better have some ideological acts that play to mass political support. Making America the great military power it was back in the early sixties and cleaning up American morality at home are tailored to do exactly that.

Military spending is scheduled to climb from about 25 to more than 30 percent of a growing federal budget, from a total authority of $214 billion in 1982 to $356 billion in 1986.[1] This includes building the B-1 bomber and the MX missile and refitting the Navy with new aircraft carriers and submarines. It does not include the booming U.S. arms export industry, like the AWACS Saudi-Boeing contract, or atomic energy and other defense-related activities. If our economy still had technology and production organization that was far ahead of the competition, and our only problem was unutilized capacity, military spending could serve to stimulate production, much as it did during World War II and the Korean War. But the conditions in the U.S. economy today are totally different: although industry is operating considerably below capacity, its main problems are its declining ability to compete effectively against imports and the high cost of credit.

Defense spending aggravates both these problems. In 1974, in his book *The Permanent War Economy* (New York: Simon and Schuster, 1974), Columbia University Professor Seymour Melman suggested that Defense Department contracting promoted built-in inefficiencies at the production end and built-in cost overruns. Melman also noted that military spending accounts for most of American industry's research and development and that the mili-

1. *The New York Times*, February 6, 1983, p. E1.

tary-industrial sector employs many of the country's most able engineers and scientists. The utilization of these resources on military products means that they are *not* available to strengthen the civilian economy.

The enormous increase in military spending also has its financial impact: it contributes to growing federal deficits. Deficits, in turn, compete with private capital and put upward pressure on interest rates. This would not be so bad for America if the deficit were invested in new consumer-goods technologies, saving energy, or even longer-gestating programs for reorganizing our transportation, health, and education systems. All these investments could make our economy/society healthier for future long-term development.

Reaganomics' faith in military spending does, in fact, represent a social investment policy. And this explains why the Administration is so wedded to that spending despite the "short-run" impediments it poses for the rest of Reagan's economic package. As a social investment policy, military spending reflects the belief that Communist expansion is the single greatest threat to America's way of life. Thus, a *precondition* of any economic/social policy has to be military preparedness and aggressive steps overseas to halt Soviet imperialism. Such steps can only be effective if the United States is *clearly* the world's most potent military power, willing to use that power whenever and wherever necessary to protect America's interests. Economic growth is meaningless if there is no security against the Communist threat. The revival of American capitalism does not make much sense if capitalism cannot protect itself on a world scale. In these terms, military spending is social investment. It is the very basis of ensuring the continuation of American institutions and therefore cannot be subject to compromise.

The Moral Majority's family policy does not play such a central role in Reaganomics. Also, it does not have any direct budget implications, so was constantly pushed into the background as the Administration struggled to carry its economic packages through Congress. But ideologically, its close identification with the Ad-

ministration's social policies provided and continues to provide
the quasi-religious foundation for antiwelfare budget cuts and
shifting income to the already successful.

The Moral Majority's concept of the nuclear family has three
fundamental characteristics: it is patriarchal; it is organized primarily for procreation and child-rearing; and it is the principal site
of reproducing America's values. The patriarchal nature of the
Moral Majority's family policy goes against the reality of increasing
divorce rates and female-headed households; it forms a bulwark
against the feminist movement and against changes in values that
might reduce male control of economic and social institutions.
This is not a minor task in America during the 1980s and—along
with the military—places the Moral Majority directly in the van-
guard of social struggle. Although feminism is mainly an ideological movement, it implies new concepts of economic structure and
relations. These may not be in direct conflict with corporate capitalism, but they are in conflict with the present corporate
managerial elite, who are almost all males. The Moral Majority is,
above all, the defender of patriarchy, and for good reason.

Consistent with its overt position on patriarchy, the Moral Majority defines the family as a *reproductive* unit. Abortion is a direct
challenge to this function and to the control over women's bodies
by a male-dominated society. Public education is also a potential
challenge to reproduction when curriculum conflicts with the fun-
damentalist values considered basic to America's revitalization. It
is no accident that the Reagan Administration's education policy
is oriented toward promoting private schooling, for it is precisely
in sending their children to subsidized private schools that families
can choose the "right" kind of value formation as an extension of
the family's role.

These precepts may seem distant from a discussion of budget
cutting or investment promotion, but they are not. They are the
underpinnings of a powerful ideology that—for an important *minority* of Americans—describes an ideal society and transcends
the importance of higher growth, lower unemployment, and
lower interest rates.

What Did Reaganomics Turn Out to Be?

"Politically," *Business Week* tells us candidly, "the Reagan Administration's program represents an agenda for the revival of capitalism . . ." (December 28, 1981, p. 76). But so did FDR's New Deal and JFK's New Frontier. Reaganomics is a *particular* agenda for capitalist revival. It creates conditions for capital investment which roll back most of the *social* constraints placed on capitalist expansion over the last generation. These constraints were built on government social welfare spending, the rights of labor to organize into labor unions, and government employment that provided social mobility for women and minorities. But more than "just" those concrete pillars of Depression and post-Depression economic development, unwritten changes also occurred in the public's view of economic morality. Full employment, while ever more elusive, is also an ever-present ideal. Security in old age, backed up by high voter participation among senior citizens and a growing percentage of the population over sixty-five, is an assumed government responsibility. Economic opportunity for minorities and women was placed on the national agenda, largely as a result of important gains by both in "cultural" equality (social racism and genderism definitely declined in the 1970s). The elimination of poverty and the provision of universal public education and training became and remain important national goals.

The Reagan capitalist revival defied this liberal social consensus. Capitalist development with greater equality was replaced by unfettered capitalist development, where business was to be given every possible profit incentive in the name of increasing economic growth.

Reaganomics is *not* an anti-big-government package: Budget cuts in social welfare programs are more than matched by increases in military spending. With the slower growth rates in the 1980s, even the Administration's lower projected government spending increases may leave government with a higher percentage of GNP than in the late 1970s. And the New Federalism—Reaganomics' answer to government decentralization—would give states control over precisely those programs that are being cut.

Income Distribution. Supply-side economics concentrates on tax cuts to the rich and to business as a means of stimulating investment and savings. Reaganomics' combination of supply-side tax cuts (a proposed 30 percent in three years) with monetarist cuts in the money supply (high interest rates) led to David Stockman's proposed budget cuts in social welfare spending. The effect of cutting tax rates across the board on personal income, plus Stockman's spending cuts, contributed to the largest income redistribution since World War II, except this time the redistribution was from the poor to the rich.

The Congressional Budget Office estimates that from 1982 to 1985, the budget and tax cuts enacted in 1981 will provide all households with a total net gain of $311 billion over the pre-Reagan tax/spending schedule. But this gain is distributed very unevenly. The 22 percent of households that made less than $10,000 in 1982 will *lose* $15.6 billion over the four years, or about $200 per year per household. The 25 percent of households that earned $10,000 to $20,000 in 1982 will *gain* $26.6 billion, or about $300 per year per household. The 35 percent of households in the $20,000 to $40,000 income category will gain $120 billion, or $960 per household per year. The 16 percent of households earning $40,000 to $80,000 in 1982 will gain $112 billion, or $1940 per household per year. Finally, that 1.2 percent of American households earning more than $80,000 in 1982 will gain a total of $69 billion, or $16,100 per household per year. These per household gains and losses represent an *annual* loss of 1.3 percent for the average under-$10,000 household, an annual 1.6 percent gain for the average $10,000 to $20,000 household, an annual 3.2 percent for those households earning $20,000 to $40,000, 4.7 percent for those earning $40,000 to $80,000, and 6.9 percent annually for those with more than $80,000 in income in 1982. These percentages do not seem large, but when cumulated and compounded, they show that a poor family will be more than 5 percent worse off in 1985 than in 1981 while a middle-class family will gain 14 percent, and a rich family will be more than 30 percent better off. These percentages alone indicate a large redistribution of income from the poor to the rich.[2]

Reagan argued that the same-percentage across-the-board tax cuts for everyone would provide equitable relief from big government, but in fact they do not. The Congressional Budget Office study shows how, by percentage, the rate cut and indexing provisions of the 1981 Economic Recovery Tax Act benefited high-income taxpayers much more than the low-income. And when budget cuts are added to the package, tax-cut gains for the poor are turned into net losses. An average low-income household (less than $10,000 in 1982) stands to lose a total of $1410 in benefit payments between 1982 and 1985, while an average high-income family ($80,000 or more) only loses $580.

The Administration was well aware of this when it pushed the Economic Recovery Tax Act and the 1982 budget through Congress. It continued to be aware of the distributional consequences in presenting more social welfare spending cuts and the New Federalism in the 1983 budget fight. As we have noted, David Stockman, in *Atlantic Monthly,* called the higher benefits to the rich the "Trojan horse" of Kemp-Roth's 30 percent tax cut. Reaganomics contends that such a redistribution is necessary to promote savings and investment and to fight inflation through lower consumer spending. While politically dangerous, the strategy hopes to buy off middle-income households with net gains that are not as high as those for the rich but still positive, and counts on higher growth rates stimulated by increased savings from income redistribution to convince the American public as a whole. Even with normal growth rates, however, 47 percent of American households (those with less than $20,000 annual income) will gain an average $70 each annually as a result of Reagan's policies, while

2. Congressional Budget Office, Human Resources/Community Development Division and Tax Analysis Division, "Effects of Tax and Benefit Reductions Enacted in 1981 for Households in Different Income Categories," February 1982 (mimeo). We used the data from Tables 1 and 10–12.

the highest 1 percent of households will be raking in an average $16,000 each, every year.

But the tax-benefit cuts are just part of the income-distribution impact of Reagan's economic policies. Economists who have studied changes in the U.S. distribution generally agree with findings that employment—as measured by the number of weeks worked —has been the most important variable explaining annual variations in pre-tax income inequality. *Higher unemployment rates generate a more unequal income distribution.* An anti-inflation policy that sharply increases unemployment has an unequalizing effect on incomes (before taking into account government taxation and spending). A monetary policy that increases unemployment, combined with a fiscal policy that cuts benefits to the poor and near-poor while increasing benefits to the rich through tax breaks, radically redistributes income. American households are not randomly distributed over the various income categories. A high percentage of the less than $10,000 income households are headed by women or minorities.

By redistributing income in this way, Reaganomics is accelerating the increase in the number and percentage of Americans who are poor. Although poverty was decreasing slowly in the 1960s and early 1970s, by the end of the decade, the trend had turned. The Census Bureau estimates that in 1979 about 26 million people were below the poverty level, and in 1981 32 million, or 14 percent of the population, were poor ($8350 in income for a family of four). The poverty rate for blacks in 1981 was 32 percent and rising. The Reagan fiscal and monetary policies have intensified an already unacceptable rate of poverty, hitting minorities and women, who constitute the bulk of the poor, especially hard. As we shall see, Reagan's cuts in government employment hit the middle class of these same two groups. So, poor and better off minorities and women are bearing the brunt of the Administration's income policies.

Investment, Savings, and Growth. Income redistribution of this magnitude can only be rationalized in America as a stimulus to economic growth. Political scientist Alan Wolfe has correctly concluded that American Keynesianism plays down the aspects of Keynes' work that are against private investment and for more equal income distribution and full employment and, instead, makes a fetish of economic growth. The American public might accept even radical changes in income distribution, higher average unemployment, and cuts in benefits to the poor—if the economy begins growing again with stable or moderately rising prices.

Growth has been hard to come by, however. After a fall in real GNP of 0.2 percent in 1980, it grew 1.9 percent in 1981, but this was entirely due to a large first-quarter increase. By the fourth quarter, the Reagan recession was in full swing, despite the Accelerated Cost Recovery System already generating substantial tax benefits to business in 1981. This included what journalist William Quirk calls (in *The New Republic*, December 30, 1981) "The Great Tax Benefit Sale," in which companies that made low profits but had large tax deductions could sell their "unusable" deductions to companies with high profits. Real gross national product fell by 2 percent in 1982. Real gross private domestic investment (GPDI)—the amount that private corporations and individuals invest each year—also rose in 1981 (by 8 percent over 1980) but fell sharply in the fourth quarter of 1981, and continued to fall in 1982. Real 1982 GDPI was 14 percent lower than in 1981 and 18 percent lower than in 1979.[3]

Supply-side economics claims that the crisis of the 1970s was caused by an overemphasis on demand and a simultaneous crushing of investment incentives as demand was stimulated by government taxes and spending. However, as University of Texas economist Harry Cleaver suggests, supply-side economics is also concerned with demand, but not with the expansion of consumer demand. Rather, the combination of stimulating investment with the reduction of government subsidies to consumption "makes clear that 'supply-side' economics is not so much concerned with limiting the growth of demand as it is with changing its *composition*. There is an *evident desire to shift the composition of demand*

3. *Economic Report of the President, 1983*, Tables B-15 and B-3.

from consumption to investment."[4] The supply-side issue for
Cleaver, then, is not demand versus supply, but *how* demand is
to expand. Direct subsidies to consumers through government
spending means that a higher fraction of national income tends to
go to wage earners; tax cuts for corporations and the rich increase
the share going to capital.

We can use Cleaver's insight to understand how supply-side
and monetarist economics can and did clash in the short run, and
the effect this may have had on investment and growth. If the
demand is to increase for investment goods like machines and
factory buildings, not only must real wages and government subsidies to consumers be cut (for example, welfare payments and
social security), but interest rates must be low enough for business to expand. Economist Milton Friedman argues that the inflation dragon must be slain first in order to restore confidence
and reinvigorate capital investment policy. Only with low rates
of inflation will capital flow into productive investments and
cease speculating on inflation. Supply-siders like Arthur Laffer
agree with Friedman in principle but see the damage that high
interest rates can bring to their centerpiece of economic growth.
Without increased growth rates, tax and spending cuts produce
high government deficits and political backlash. And high deficits put upward pressure on interest rates because of the amount
of capital that has to be devoted to financing the debt itself. Savings in 1982 flowed into government debt financing rather than
into private investment.

And what about the savings rate—that crucial figure that is
supposed to fuel the supply-side expansion? Although monetarist
high interest rates hit investment hard, they should have stimulated people to save. As early as 1980, Stanford neoconservative
economist Michael Boskin was suggesting that higher interest
rates would significantly increase savings.[5] Indeed, in the fourth

4. Harry Cleaver, "Supply-Side Economics: The New Phase of Capitalist Strategy
in the Crisis," Department of Economics, University of Texas, 1981 (mimeo), p. 5.
5. Measurements of household savings in the United States are skewed by the
fact that so many American families save by owning a house, which does not show
up in the statistics as savings.

quarter of 1981, the savings rate did increase from 6.5 to 7.5 percent of disposable personal income but then dropped back to 6.8 percent for 1982, only slightly higher than the 6.4 percent for 1981. This increase in personal savings was just enough to finance the increase in federal debt service. The rise in savings in 1981 over 1980 was $24 billion, while the increase in net interest paid by the federal government in 1981 was $16 billion. In 1982, debt service increased by $16 billion and personal savings by $11 billion.[6] Again, while the savings rate increased somewhat, the hoped-for bonanza was not forthcoming, especially in light of the whopping deficits and continued high interest rates government paid on that debt.

Inflation. If everything else was going wrong, Reaganomics did show that a tight money policy could slow inflation. Price increases slowed in the spring of 1982, thanks largely to continued reductions in gasoline consumption, a slowdown in the rise of housing prices, and the average interest paid in buying homes (rental units were no longer included in the consumer price index). Clothing and auto prices fell as well. The real question that faces monetary policy is whether the tight money used to bring down inflation is sufficient to control inflation permanently. The "rational expectations" model promoted by Friedman's disciples at the University of Chicago predicts that it is. In that model, an important part of inflation is the existence of inflation itself. Expected price increases are built into employer and labor decision-making. Once prices begin to level off, labor will ask for lower wage increases and investors will not plan on price rises. Increased price stability promotes investors to make longer term investments.

But there are alternative arguments: For example, the present oil glut was caused by U.S. monetary policy only insofar as high interest rates have caused a growth slowdown in all industrialized countries except Japan and thus a much slower increase in overall demand for petroleum. As soon as economic growth picks up even slightly, demand will increase and also prices. Home prices fell

6. *Economic Report of the President, 1983*, Tables B-23 and B-76.

only temporarily because of prohibitively high mortgage rates. If mortgage rates decline even temporarily, prospective home buyers now sitting on the sidelines will jump in and raise prices again, including what they pay monthly on their mortgages. Health-care price increases have not slowed down significantly and will continue to rise. Food prices will also continue rising. All in all, control of inflation will necessitate intermittent tight-money policies and this will slow down growth.

There are also counterarguments: Oil prices will stay low for quite a while, since prices have dropped even while two oil-producing nations, Iran and Iraq, have had unusually low production because of their war. Speculation in real estate was a principal contributor to rising real-estate prices; with higher interest and lower inflation, that speculation will decline sharply and the home market will stabilize. More rational labor policies (i.e., government anti-unionism) will keep wage increases modest. Stabilizing energy prices combined with lower wage increases will keep food price increases moderate.

Unemployment. The other half of Reaganomics' price stabilization has been the highest rate of unemployment since before World War II. By the winter of 1982–83, the unemployment rate had reached more than 10.5 percent. There were almost as many unemployed Americans (11 million) as in 1933 (12.8 million), at the height of the Great Depression.[7] Unemployment, business failure (there were 15,829 bankruptcies in the first eight months of 1982 alone—more than at any time since 1932), and mortgage foreclosure (100,000 in May 1982) became characteristic of Reaganomics as inflation slowed. For monetarists, this was the necessary price for convincing investors that inflation was indeed down and

7. These unemployment statistics tend to underestimate some aspects of unemployment by not measuring the duration of unemployment. Paul B. Manchester, the staff economist with the Joint Economic Committee of Congress, devised an index that multiplies the number of people unemployed by the average number of weeks unemployed. For example, although Republicans were pleased that January 1983 unemployment fell to 11.4 million, that figure failed to show that duration of unemployment had risen to 19.4 weeks, making January's index 221 million weeks, almost double the 117 million weeks average for 1975 and the worst month in history (*The New York Times,* February 6, 1983, p. F1).

that long-term interest rates would fall. Only that knowledge, according to the rational expectations model, would stimulate long-term, productive investment.

But even if the model works—and there are serious doubts that it will—the result will be not only that certain groups will pay for the decline in inflation and a small, already wealthy minority will not, but that for the model to continue working, *these same groups will have to continue paying.* Real wages per employed person already fell 13 percent between 1973 and the end of the Carter Administration, and after six months of leveling off under Reagan, they started down again. Between November 1980, when Ronald Reagan was elected, and the fall of 1982, average individual real wages fell another 2.5 percent. Under Carter, most of the decline occurred in disastrous 1980, when a recession with high inflation bit hard into consumption power. Under Reagan, the erosion has been slow and steady.

But worse, in 1982, high unemployment rates led to a decline in total real disposable income, which means that not only were individual weekly incomes down, but so—for the first time since 1974—was the amount earned by all the people working in a family, since fewer family members could find jobs. And this is precisely what the Administration sees as necessary for U.S. companies to become competitive in world markets and for profits to rise. The tremendous pressure generated by greater than 10 percent unemployment and an anti-union mood has worked to reduce wage costs in industry after industry. On the other hand, top executive salaries are way up. In a survey of twenty-five corporate presidents and chairmen of the board, the *San Francisco Chronicle* (June 6, 1982) found that even with corporate profits falling in 1981–82, executive salaries went up 12 percent, to an average $509,000 per year in 1982. Nor should labor expect rapid wage increases in a potential Reagan expansion. One of the benefits to business of high unemployment rates, union-busting, and reduced social welfare spending (for example, on unemployment insurance and family assistance) is to reduce *future* wage increases once GNP begins to grow.

Although unemployment is widespread, it is also much greater among minority youth, youth in general, and in the upper Midwest. The Reagan economy has seen northern labor migrating in search of jobs in Texas, Oklahoma, and Louisiana—industrial workers heading to the oil fields and the oil regions—often futilely or only finding short-term work. The Reagan years have also seen the institutionalization of the "underground" economy—the drug dealers, the cash-only merchandise sales and labor contracts, the barter arrangements between advertisers and television networks, the cash-payment subcontracting by large corporations with small-scale, low-cost jobbers often employing illegal aliens, the traffic in stolen goods. *Business Week* (April 5, 1982, pp. 64–70) estimates this unreported economy as representing 15 to 20 percent of GNP. For many young and minority Americans without work, entering the underground is the only possibility for earning income. Unemployment rates of 50 percent in official labor markets simply don't lend themselves to meaningful job searches.

Labor is not the only constituency that is hurting. Much closer to Republican hearts is small business, hanging and slowly turning in the wind on the rope of high interest rates. But the longer-term and less obvious effect of Reaganomics on small business is to accelerate the business concentration already taking place over the last twenty years. Tight money has crippled small firms. Permissive antitrust policies have cut back the capital available to small firms, as large corporations have absorbed billions of dollars in loans to finance acquisitions and millions more in lines of credit, pending the outcome of merger battles. The Small Business Administration's loan programs have been severely cut. The Economic Recovery Tax Act gives large, capital-intensive firms an overwhelming advantage in the marketplace. The Administration has encouraged large corporations to buy out small and medium-sized firms, as well as each other.

Despite these policies, many small-business owners have been loyal to the President, and continue to see him as one of their own. He *has* reduced the enforcement of many regulations on small business. But more important, his wage and inflation policies can be particularly helpful to more labor-intensive, competitive enterprises in the longer run, especially when (and if) interest rates fall and the economy begins expanding.

The Reagan social investment program—military spending—is the fly in the small-business ointment. Military spending increases do more than just help to keep interest rates high through large federal deficits. Such spending competes for engineers, technicians, and many other skilled labor categories, driving up the price of those types of employees. Many small businesses in technology-related industries are forced to pay higher wages for a whole range of skilled workers whose job alternatives lie in defense industry. Military spending also strengthens certain unions—like the Machinists' Union and the United Auto Workers—unions that politically oppose Reaganomics and are powerful actors in the union movement as a whole.

But, at the same time, military spending combined with cuts in government employment is a boon to small businesses seeking qualified, less technical college-educated personnel. The Administration claims that the planned elimination of 300,000 federal jobs will be offset by 1984 through an increase in defense-industry employment. Yet the people who stand to lose their jobs from these cutbacks are not the ones being hired by defense contractors. Government employment primarily benefits professional women (both white and black) college graduates and professional minority men; about 50 percent of these two groups worked at all levels of government in the 1970s (see Chapter 6). Military contractors will hire some women and minorities, but few of them at the professional level. Large corporations have a dismal record on this score. They are dominated at the highest echelons by white males, and there is no reason to believe that, in the current political atmosphere, this will change. It will be small business that will have to employ these highly educated minorities and women, and at much lower wages than government paid them. Small business in certain nonengineering industries and services may therefore benefit by the shift from direct government employment to military contracting.

For the social mobility of women and minorities, the implications of shifting Federal spending from social welfare to military contracts are clear: this 50 percent of the labor force is being pushed into unemployment or into taking lower-paying, lower-skilled jobs. Military production tends to favor white, male, higher-skilled labor. The militarization of the economy relative to the expansion of other government services, or even other private goods and services, means greater discrimination in the labor force; to put it bluntly, it represents increased sexism and racism. Minorities in the military are principally employed as soldiers, although for low-skilled whites and minorities, military service is the most important form of post-secondary-school vocational training.

Military spending also tends to favor large corporations that operate on a cost-plus, cost-overrun basis and have difficulty producing consumer goods or machinery competitively. There are exceptions, like Boeing, but other companies—McDonnell-Douglas, Grumman, General Dynamics, and Northrup, for example—are so heavily involved in military contracts that their whole organizational structure has been converted into Pentagon capitalism.

The bottom line of Reaganomics is that it favors a small, already well-off minority of Americans at the expense of the bottom half of families on the income scale. The Administration has also put enormous resources at the disposal of large corporations in the form of accelerated depreciation, and it has changed the conditions of using those resources by cutting enforcement of pollution controls, rolling back health and safety regulations, and siding with business against organized labor. Women, blacks, and Hispanics are losing the economic and cultural gains they made in the last two decades. Labor unions are more on the defensive than at any time since the 1920s. Reaganomics hopes to change the social conditions of U.S. production in order to raise profits and promote investment. All these sacrifices, it is argued, will result in higher growth and—in the longer run—the "trickle-down" of higher incomes and better jobs now going increasingly to the white upper middle class.

Why Reaganomics Will Not Work

If the trade-off of fewer social benefits for more corporate profits and greater militarization of the economy is to be made palatable to the majority of Americans, they must gain increased purchasing power. If this does not happen, Reagan's program will be politically bankrupt, and the question he asked in the 1980 Presidential debates—"Are you better off now than you were four years ago?"—will come back to haunt him in 1984.

American labor's real average weekly earnings declined sharply between 1973 and 1980, and after two years of a Republican administration, real earnings have continued to fall. The average wage earner receives about the same gross weekly pay as he or she did in 1961. But since taxes are based on nominal income, workers have been pushed into higher tax brackets at the same time that they have *lost* pre-tax consumption power. Their real take-home pay has been falling faster than real gross earnings. The Reagan tax and budget cut is designed to solve this second problem, at least for those households with more than a $10,000 annual income in 1982. As we have noted, under the Administration's tax package, a household earning $15,000 in income in 1982 will get a net gain of $300 per year from 1982 to 1985. Yet that same family would only have to lose 2 percent annually in real earnings—about the average since 1973—in order to offset completely the tax gains.

To turn this process around, Reaganomics must produce much higher growth rates. It planned to achieve this by cutting inflation sharply, restoring business confidence in government economic policies, and redistributing income upward and to business, to induce more savings, more investment, and greater productivity, all of which was supposed to lead to higher growth rates with stable prices, a balanced federal budget, and increased wages.

Unfortunately for those who dreamed of a neoconservative dynasty based on high profit rates and permanent prosperity, Reaganomics has run into both "internal" and "external" contradictions. The internal contradictions arise from its illusory economic assumptions. The external problems come from the fundamentally antidemocratic nature of this brand of supply-side economics, especially when it is combined with tight money.

The supply-side hypothesis that lower income taxes will stimulate people to work harder, produce more, and save more is not supported by the facts. For example, a family making $30,000 a year in 1982 would have been a principal beneficiary of the 1981 economic recovery package, receiving $340 in net benefits in 1982, up to $1500 in 1985. But a continuing decline in real income, plus the possibility of being driven into higher tax brackets by even a moderate inflation, would force this family to use its tax savings to maintain its current standard of living.

With high unemployment, the fear of being laid off might prod some people into working harder, but that does not result in increased savings. Indeed, there is considerable evidence that economic insecurity reduces productivity by heightening tensions between workers and their bosses. As for high-income groups, there is no certainty that tax breaks will produce harder-working executives or that the already rich will not use the extra money to buy luxury goods.

Michael Boskin's highly touted predictions that higher interest rates would produce significantly higher savings rates also fell through. One of the reasons that savings did not increase as much as Boskin predicted is that increased interest was accompanied by declining real wages. As Milton Friedman himself argued twenty years ago, family savings and consumption plans are made on the basis of "permanent" income—lifetime income flows people expect to realize because of their education and training. With real wages declining sharply after 1973 and continuing into 1982, families were still trying to maintain consumption patterns developed in the 1960s and early 1970s. Tax cuts were used to pay off personal debts rather than buying Treasury certificates or opening IRA accounts.

The supply-siders' theory that tax savings would be plowed back into productive, job-creating activities has also not been supported by the facts. Many corporations used their anticipated savings to establish new lines of credit to acquire other companies. Oil companies, which account for more than 30 percent of all private profit, are seeking to monopolize other resources by buying into coal, copper, and shale. Consolidation rather than expansion is the dominant corporate strategy in response to Reagan's incentives. Capital flight continues as manufacturers move abroad and south. The major source of new capital is public investment in defense industries.

Also implicit in the supply-side recipe for economic abundance is the proposition that corporations will pass on to the consumer lower costs from lower taxes and improved productivity rather than increase their own profits. That prospect is unlikely, however, since any new savings from lower taxes will be offset by high interest rates. But even if the 1982 preelection interest-rate declines hold in the longer run, many businesses would like to return to the "normal" profits of 15 percent that they earned during the 1960s, as opposed to the 10 percent rate of the 1970s. Reestablishment of high profits is the heart of Reaganomics, and it can only mean continued "profit-push" inflation.

High interest was supposed to have been a short-run "shock treatment" to halt price increases and place the economy on a noninflationary growth path. The Fed's monetary policy assumes that the main cause of inflation is excess demand. The Fed may be right in assuming that strangling demand will reduce price increases, but the economy will have a difficult time recovering. And a sharp decline in demand will only have a permanent effect on inflation if Reaganomics is correct in its assumptions about inflation depending largely on *expectations* of inflation. If there are other reasons for the steady rise in prices since the late 1960s—such as profit-push and the conflict between wage earners and corporations over the distribution of gross national product—the "shock treatment" will not work, at least not in a democracy.

The Arthur Laffers and David Stockmans know how crucial lower interest rates are to Reaganomics' success. Monetarist and supply-side solutions clash in the short run, especially when the period of tight money stretches into depression proportions. Supply-side tax reduction cannot stimulate investment and growth if credit is restricted. Budget cuts have negative political impact without a corresponding spurt of growth to increase middle-class incomes and cut unemployment to reasonable proportions. The tax-revenue rush predicted by supply-siders and Stockmanists never materialized, leaving the economy with huge federal budget defecits that compete with private capital for savings and keep pressure on interest rates.

The supply-side creed's most fundamental article of faith is that large private corporations are fundamentally efficient. Once government regulations are lifted and taxes lowered, the line goes, these corporations will expand sales, hire more workers, and beat their foreign competitors. Reaganomics is based, to a great extent, on the belief that only large corporations can revitalize the American economy. Yet costly mistakes by the managers of some of these corporations—for example, in the tire, automobile, and steel industries—have been a major cause of the nation's economic decline. In a widely discussed article published in *Harvard Business Review* in 1981, professors Robert Hayes and William Abernathy concluded that we are "managing our way to economic decline."[8] Almost half of all new jobs in the 1970s were created by small businesses, particularly those in the service sector. These are precisely the firms that are hit hardest by high interest rates and tight money, and the firms that benefit least from the new tax laws.

And, finally, the internal contradiction of military spending: Reagan's social investment policy is to make the world safe for democracy. But raising military spending not only increases the investment going into the production of goods that cannot be consumed, automatically creating inflationary pressures, but building armaments requires cutting private consumption spending sharply to take the heat off interest rates. It also means reducing overall real wages so that total demand is held in check with-

8. Robert H. Hayes and William J. Abernathy, "Managing Our Way to Economic Decline," *Harvard Business Review*, July-August, 1980, pp. 67–77. See also: Paul Solman and Thomas Friedman, *Life and Death on the Corporate Battlefield* (New York: Simon and Schuster, 1983).

out resorting only to high interest. This means squeezing unions and forcing workers to accept lower wage settlements.

By the summer of 1982, the results of combining supply-side with monetarist economics had the business community moving against the supply-siders. From Wall Street's point of view, the potential of huge federal budget deficits until 1984 and 1985 portended either continued high interest rates and perhaps even depression, or continued high inflation. The tax breaks had not stimulated economic growth—precisely, the argument went, because interest rates had to stay high to hold down inflation. The response was the Tax Equity and Fiscal Responsibility Act of 1982, which raised taxes by $98 billion, in part through medical and casualty tax deductions, in part through consumer (excise) levies on cigarettes, air travel, and telephone services, but mostly through increases in business taxes. Supply-siders opposed such revenue-raising measures tooth and nail, and that severely split both Democrats and Republicans over the act. Its passage signaled a partial return to more traditional Republican, corporate-conservative economics, in which monetarist policies prevail. According to a Congressional Budget Office memorandum of July 1982, the personal tax increases and social welfare cuts in the act hit hardest those households with incomes of less than $10,000 and those with more than $80,000; but this is misleading. In fact, the lowest-income families will lose an additional $120 per year, raising that loss to about $320 annually; families earning $10,000 to $20,000 per year will lose $80 of their previously enacted $300 annual tax cut; those in the $20,000 to $40,000 range will lose about $110 of their $960 gain; those in the $40,000 to $80,-000 range will lose about $120 of their previous $1940 cut, while the $80,000-plus families will lose only $1000 of their previous $16,000 annual gain. So the bottom 47 percent of income earners still come out on the short end of the stick, and the concept of lower income taxes for the rich and corporations combined with cuts in social welfare spending—essentially the supply-side, Stockman-adjusted approach to economic development—comes out relatively unscathed.

It is this concept, along with Reagan's devotion to military spending, that made the President veto Congress' supplemental spending measure in September 1982, and that, in turn, led to a major political loss when the veto was overridden. Although the President based his veto on the "budget-busting" aspects of the measure, the real conflict was over spending *priorities,* Reagan wanting more military appropriations and Congress more social welfare.

This brings us to Reaganomics' external contradictions. Supply-siders assume that higher economic growth will filter down into more jobs for the poor and near-poor. Budget cuts will be replaced by jobs and steady income for those who formerly were on welfare. Private services will replace government handouts. But there is serious doubt that even very rapid economic growth would reach down into suffering cities and poor rural areas. Budget cuts to the poor are cuts in income, and they are unlikely to be replaced by employment in low-paying private enterprises. At some point, the reaction to such cuts will hurt the Reagan Administration politically.

At the same time, political resistance has prevented the kinds of budget cuts necessary to support rising military spending and falling taxes for corporations and the rich. Social security has not been significantly reduced, although several attempts have been made to do so. The threat of cuts in social security benefits was a key factor in many Congressional races in the November 1982 midterm elections. Threatened student-loan-program cuts brought students out against the government for the first time since the early 1970s. Democrats in Congress got the word in 1982 that taking a stand against the Economic Recovery Tax Act, round two, would be popular with their constituencies. The Reagan budget fight had little resemblance to the Democrats' collapse the previous year. By the fall of 1982, even many Republicans found it necessary to separate themselves from the President's policies on social welfare cuts and military increases. The veto of the supplemental appropriations bill was, more than anything, a response to constituencies' increasing hostility toward the Administration's emphasis on military spending over social welfare.

The most important contradiction, therefore, lies in Reagan's assumptions about Americans' acceptance of his stance on social issues. As early as September 1981, the AFL-CIO—historically not the most militant of labor organizations—organized a mass demonstration against the antilabor, antipoor aspects of the Reagan program. Women's groups became increasingly anti-Reagan and anti-Republican as the extent of Reaganomics' and the Moral Majority's war on women became clear. Environmentalists had a ready-made villain in James Watt and were able to enlist masses of new recruits. Congressional positions against increased military spending were politically popular as early as spring 1982, when the business community realized that without reducing this spending, interest rates would stay high. Well-organized resistance by the Catholic Church and student groups to Reagan's foreign policy in Central America effectively prevented direct American military intervention in El Salvador's civil war. And the nuclear-freeze movement sprang from the grass roots to become the most effective organization opposing Reaganomics' militarization policy.

Reagan's willingness to sacrifice the welfare of the vast majority (women, minorities, labor unions, and the aged) to the interests of corporate America in return for the promise of economic growth and American world power almost spontaneously re-created the New Deal Democratic coalition. Reaganomics made the lines between the people and the corporations as clear as they had been in fifty years. Support for the President's promise of corporate investment and growth means lower real wages, lower social benefits, a more polluted environment, rape of the wilderness, increased militarism and the threat of nuclear war, the reduction of women's rights, and high unemployment. As soon as people were forced to think about it in these terms, resistance *had* to set in.

However, alternative economic policies do not follow spontaneously. Corporate America is weakened but still powerful. Government has earned a bad reputation, failing time and again to resolve a long economic crisis. There is a workable alternative to Reagan's "cowboy capitalism," to use consumer advocate Mark Green's phrase, and to the state capitalism proposed by investment banker Felix Rohatyn and by economist Lester Thurow. But before we outline such a proposal, we will analyze what happened in the U.S. economy after World War II, the role of government in that economy, and how Reaganomics came to power. With that analysis, the democratic alternative should make real sense.

3 Is Government Really the Villain?

To Americans growing up in the early 1960s, just about anything seemed possible. We had the highest standard of living in the world, we dominated world trade, and our productivity and profits were rising. We thought we could eliminate poverty, stimulate economic growth with stable prices, end racial discrimination, keep the rest of the non-Communist world safe for democracy, and even conquer space—all at the same time. We also had a young President and an administration that reflected the nation's exuberance, success, and self-confidence.

Economist John Maynard Keynes' vision of harmonious capitalist development, in which labor could increase its wages and business its capital, seemed to have been attained. The Keynesian solution to the Great Depression was for government to take a much greater part in the economic system. Government would stimulate employment by injecting more money into an underutilized economy. This money in the hands of the employed would create demand for goods and get the factories producing again. Although it really took World War II to put Keynes' ideas to work, the American people came out of the Depression with a new economic philosophy: government was now economic manager, employer of last resort, and buffer against the market's inequities.

In taking responsibility for correcting the boom-and-bust aspects of capitalist economic development, government also became an important arena for working out who in our society gets what. Before the New Deal, most of those conflicts were settled in the production sector, with the government's role restricted largely to legal mediation, law enforcement, and some public education. Of course, the U.S. legal structure favored property rights over worker organizations, kept women and minorities from voting, and—apart from occasional trust-busting—promoted the monopolization of such industries as railroads, energy, automobiles, and steel against the interests of small business and family farmers. There were, nonetheless, monumental electoral-political conflicts over economic policies. Who was in charge of this "limited" government was still an important issue for labor, big and small capital, farmers, and women.

The New Deal and Postwar Development

With the New Deal, government necessarily became more pro-people. So-called free-market capitalism, already dominated in the 1920s by huge corporations employing thousands of workers, had crashed. In 1932–33, 25 percent of the labor force was unemployed. Purchasing power per capita had fallen by half between 1929 and 1933. Banks were failing and workers were marching in the streets. Government intervened to save business, but in doing so had to respond to labor organizations' demands for a greater say in the workplace. In 1935, Congress passed the Wagner Act, which recognized labor unions as legal bargaining units. In 1935, it also passed the Social Security Act, and in 1938, the Fair Labor Standards Act, providing for a minimum wage and maximum working hours. President Roosevelt went much further in extending government powers over the economy than previous administrations, including bringing the public sector into direct ownership and control of energy production and direct involvement in regional economic development (the Tennessee Valley Authority).

None of this did much for the economy (unemployment was at 18 percent in 1938), but it did instill a confidence in Americans that the government was trying to do something for *them.* They were right. Roosevelt's victories in 1932 and 1936 were not just a mandate to save jobs but to alter the nature of an unequal and harsh economy. Conditions in the private sector were changed by union-legalizing legislation—a change that produced rapid wage growth after World War II. That many unions later became impersonal bureaucracies separated from their membership does not negate their importance in extending worker rights during the 1930s, 1940s, and even today. But the most significant change initiated by the New Deal was the direct economic role played by government. Government became a source of minimal guarantees against poverty and starvation for which the private sector was unwilling to take responsibility. The Roosevelt government also acted to equalize the distribution of goods and services, both during the Depression and World War II: between 1932 and 1944 individual income inequality declined more than at any time during this century.

All this became part of a national development policy that set the conditions for economic growth after World War II. Labor and business had to behave differently toward each other even though their underlying antagonisms remained. The mass of American voters saw in the government not just a legal structure and a provider of public education but a source of economic security and management. For some groups, such as women and minorities, government also became a source of social mobility, a last resort for realizing the American dream. The New Deal expanded government into an official and legitimate battleground for human rights in an economic system based on property rights. It also brought government deeply into the production and distribution system as an allegedly "disinterested" third party arbitrating capital/labor demands for greater portions of national output. And finally, it made government the direct focus of demands by social movements for a "fair social share" through better access to good jobs, the reduction of wage discrimination, and provision for greater access to education and training.

The New Deal, no matter what its critics may say about it, promoted the growth of private enterprise under changing mid-twentieth-century social conditions. Government intervention in the economy reflected those changing social conditions. And New Deal policies served business interests as much as or more than labor and consumers. The New Deal implicitly recognized that capitalist development could not continue as a *social* organization without some mitigation of its worst effects on the labor force. With that recognition, necessary for the very legitimacy of private enterprise and of governments that uphold and promote private enterprise, the public sector increasingly became the battleground on which economic growth and distribution issues were fought.

There is also another, less pleasant, part of the story. In addition to its role in supporting the demands of social movements for increased economic and social participation, the New Deal became associated with war and empire. American military power in World War II defeated fascism in Europe and Japanese imperialism in Asia, but postwar policies mixed protecting democracy in Europe and Japan and decolonizing Africa and Asia with the expansion of U.S. capital investment and political influence in the Third World, often at the cost of blocking social and political change in those poverty-stricken countries. The Cold War made the United States the champion of right-wing dictatorships as anti-Communist bulwarks, and the opponent of any leader who even hinted at controls on U.S. investment.

Further, the development of the atomic bomb and its awesome destructive power revealed at Hiroshima and Nagasaki made the U.S. government paranoid that anyone else might have access to such weapons. This combination of anticommunism, the temporary monopoly of atomic weaponry, and the United States' new role as leader of Western Civilization gave postwar New Deal governments distinctly imperial trappings. American leadership assumed the legitimacy of its military interventionism on a world scale.

Many writers claim that such a role was consistent with post–World War II New Deal domestic policy. Military expansion had, after all, been the direct solution to the Depression. Economist

Harry Magdoff has shown that postwar military spending largely accounts for the difference between a 17 percent rate of unemployment in 1938 and the 5 percent average between 1948 and 1973. Other economists, like Samir Amin, have contended that without the profits from U.S. Third World investments and U.S. control over Third World resources, American workers would have had to take lower wage increases in the 1950s and 1960s. The Korean War and military spending increases in the early sixties did help governments solve recessions and promote economic growth. They proved the point that war is good for business (and for labor, if we exclude the fifty thousand Americans who died in Korea and the hundreds of thousands wounded). But American Empire, the nuclear arms race, and support for repressive regimes abroad are expensive propositions, both financially and morally. They are, in principle, inconsistent with America's democratic values. Eventually, Empire and militaristic anticommunism contributed to the demise of the New Deal accords.

Who Killed Liberalism?

In the twenty years after the early sixties, the enthusiasm of that era not only died but American economic reality changed. While we are still the world's greatest economic and military power, we no longer dominate the economic game. Many of our industrial products have difficulty competing even in domestic markets, and there is no longer much talk of sustained, controlled economic growth while we eliminate poverty and discrimination. The purchasing power of an average worker's wages has fallen about 16 percent in nine years, back to the same level as in 1961. The members of an American family have to work longer collectively each year just to stay even. Since 1970 we have had four recessions, two of them major, three under Republican Presidents. The unemployment rate has been higher in each succeeding recession, and even in 1982 inflation continued through the depth of the downturn. The percentage of Americans living below the poverty level stopped decreasing and began increasing by the end of the decade: between 1979 and 1981, an additional 6 million Americans joined the ranks of the poor, swelling that number to 14 percent of the population.

It was not unnatural that when the New Deal formula began to unravel in the early 1970s, government was at the center of the controversy. Business argued against too much regulation, even though most government regulatory agencies are run by representatives of big business and serve to regularize business relations more than protect consumers or workers. Consumers argued (and voted) against high taxes, even though they simultaneously fought against cuts in public funds or services that affected their particular interests. The public saw in huge government bureaucracies the specter of Big Brother—taking away income, tapping phones, supporting the lazy, crushing individual initiative, and diminishing individual rights. At the same time, social movements of minorities and women demanded greater economic participation and social rights through government intervention, and youth led the assault on war and covert intervention as an instrument of U.S. foreign policy.

The conservative answer to these difficulties is deceptively simple and accepted by a significant part of the American public: government bureaucracy and inefficiency caused the golden age of post–World War II economic growth to end. If the government would just get off people's backs and free enterprise were once more allowed to spread its wings through less government interference, America would regain the growth track. Private enterprise and the market system create—through the workings of Adam Smith's mysterious "invisible hand"—the best sort of society, one in which individuals have the liberty to do what they want and, acting as individuals, somehow produce the greatest social good. Government interferes with this process.

The failure of Reaganomics is due largely to insisting that the facts of America's economic crisis fit this conservative ideology about the relationship between government and the individual. The economic history of the postwar period and government economic and social involvement is much more complicated than the simplistic notion of government bureaucracy-against-the-people suggests. The U.S. government did not "just grow." The increase in government expenditures came about primarily in response to demands that the public sector do something about stimulating economic growth and simultaneously provide basic levels of human services to all Americans. The public sector was also called upon to help fulfill the American dream for all those who wanted to own a home or go to college, and for all those college-educated women and minorities who could not get professional jobs in the private sector. The government built highways to stimulate the automobile industry and allowed mortgage interest tax write-offs to make home ownership cheaper. The private sector has provided jobs, but the public sector has had to school the young, take care of the aged and the indigent sick, support the average 6 percent unemployed, feed the poor, subsidize private production, maintain consumer demand, employ at decent wages those higher-educated Americans who are discriminated against in private industry, protect consumers and workers against greedy entrepreneurs and corporations, and defend Americans against the perils of an alleged worldwide Communist revolution.

The relationship between private-sector control of the economy and increasing public services was—not surprisingly—a happy one as long as the economy grew at a reasonable pace, interest rates remained low, and profits were rising. Then, the profit rate of nonfinancial corporations fell sharply in the late 1960s—specifically from 1966 to 1968—and the economy destabilized after 1973. Someone had to be blamed. Government is a perfect villain. There *is* bureaucracy and some inefficiency at all levels of government. There *are* some government programs that are pork-barrel, boondoggle, and wasteful. There are also lots of tax loopholes, unnecessary regulations, and insider deals at the public's expense. Almost everyone in the country has some firsthand contact with government—either through the schools, the army, social security, unemployment insurance, the police, or taxes. The public sees government on the one hand as a necessary intermediary between consumers/workers and private enterprise, but on the other as a wasteful, powerful giant eating into people's hard-earned wages.

With a progressive taxation structure, the inflation of the 1970s drove up income taxes faster than nominal wages. At the same time, nominal wages were not rising as fast as the prices of consumer goods, so people's purchasing power fell even before taxes. Many were paying higher taxes on wages that could buy fewer goods. This "double taxation" through inflation and increasing tax rates made most middle-income Americans see increased government spending as the culprit behind their financial woes. Not only did income-tax rates rise but skyrocketing real-estate values in the 1970s also raised property taxes. People who had owned their homes for years found themselves forced to pay much higher property taxes out of incomes that seemed to be shrinking. Owners of apartment buildings passed these taxes on to their tenants in constantly increasing rents. In some states, notably California and Massachusetts, homeowners and tenants rebelled by passing statewide initiatives limiting property-tax increases.

In this atmosphere, it was not difficult for business and politicians to exploit antigovernment feelings and pin the rap on public spending for everything bad that had happened in the United States since the halcyon days of the early 1960s. The failure of American management to compete with the Japanese was somehow blamed on government regulation; unemployment and inflation was blamed on an expansionist liberal government run amuck. Are these accusations valid? We don't think so. The facts behind public-sector growth in the last fifty years and especially after World War II show inefficiency but not independence. Almost everyone in America has demanded increased public spending in some form, not only the poor and labor but private business and a middle class demanding better public schooling for its children, mortgage interest tax write-offs, and more freeways to get from suburbs to downtown.

In order to keep the economy growing and keep everyone "happy," the government increased outlays in the 1970s, hoping that somehow induced growth would outpace spending. The result was that neither business nor labor was satisfied, labor because real wages and benefits fell and business because profit rates were not as high as in the past and the prospects for long-term growth with stable prices were rather grim. Short-term speculation became a "better investment" than long-term industrial growth. Once (big) business stopped believing in the New Deal model, that model became unworkable. Indeed, once big business stops believing in any government economic management model—especially one that depends on business for its legitimacy—can that model continue to function?

Public Spending and Social Demand

Let's take a brief look at what has actually happened to the public sector in the last five decades. As shown in Table 3-1, total government spending in the United States increased from $31 billion (1972 dollars) in 1929 to $523 billion (1972 dollars) in 1982. That is, when the fivefold increase in prices between 1929 and 1982 is corrected by measuring everything in the constant purchasing power of 1972 dollars, local, state, and federal governments in 1982 spent about fifteen times the amount they spent in Herbert Hoover's day. Since the U.S. population almost doubled in those fifty years, government spending increased more than eight times per capita, from about $250 to $2260 per capita, always counting in 1972 dollars. So the growth of the public sector has been enormous in the last fifty years, almost any way we measure it.

But there are important details about this growth that cannot be overlooked: First, the U.S. public sector, unlike public sectors in other industrialized countries such as France, Great Britain, Germany, and Italy, grew during this period *without* entering directly into the production or distribution of goods and services (except for the unique case of the Tennessee Valley Authority). Second, as Table 3-1 also shows, most of the growth in government spending occurred between 1929 and 1953, and resulted primarily from a large increase in social welfare spending during the Depression and military spending jumps during World War II and the Korean

Table 3-1 Total and Per Capita Government Spending in the United States, 1929–82

Year	Total govt. spending (in billions of dollars)	Total govt. spending (in 1972 billions of dollars)	Govt. spending per capita in 1972 dollars	Govt. spending as a percent of GNP
1929	10.3	31.4	258	10.0
1933	10.7	42.6	339	19.1
1940	18.4	63.3	479	18.4
1945	92.7	244.5	1748	43.6
1948	50.5	95.3	650	19.5
1953	101.6	172.7	1078	27.7
1955	98.0	161.1	971	24.5
1959	131.0	193.8	1090	26.8
1966	213.6	278.3	1416	28.2
1973	405.3	383.5	1823	30.6
1977	624.0	446.2	2057	32.5
1979	753.2	462.7	2097	31.2
1980	869.0	490.0	2149	33.0
1981	979.7	506.1	2230	33.5
1982	1084.5	523.3	2256*	35.5

Source: Economic Report of the President, 1982, Economic Report of the President, 1983, Tables B-1, B-3, B-28, B-75. Implicit GNP price deflators were used to calculate real government spending in 1972 prices (see Table B-3). This tends to somewhat underestimate real spending in earlier years and overestimate in later years. So, for example, if the price deflator for "government purchases of goods and services" had been used, per capita spending would have been $388 in 1929, $1307 in 1953, $1806 in 1973, and $2103 in 1982. This would strengthen our case that government spending increased much more rapidly between 1929 and 1953 than between 1953 and 1981.

*Estimated.

War (1950–53). By 1953, total government spending per person had increased fourfold, to almost $1100, about one-half of what it is today. Third, since 1953, total public spending has been increasing only slightly more rapidly than the gross national product except in recession years, and most of that increase (from 27 to 31 percent of GNP) came during the Vietnam War. In fact, since the early 1970s, the total of local, state, and federal spending has been rising at about the same rate as GNP, except for the recession years of 1974–75 and 1980–82, when government spending continued to increase as real GNP growth fell.

So why all the fuss about increased government spending? If the public sector is only growing at about the same rate as the total economic output, why is its spending seen as outrageously out of line? To answer that question, we have to consider *who* is hurt by increased government spending (and its counterpart, increased taxes) and who benefits. As a first step, we can divide the public-sector budget into two parts—social welfare spending, which includes education, social security, health care, unemployment, welfare, and housing, and nonsocial welfare, which includes military spending, police and prisons, highway construction, interest on the national debt, and subsidies to agriculture. Table 3-2 shows how social welfare expenditures increased rapidly during the Depression as a percentage of total government spending, then decreased to the 1929 level after World War II, were pushed to their lowest relative level during the Korean War (26 percent of the total), and steadily increased to an all-time high percentage (58 percent) in 1977.

The last fifty years have therefore not been at all uniform in the *way* government spending has increased, and these differences are crucial as to *who* gets the benefits of the spending and *how* government benefits reach the public. During the Depression, government funds went increasingly for transfer payments to the unemployed. With World War II the funds went directly to employ people in the armed forces and in private corporations producing military hardware. The Korean War accentuated this trend. Social welfare spending grew less rapidly between 1948

Table 3-2   Government Social Welfare Spending, 1929–80

Year	Total social welfare spending (in billions of dollars)	Social welfare spending as a percent of total government spending
1929	3.9	39.0
1935	7.9	51.0
1940	8.8	47.8
1945	7.9	8.5
1948	18.7	37.0
1953	26.0	25.6
1955	32.6	33.3
1959	49.6	37.9
1966	87.9	41.1
1973	213.9	52.8
1977	361.6	57.9
1979	430.7	57.8
1980	493.4	56.8

Source: Social Security Administration, *Social Security Bulletin* (1953, 1955, 1960, 1969, 1975, 1979, 1981), generally September issue. Revised 1979 and 1980 data directly from Social Security Administration.

and 1953 than gross national product. But since 1953, the opposite has been true, especially between 1953 and 1973, when social welfare expenditures per capita—even corrected for inflation— rose 5 percent annually while gross national product per capita increased only at 2 percent per year. In the meantime, military expenditures as a percent of GNP fell between 1953 and 1960, increased again beginning with the Kennedy Administration until the winding down of the Vietnam War in the late 1960s, when they decreased until the 1981 Carter budget (and, in turn, were increased even more by the 1981 and 1982 Reagan budgets). So government investments in the young and transfers to the old and sick, the unemployed, and the poor increasingly dominated government spending from 1953 to 1979. And spending that directly benefits private enterprise declined as a percent of total government spending.

What about the *components* of social welfare spending? If we identify spending on public education as tending to benefit mainly middle- and upper-middle-income families, since their children stay in school longer, and if we identify welfare, unemployment insurance, health care (Medicare and Medicaid), social security, and housing as benefiting lower-income Americans, how have these percentages changed between 1953 and 1979? Table 3-3 suggests that during the period between 1950 and 1979, the percentage of spending on education rose and then fell sharply, due to the baby-boom bulge, while social security and unemployment insurance, public aid (welfare), and health care rose steadily in relative terms.

The growth of the U.S. public sector since World War II, particularly the increase in overall social welfare spending since 1953, means that a higher percentage of gross national product now goes directly into transfer payments and education than was true twenty years ago. The increase—8 percent of GNP in 1953 to 18 percent in 1979—appears to have gone more and more to lower-income families in the form of social security and various kinds of welfare payments. Even these rough figures show, then, that the public sector bureaucracy set up in the 1930s to combat economic depression has been responsive in the past generation—long after the Depression—to the demands of those who have not been participating "fully" in the private economy. The problem shifted from one strictly concerned with unemployment (and the threat of starvation) in the 1930s to a problem of unemployment and *poverty* in the 1950s, 1960s, and 1970s. Once the United States emerged victorious from a world war, the idea that everyone in the society had a *right* to a decent standard of living took hold.

The growth of the public sector is therefore not primarily the result of a government bureaucracy seeking to increase its power, as is often claimed in conservative ideology. Social welfare expenditures increased in response to real demands—demands that originated in social movements and that were translated into law by Congress, state legislatures, and local municipalities. These social movements take the form of labor organizations, middle-class parents' movements, the civil rights movement, and senior-citizen organizations. They turn to the public sector for general increases

Table 3-3 Social Welfare Spending by Program, 1950–79 (% of total Social Welfare Spending)

Year	Social insurance	Public aid	Health/ medical	Veterans	Education	Housing	Other	All health/ medical*
1950	21.0	10.6	8.8	29.2	28.4	0.1	1.9	13.0
1960	36.9	7.6	8.5	10.5	33.7	0.3	2.2	12.2
1965	36.4	8.1	8.1	7.8	36.4	0.4	2.7	12.4
1970	37.5	11.3	6.8	6.2	34.9	0.5	2.8	17.4
1975	42.4	14.0	6.1	5.9	27.9	1.1	2.6	17.5
1977	44.5	14.6	5.7	5.3	26.1	1.2	2.6	18.6
1978	44.4	15.1	5.8	5.0	25.7	1.3	2.7	19.3
1979	45.2	15.1	5.1	4.8	25.3	1.4	2.5	20.1
1980	46.5	14.7	5.7	4.4	24.4	1.4	2.8	n.a.

Source: U.S. Department of Commerce, *Statistical Yearbook, 1981,* Table 518. Data for 1980 from SSA.

*Sum of the health and medical components of all the various programs, particularly Health/Medical, Social Insurance, Public Aid, and Veterans.

in benefits for youth, the aged, and the poor. And, as Boston University's Frances Fox Piven and Columbia's Richard Cloward have argued, increased government intervention strengthens workers' market leverage, particularly those lower-paid workers who are likely to find themselves unemployed and susceptible to competition from the unemployed.

Of course, the demands were met in an ideological climate that committed American society to eradicating poverty and softening the worst injustices of capitalist development. This ideology was not just the result of believing that the economy could *afford* to achieve such goals. The Keynesian and New Deal heritage make the goals consistent with overall U.S. economic development: Keynesian theory dictates that the principal impediment to capitalist development is lack of consumer demand; social welfare expenditures increase demand at the same time that they are politically essential for keeping the social peace. Yet once the commitment is made to eradicate poverty, to provide security against the fears of old age, unemployment, and sickness, and to educate youth, this spending becomes an integral part of the social context in which people live out their lives. For many members of American society, it even determines how they survive from day to day. This is why David Stockman could argue in his candid *Atlantic Monthly* interview that *entitlements,* such as social security, veterans' benefits, and unemployment insurance, are politically almost untouchable. They are built into the system. And they are built into the system for all of the right reasons: the mass of Americans *want* these entitlements because the private sector has not been willing or able to provide the training, job security, basic human services, or old-age security for the great majority of American wage earners. Although there may be inefficiency in the provision of entitlements, the concept and political demands behind them are integral to American democracy.

There is another function of public-sector spending that cannot be overlooked: both nonsocial welfare and social welfare spending employ people. Approximately 16 million were employed directly in federal, state, and local government agencies in 1980, and another 8 million depended indirectly on military, health-care, and research and development subsidies to the private sector and contracts with individual private firms. Those directly employed were *not* a representative cross-section of American workers. Government employees tend to have more schooling and are more likely to work in professional jobs than private-sector workers. Women, blacks, and ethnic minorities are also "overrepresented" in such government professional jobs compared to the private sector; they also get paid relatively more in government work than in the private sector. About 40 percent of white women professionals in the labor force are employed directly in federal, state, or local government. The figure is the same for black men professionals, and rises to 60 percent for black women professionals. All this adds up to government employment that provides social mobility for women and minorities of both sexes—a social mobility that would probably not have occurred (or would have occurred only with much greater social conflict) if these groups could have found employment only in the private sector.

Again, this pattern of employment in the public sector did not occur spontaneously. In some cases, such as the teaching profession, the employment of women was the logical extension of women's child-caring role in the home. Women teachers also work for lower pay than male teachers, and hard-pressed school districts long ago found it more economical to hire women to teach primary school. But the high percentage of women and minority professionals throughout the public sector cannot be explained solely by cultural "logic" or the government's hiring of women and minorities as low-cost labor, for government jobs parallel bureaucratic positions in the private sector and government pay scales discriminate much less against women and minorities than do similar jobs in the "free market." In the postwar period, government was the principal job market that provided at least some equal opportunity to women and minorities. It did so because of social pressure from these large, discriminated-against groups for greater participation in the fruits of U.S. economic development, fruits that they could not harvest in white male-dominated private enterprise.

Government spending to the tune of 33 percent of gross national product, and direct plus indirect employment of 25 to 30 percent of the labor force, plays a crucial role in softening the effects of recessions. As the economy turns down, government spending usually does not decrease, even while the private sector is laying off labor. So a significant block of the labor force is (or was) relatively immune to recession. As tax revenues from private-sector incomes and profits decline in recessions and government salaries and transfer payments rise (unemployment compensation and welfare increase, for example), government debt also rises. In the past, when prices and interest rates tended to remain stable or even fall in recessions, an increase in government debt was consistent with a countercyclical policy that offset declining incomes in the private sector and eventually led to economic recovery. During the ensuing recovery, government deficits were reduced sharply as taxes rose relative to expenditures.

This process still works. Indeed, supply-side economics depends on it: a decrease in tax rates is supposed to generate such a stimulus to the economy that tax revenues will begin to catch up with government spending, eliminating federal deficits, reducing the demand for capital, lowering interest rates, and turning the economy "back" to the private sector. Paradoxically, the last two serious recessions (1974–75 and 1981–82) have been especially severe because the public sector did not allow government spending to play as strong a part in stimulating recovery as it had in the past. Although public debt increased rapidly in both these recessions, the Federal Reserve increased interest rates to combat an inflation that slowed but *continued through the recessions.* Reducing inflation rather than pursuing economic recovery became—at least for a time (until the impending 1976 election forced the issue)—the main goal of Republican government economic policy. Higher interest rates on the money that private banks borrow—known as the prime rate—reduced the economic growth stimulus of increased debt.

Something happened in the late 1960s and early 1970s that altered the possibilities for government policies to be effective in meeting the needs of economic growth and reducing poverty at the same time. One argument is that President Johnson tried to finance a war in Asia and keep things under control at home through the War on Poverty, but in doing so began an inflationary spiral that traditional Keynesian policy could not handle. This explanation again places all the blame on government policy, especially government spending. In reality, the events are much more complicated.

Certainly continued poverty in the richest country in the world cannot be blamed only on public policy, especially when public spending has been much more effective in increasing low incomes than private investment and employment. And although war-making power is restricted to the federal government, it would be difficult to separate government military policy from the general anti-Communist ideology pushed so heavily by U.S. private corporations and most labor unions. Many of the largest of these corporations—those President Eisenhower had in mind when he referred to the "military-industrial" complex—also have a direct economic interest in military expansion.

The corporate sector, therefore, while blaming the bureaucracy and the poor for economic problems, is itself implicated in the present crisis. Business has failed to reduce poverty and continues to discriminate against minorities and women, thereby pushing those groups to demand public-sector support. In the past thirty-five years, business has stood by and even cheered while the government expanded military spending and engaged in major wars, all at the expense of much-needed public-transit systems, urban renewal, alternative energy sources, and improved health care. The present lack of these goods and services is hurting private enterprises themselves.

But there are other aspects of corporate expansion that are as important as government spending in understanding the present crisis. There have been significant structural shifts in the American economy besides the rapid increase of social welfare spending relative to nonsocial welfare spending. These shifts began long before the 1970s and have to do with the kind of goods and services American capital is producing and where it is producing them. There have also been drastic changes in who pays taxes and how much workers earn and save. All of these factors have contributed to the decline of New Deal policies, especially since these policies did not take into account these changes as they were occurring.

4 The Changing Structure of American Capitalism

Reagan's advisers have on occasion likened their mission to JFK's New Frontier. Whatever the political payoffs of such nostalgia, it betrays an unwillingness to accept the full implications of recent U.S. economic history. Our political economy has changed drastically in the last thirty-five and even ten years. Massive numbers of married women and grown-up postwar babies entered the labor force in the 1960s and 1970s. An unsuccessful war in Asia severely eroded American dominance of world markets. Oil producers raised prices of crude oil tenfold in six years. Entire industries faded or moved from traditional locations. Inflation and unemployment occurred simultaneously as "stagflation" became a new reality. Productivity increases slowed dramatically in every economic sector.

The deception of political nostalgia is that it makes people believe in something that no longer exists, or perhaps never existed. Historical events have irreversibly affected where and how money is made in the economy, where people are employed, and how much they are paid. We are not the economy and society we were in 1960, 1930, or 1920, and wishing we were is not going to make it so. Neither are policies based on such wishes going to work, as Reaganomics has made painfully clear.

One thing we do have in common with the past is that our economy is in crisis—crisis has occurred before. In the past we have emerged from crisis, but only when its nature was understood and accepted. To solve this one, we have to analyze events *since* the JFK era rather than harking back to solutions that worked twenty years ago. The simplistic notion of blaming government for interference in an otherwise dynamic private sector avoids precisely that reality. It conveniently ignores structural changes in the private sector itself and how those influence our present economic development. It also avoids dealing with government policy as historically *part* of those changes and inseparable from them.

Before turning to government's role, however, we will outline our analysis of economic change in the postwar period. We conclude that the big private corporations which dominate our economy are more responsible for the present crisis than government or labor unions. Adam Smith notwithstanding, profit maximization by large, economically powerful, private corporations has not maximized the public good. Corporate investment and employment decisions have produced dislocation, discrimination, declining real wages, high unemployment, pollution, poor transportation systems, and run-down, crime-ridden cities—social costs that the American public, not the corporations, have to bear. The costs have become so great that it is time to think seriously about developing an alternative to big private businesses as our principal investment planners.

Postwar Economic Growth, Employment, and Wages

What actually happened when World War II ended and we moved back to a peacetime economy? Many people thought there would be another Depression. But the war had injected huge amounts of money into the economy and built an enormous manufacturing capacity, largely using public funds.

Economic growth in the postwar period averaged a 2.4 percent annual increase in gross national product per capita between 1948 and 1973 and 1.5 percent between 1973 and 1981. Consumption power, which economists call "real wages," rose 60 percent between 1948 and 1973, but has since fallen 16 percent. Productivity, which we measure here as gross national product per employed worker, also increased 2.4 percent annually between 1948 and 1973, but only 0.2 percent per year between 1973 and 1979, and fell between 1980 and 1982. So it appears that the rate of growth of per capita income, real wages, and productivity all increased at about 2.4 percent per year for twenty-five years, making average Americans about 60 percent better off materially. Since 1973, though, many of these indicators of progress have become stalled: real wages have fallen drastically, productivity increased at a lower rate and then began to fall, and economic growth has been the lowest since the late 1950s. What is going on?

Before answering that question, we should dispel the notion that economic growth in the postwar period was even. It was not. Table 4-1 shows that after the low per capita GNP growth in the 1930s (0.8 percent annually) and the World War II boom (4.5 percent annual rate), the economy continued to grow rapidly, fueled by the Korean War, but then slowed down sharply for the rest of the 1950s. There were recessions in 1949, 1954, 1958, and a milder downturn in 1960. Total GNP growth was only 2.4 percent annually from 1953 to 1959, and GNP per capita growth was only 0.6 percent per year. Beginning in the early sixties, however, the economy boomed again in the longest sustained economic expansion of the century (1960 to 1969). The expansion was fed by increases in government spending that raised the public sector's percentage of GNP from 27 to 31 percent.

There were also demographic cycles under way that had important effects on economic growth, wages, and productivity. The rise in the birth rate after the war resulted in an average 1.8 percent annual increase in population for fifteen years, between 1947 and 1962.

Women who had been pulled into the labor force during World War II returned home to bear and care for children, withdrawing from the wage economy (day-care centers were not on the national agenda). Even so, women's labor-force participation did increase throughout the 1950s, and the growth of employment

Table 4-1 Growth Rates of Real Per Capita GNP, Real Wages, and Productivity; Average Unemployment and Savings Rates, by Period, 1929–82 (%)

Years	Annual real per capita GNP growth	Annual growth in real wages	Annual growth of productivity GNP/emp. person	Average unemploy-ment rate	Average savings rate
1929–40	0.8	n.a.	0.8	n.a.	n.a.
1941–47	4.5	n.a.	1.9	3.9	16.5
1948–53	3.2	3.2	3.9	4.0	6.2
1954–55	0.8	3.0	1.9	5.0	6.3
1956–59	0.5	1.7	1.4	5.2	7.0
1960–66	3.1	1.7	2.8	5.3	6.2
1967–73	2.5	1.0	1.3	4.6	7.5
1974–79	2.0	−1.4	0.2	6.8	6.7
1980–82	0.0	−3.0	−0.3	8.1	6.2

Source: Economic Report of the President, 1982; 1983, Tables B-23, B-2, B-29, B-37, B-39. Productivity is measured by real GNP growth (column 1) minus growth of the employed labor force in the same period. Average savings rate is measured by personal savings as a percent of personal disposable income.

was limited largely to that increased participation, those men born in the 1930s and early 1940s—a period of low population growth —plus that small and diminishing group of rural workers displaced by machinery and corporate takeovers in agriculture. While population was growing at almost 2 percent per year, employment was increasing at less than 1 percent annually until the early 1960s.

These demographics created a situation of relatively low unemployment and real wages increasing more rapidly than productivity. Labor unions grew in strength. Looking again at Table 4-1, we can see that although productivity rose faster than real wages between 1948 and 1953 (both increases were very high—3.2 percent annually for real wages and 3.9 percent for the change in GNP per person employed), between 1954 and 1959 real wages rose much more than productivity. Unemployment rates by today's standards were also low, averaging 4.6 percent for all workers and 8.2 percent for blacks between 1948 and 1959. The 1950s were therefore a period of relatively slow GNP *per capita* growth, but were simultaneously marked by historically low unemployment rates and a growth in real wages that was as high or higher than productivity increases.

The demographic trends reversed in the 1960s. Population growth dropped sharply during the decade to 1 percent per year by 1968. As the children of the late forties and their mothers released from child-caring began entering the labor force, employment grew more rapidly than population for the first time since World War II. Real wages continued to increase rapidly until 1966, but less than productivity, which shot up by almost 3 percent annually. By the end of the decade and the early 1970s, employment increases began to swamp population growth: between 1966 and 1973, the labor force was growing by more than 2 percent per year, and increased by 2.3 percent annually between 1973 and 1980. Real wage increases between 1966 and 1973 fell to 1 percent a year while productivity increases also fell to 1.5 percent annually. Yet productivity was still rising faster than wages. And because of the sustained growth fueled by government spending, unemployment rates remained low despite rapid increases in employment during the late 1960s. The stage was set for the crisis that followed as the economy weakened.

In many ways, the 1960s—particularly the *early* 1960s—were an anomaly in America's recent history. Population growth had been high for more than a decade, which meant rapidly expanding domestic markets. The United States was at the height of its power, both economically and militarily, which meant that it could count on expanding its world markets as well. New entrants into the labor force were increasing slowly, so expanding production could absorb them. The age structure of the population was such that the biggest increase in public spending was on education, an expense gladly borne by the majority of Americans because they were spending on their own children, and the intake of social security taxes was greater than the payout. Real wages were still rising rapidly (although not as rapidly as in the previous decade), so paying more taxes even for the elimination of others' poverty and for massive increases in military spending was acceptable. Expanding markets, cheap energy, government subsidies for research and development, stable prices, and low interest rates all made for a high incentive to invest in increased industrial capacity. It was also during this period of continued increases in real wages that personal savings rose from about 6 percent of disposable income in 1959–60 to more than 8 percent in the early 1970s.

Wages and Employment. Changing demography contributed to important developments in the 1970s. Rapid increases in those of labor-force age, smaller families, and increasing female labor-force participation (based in part on a rejection of traditional female roles) put downward pressure on wages and increased unemployment rates. This pressure began well before 1973, but since that year, real wages have fallen at a rate of about 2 percent annually, while employment has grown at a rate of 2.3 percent per year. Between 1974 and 1981, unemployment averaged 6.9 percent for all workers and 12.5 percent for black workers. The economy therefore absorbed many more workers in the 1970s than at any time since the war, but at a cost of much lower wages per worker and increasing average unemployment rates. Part of the decrease in wages came from a lower average number of hours worked per week per worker. In the late sixties, the average employee in private industry worked 38 hours, while by 1981, that figure had dropped to 35 hours. All this combined to limit the growth of *total* real wages and salaries paid out by private industry and government to 0.4 percent annually for the seven years after 1973. Put another way, the rapid growth in the labor force slightly more than offset the decline in real wages paid per worker to produce a total increase of less than 3 percent in purchasing power in the period from 1973 to 1980 for all wage and salaried workers added together. Government employees did much worse than those in the private sector. If we subtract government workers' wages and salaries, the increase improves slightly to about 5 percent for labor in the private, nonfarm sector.

This change in the labor market was matched by a return to the multi-wage-earner family. Americans kept up their standard of living by increasing the number of people in each family who worked. Participation of women in the labor force increased to more than 60 percent. Real wages of each person working decreased, but the pre-tax *family* wage kept pace with inflation, as long as there was more than one wage earner in a family. Yet, the number of single-wage-earner households also increased, which meant that many Americans became increasingly worse off because they lived alone or were single-parent heads of household. On the one hand, then, in the 1970s we observe divorce rates increasing, but on the other, the pressure to live in a unit with more than one wage earner was also increasing.

Yet the labor force is anything but homogeneous. The different segments of the 90 million Americans on wages or salaries did not get hurt equally by the inflation of the 1970s. As we would expect, certain unionized labor groups like chemical workers—closely tied to the rapidly expanding petroleum industry—coal miners, and autoworkers all had wage increases higher than inflation. But other unionized workers, such as those in the construction industry, suffered losses in buying power even though—on average—they started out and ended up with much higher than average weekly earnings. Clerical workers lost the most: their real earnings fell by about 18 percent between 1973 and 1981.

With this type of division in the work force between labor that gets hurt by inflation and the much smaller group that is able to ride out inflation successfully, it is easy to see how the smaller group would be in favor of a federal policy that paid less attention to inflation and more to economic expansion, while the larger group would push hard for an anti-inflationary policy, even if that meant increased unemployment. The fact that certain unions were able to keep their members ahead of inflation while most of the labor force suffered also helped create resentment toward unions in general, even though many unions were not able to protect their members at all. Autoworkers' and air controllers' wages, for example, seem extraordinarily high to other wage earners; few can empathize with the hard knocks those unions took in 1981–82, mainly because most of the labor force fared much worse in the 1970s. The division within the work force, therefore, makes relatively easy union-busting by business and the present federal government, at least much easier than if unions had paid more attention to the condition of the labor force as a whole rather than just their own membership.

The increasing number of women working for wages tended to exacerbate such wage differentials. While women's percentage of the labor force has edged upward gradually throughout the end of the nineteenth and first half of the twentieth century, the pace of this change increased significantly after 1940 and even more after 1960. It took seventy years (from 1870 to 1940) for women to increase the "first" ten percentage points in the labor force, from 14 to 24 percent. Then it took about twenty-four years (from 1940 to 1964) to increase the next ten percentage points, from 24 to 34 percent. And it appears that the next ten points, up to 44 percent, will be achieved in twenty years—by 1984 (see Table 4-2). This translates into far smaller increases in the number of men than women coming to work each year: 40 million men working in 1948 became 56 million in 1982; but 15 million women in 1948 became 43 million in 1982.

Table 4-2 Comparison of Males and Females in the U.S. Labor Force, 1870–1982 (%)

Year	Males in labor force*	Females in labor force*
1870	85.6	14.4
1880	85.0	15.0
1890	82.8	17.2
1900	81.7	18.3
1910	78.8	21.2
1920	79.6	20.4
1930	77.9	22.1
1940	75.6	24.4
1948	71.5	28.5
1953	69.4	30.6
1955	68.6	31.4
1959	67.2	32.8
1966	64.4	35.6
1973	61.5	38.5
1979	58.3	41.7
1981	57.2	42.8
1982	56.5	43.5

Sources: U.S. Department of Commerce, Bureau of the Census, *Historical Statistics of the United States*, Part I, p. 129; *Economic Report of the President, 1983*, Table B-30.
*Until 1940, the labor force included all those ten years old or older; after 1940, sixteen years old or older.

Why were married women reincorporated into wage labor after being relegated to housework in the mid-nineteenth century? University of Chicago economics professor Gary Becker and other conservative economists think it was due to women's rising relative wages. Feminists like Heidi Hartmann, though, argue that women's continued *low* wages made them increasingly attractive to industry despite resistance from male workers, and that new (low-wage) jobs opened up for women in services. Women's relative wages did *not* rise between 1948 and 1981, so that incentive could not have brought them out in such large numbers. Also, the end of the baby boom in the early 1960s (and a higher marriage age) did allow older women to reenter the labor force and kept younger women in longer. But the most important causes of increased labor-force participation appear to be the legitimation of wage work by married women (a legitimation instigated by World War II and supported by a new postwar image of the "professional" woman), and, as Hartmann and others claim, relatively low female wages and the expansion of the service sector, which made clerical and sales jobs available in great numbers and induced employers to hire women into them.

So, while women now enter some traditionally male occupations, the great majority of them work in a limited group of "female" jobs, mostly in the wholesale/retail trade and various kinds of services. And women earn wages that are much lower than men's. The ratio of female to male wages has changed little despite the women's movement. In fact, it has become less equal: in the 1930s the average ratio of female to male wages was about 0.63, and in the 1960s and 1970s, the ratio was about 0.55. Even if we correct for differences in education and age between women and men in the labor force, this ratio remains at about 0.55, although it does fluctuate between public and private employment; in 1970, women earned about one-half the wages earned by males in the private sector and about 70 percent of what males earned in the public sector.

The Structure of Employment. Employment grew rapidly in the 1960s and 1970s, but more and more of this growth was in wholesale/retail trade and services, especially private services. Table 4-3 shows just how drastic these shifts in employment have been. Between 1948 and 1973, 4.5 million people entered manufacturing, and 17 million entered wholesale/retail trade, services, and finance/insurance/real estate—what we can call, in general terms, private commerce and services (private c&s). Since the late 1960s, manufacturing employment has hardly grown, but c&s jobs have continued to expand rapidly, increasing by 11 million between 1973 and 1982. As late as 1955, one out of three Americans worked in manufacturing (the figure had been as high as 38 percent in 1945); in 1966, the figure was still at 30 percent. But by 1982, only one out of five worked in manufacturing. This trend is supposed to continue, with almost all new jobs in the 1980s created in c&s.

Table 4-3 Nonagricultural Wage and Salary Workers, by Sector of Employment, 1929–82 (in millions)

Year	Total	Manufacturing	Mining	Construction	Transportation/ utilities	Wholesale/ retail trade	Finance & insurance	Private service	Government
1929	31.3	10.7	1.1	1.5	3.9	6.1	1.5	3.4	3.1
1933	23.7	7.4	0.7	0.8	2.7	4.8	1.3	2.9	3.2
1940	32.4	11.0	0.9	1.3	3.0	6.8	1.5	3.7	4.2
1945	40.4	15.5	0.8	1.1	3.8	7.3	1.5	4.2	5.9
1948	44.9	15.6	1.0	2.2	4.2	9.3	1.8	5.2	5.6
1953	50.2	17.5	0.9	2.6	4.3	10.2	2.1	5.8	6.6
1955	50.6	16.9	0.8	2.8	4.1	10.5	2.3	6.2	6.9
1959	53.3	16.7	0.7	3.0	4.0	11.1	2.5	7.1	7.1
1966	63.9	19.2	0.6	3.3	4.2	13.2	3.0	9.5	10.8
1973	76.8	20.1	0.6	4.1	4.6	16.6	4.0	12.8	13.7
1977	82.5	19.7	0.8	3.8	4.7	18.5	4.5	15.3	15.1
1979	89.8	21.0	1.0	4.5	5.1	20.2	5.0	17.1	15.9
1981	91.5	20.3	1.1	4.3	5.2	20.7	5.3	18.6	16.0
1982	89.6	18.8	1.1	3.9	5.0	20.5	5.4	19.0	15.8

Source: *Economic Report of the President, 1983*, Table B-37.

The implications of this shift for understanding our present situation should be fairly obvious. The manufacturing sector as a whole is no longer the dynamic element in our economy as far as employment is concerned. There *are* rapid-growth parts of manufacturing, like high-technology industries. And there is always the possibility that high tech will expand so much that it will become to manufacturing what the automobile industry was in the 1950s. It is also true that part of the growth in services comes from manufacturing industries separating their service divisions into new enterprises, such as General Motors Acceptance Corporation (GMAC) handling the finances for General Motors. But these caveats concerning the statistics do not change the fact that in the near future business services, health care, and wholesale/retail trade will be the great employment generators if the present development pattern persists. We are rapidly becoming a service economy. Twice the number of people now work in private- and public-health care alone than in construction. Three times more people work for McDonald's making hamburgers than are employed by U.S. Steel. So what happens in services will have a lot to do with labor-management relations, wages, and productivity.

Shifts in the labor market and the large drop in real wages after 1973 were important contributors to the demise of the New Deal accords. These policies worked well when real individual wages were rising and the principal uses of tax dollars were for educating white workers' children and the subsidization of corporate innovation and growth. As real wages fell and families worked more hours to purchase the same commodities (or worked the same or less hours and suffered consumption loss), taxes became less acceptable, especially since they were used increasingly for supporting the poor, the sick, and the aged. Middle-income families were and are mainly concerned with maintaining their standard of living in the face of inflation, which means trying to reduce their taxes and raise their wages.

Productivity, Profits, and Investment

This leads to the other side of the private-sector problem. The labor force grew slowly in the 1950s and early 1960s, and very rapidly in the late 1960s and 1970s. Real wages fell after 1973. But if the labor force was growing so quickly in the 1970s—and we should add that it was a much more highly educated labor force than was working during the 1950s' GNP expansion—why didn't GNP growth rates also increase? The stock answer, of course, is that productivity increases slowed down and have now turned negative (Table 4-1). Yet that answer only tells us that output growth is lower because the amount that each person produces is growing less rapidly than before. We have to know *why* productivity declined, not because productivity itself is necessarily the crucial issue for U.S. economic and social development, but because analyzing this decline helps us to understand what is happening in our crisis-ridden economy.

Does the cause lie in the labor force itself? If the labor force is more educated, its productivity should be higher, not lower. It is possible that each worker is less willing to work hard, and there have been many claims that the labor force is lazier today than it was ten years ago. However, in *Accounting for Slower Growth* (Washington, D.C.: Brookings Institution, 1979), Edward Denison, a leading analyst who has long grappled with the productivity problem, argues that less effort by workers is not the root cause of declining productivity growth. Denison cannot come up with an exact answer to the productivity puzzle (he believes that a number of small effects may have combined to produce slower growth), but his analysis and others suggest that changes on the investment side of the economy in the 1970s are now causing our economic problems.

Productivity and Employment Structure. George Gilder, author of *Wealth and Poverty* (New York: Harper & Row, 1980), is only partly right when he argues that massive restructuring of American employment has lowered productivity growth. Since

Table 4-4 Real Gross National Product Per Employed Person (RGNPPEP) and Growth in RGNPPEP, by Sector, 1948–80

Year	Manufacturing (1972)	Wholesale/retail trade (1972)	Private services (1972)	Government services (1972)
1948	7782	8387	11,058	12,140
1953	9206	9206	10,810	14,591
1955	9804	9819	10,903	13,869
1959	10,251	10,396	11,380	12,840
1966	13,276	11,841	11,484	12,676
1973	16,104	12,717	11,225	11,391
1979	17,523	12,282	10,444	10,931
1980	17,291	11,912	10,251	10,816
RGNPPEP Annual Growth Rates, by Sector (%)				
1948–53	3.4	1.9	−0.4	3.7
1954–55	3.2	3.3	0.4	−2.6
1956–59	1.1	1.4	1.1	−1.9
1960–66	3.8	1.9	0.1	−0.2
1967–73	2.8	1.0	−0.4	−1.5
1974–79	1.4	−0.6	−1.2	−0.7
1980	1.0	−0.9	−1.3	−0.7

Source: Economic Report of the President, 1982, Tables B-11, B-37.

the early 1950s, most of the increase in the labor force has been absorbed into the service sector, as we have shown in Table 4-3. And Table 4-4 shows that after 1959, productivity growth in manufacturing was much more rapid than in either wholesale/retail trade or services. But by the 1970s, declining real wages were partially matched by a decline in productivity increases in all sections, including manufacturing. The increase in manufacturing-sector GNP per employed worker slowed down from 3 percent annually from 1948 to 1973, to 1 percent after 1973. Services —where about 80 percent of new workers find jobs—were particularly hard hit. The contribution to GNP of each employed worker in private commerce and services (which include wholesale/retail trade, banking/insurance/real estate, and nongovernment services) increased only by 1.2 percent per year between 1948 and 1973, and decreased 0.6 percent annually from 1973 to 1980. If we exclude the banking/insurance/real estate component of that sector, the annual growth rates are 1 percent between 1948 and 1973 and −1.2 percent from 1973 to 1980, reflecting the rapid growth of banking and real estate after 1973. So output per worker in that part of the economy which already employs about one-half the private labor force is decreasing.

Thus, the *increased* annual shift of the labor force from "high productivity growth" manufacturing to "low productivity growth" wholesale and retail trade and services therefore does have some effect on average productivity increases from year to year even if output per employed worker *within* manufacturing had also been falling from 1973 to 1980.

The expansion of private commerce and services relative to traditional employment in manufacturing and construction is not a temporary phenomenon. Employment in wholesale/retail trade and services can be expected to continue increasing at a rapid rate. The U.S. Labor Department predicts that most new jobs in the 1980s will be in those sectors. Since the growth of jobs in government may have ended, what happens in private-sector commerce and services will be important for productivity and wage growth, especially under an anti-public-employment conservative or neoliberal economic policy.

Productivity and Capital Structure. In 1981 *Business Week* agreed that the main trends in the U.S. economy changed dramatically between the 1960s and 1970s, in what it called a significant *restructuring* of private-sector growth. This restructuring involved a shift in manufacturing from old-line industries to high technology, a shift in profits from agriculture and old-line manufacturing to the energy sector, highly differentiated rates of investment in different sectors, and a rapid shift of output and employment growth from the U.S. Northeast/upper Midwest to the South and West. According to *Business Week*, the sectors of the U.S. economy have "spun apart." It claimed that this has been due largely to rising energy prices since 1973: High-energy-consuming old-line industries and agriculture have had their profits eroded, and have had to restructure the methods of producing the goods and services that the public demands; high energy prices have jacked up profits in the energy-producing enterprises, concentrating capital there rather than in manufacturing, agriculture, and services. As a result, labor is replacing capital, and productivity growth is declining. The conclusion of this process, said *Business Week,*

> depends on what happens to energy prices. Right now the entire industrial world has gained a breather on oil prices. But even if price rises in the future prove to be modest, as most experts forecast, the forces for restructuring have already been set in motion by past oil price increases, and it will take years for them to work through the economic system. (June 1, 1981, p. 62.)

Edward Denison disagreed. In *Accounting for Slower Growth,* he contended that energy price increases lowered U.S. productivity growth in the post–1973 period by only 0.1 percentage points, a small amount relative to the overall decline. But even if Denison were correct in his estimate of the direct effect of higher energy prices on productivity, *Business Week* showed clearly that high energy prices have concentrated capital in energy-producing companies. Between 1964 and 1981, the percentage of all nonfinancial corporate profits concentrated in oil and gas alone rose from 21 to 36 percent. Although this fraction is projected to fall in the eighties as oil prices rise more slowly (or even fall), it will still stay above 30 percent.

The energy industry's share of capital spending in the mid-sixties was 16 percent, and only 21 percent as late as 1976; but in 1981, as much as 30 to 35 percent of business investment came from this source (*Business Week,* June 1, 1981). So oil and gas companies will continue to play a dominant role in determining U.S. development. Their investment policies will be instrumental in Americans' lives for decades to come. Add to this the fact that financial corporations increased their share of domestic corporate profits from about 10 percent in 1965 to 18 percent in 1980 *(Economic Report of the President, 1982),* and it is obvious that capital markets underwent a drastic shift in the 1970s. These shifts have placed enormous economic power in the hands of oil/gas producers and financial institutions.

The current debt crisis has revealed that an important source of the financial sector's profits was Arab oil money placed in U.S. banks and then lent at high interest rates to Third World newly industrializing countries (NICs) such as Mexico, Brazil, and Argentina. This sheds new light on the investment policies of U.S. financial institutions and the double role of rising oil prices in the U.S. economy. On the one hand, increases in oil prices increased costs of production and contributed to reduced demand for consumption goods (the increases acted as a tax on consumers)—both factors tended to reduce profits for industrial and agricultural producers. On the other hand, higher oil prices raised profits for oil and gas producers (as well as other energy producers) and for banks, since banks obtained a large new source of capital just as personal savings growth slowed down. The large banks assumed correctly that the U.S. government would bail them out in case of a foreign government threat of default (as they are now being bailed out through increased U.S. contributions to the International Monetary Fund). So they could afford to take the high risks associated with foreign loans and get the high interest rates associated with such high risk loans. These loans, in turn, financed increased economic growth in the NICs, increasing demand for U.S. industrial exports and contributing significantly to the U.S. growth rate in the late 1970s.

Higher oil prices were therefore crucial in shifting capital from one sector to another. For the banks, they indirectly formed the basis of increased profits. The fact that so much of the newly available capital was being invested abroad lowered the potential capital available domestically. Banks thus have a vested interest in high oil prices—the present glut and falling oil prices, combined with the inability of the NICs to repay their loans, has all the makings of a world financial crisis.[1]

Business Week seems to underplay the fundamental structural problem wrought by these recent changes. Capital has become concentrated *outside* the job-creating sectors. Oil/gas industries and financial institutions (including real estate) employ a very small fraction of the American labor force (about 6 to 7 percent). Even if we add another 5 percent of the labor force which is indirectly employed by those industries because of the construction and services they require, it is obvious that investment of this capital *outside* the sectors themselves has much more of an impact on jobs and growth than what takes place inside.

If, for example, oil companies decide to invest more abroad or speculate in real estate or invest more in the Southwest, these decisions have enormous repercussions on the availability of jobs and the kinds of jobs available. Similarly, private financial institutions are wielding increasing power over the economic development process. *Who* has the capital in the American economy has therefore changed drastically in the last decade, and this change will have profound effects on the economy's future development and productivity growth.

Productivity and Investment. MIT economist Lester Thurow has argued that productivity is declining because "veins of ore," particularly the labor shift from agriculture to industry, are running out. Energy itself is becoming more expensive to mine. Thus, American society must find new, highly productive veins, such as high technology and its application to manufacturing and services, and this will revitalize the economy. True enough. Some veins are running down: energy sources are becoming more expensive to extract, and we have placed constraints on working conditions and

1. The fact that manufacturing and agriculture were hurt by rising oil prices whereas oil and gas plus finance profited from it does much to explain why Denison's data show such a small overall effect on productivity of the oil price increase, and why other economists like Harvard's Dale Jorgenson, who concentrate on manufacturing industry, can claim that the oil price increase is crucial to understanding productivity declines.

Table 4-5   Profit Rate of Nonfinancial Corporations and Real Investment, 1955–81 (%)

Year	Rate of Return on Stockholders' Equity*		Real Investment (as % of GNP)
	Before Tax	After Tax	
1955	13.1	6.2	9.3
1959	10.5	5.1	8.8
1962	11.2	6.1	9.0
1965	15.4	9.5	10.5
1966	15.5	9.6	11.0
1967	13.4	8.2	10.4
1968	13.8	8.0	10.4
1969	12.5	7.1	10.7
1970	8.8	4.7	10.5
1972	10.5	6.2	10.2
1973	12.8	8.3	11.0
1977	10.2	6.3	10.2
1979	10.2	6.6	11.5
1980	8.4	5.5	11.3
1981	7.7	5.1	11.4

Source: Economic Report of the President, 1983, Table B-88.
*Corporate profits corrected for inflation effects divided by the net worth of physical capital valued at current replacement cost. Samuel Bowles and Herbert Gintis, "The Crisis of Liberal Democratic Capitalism: The Case of the United States," Politics and Society, Vol. II, no. 1 (1982), pp. 51–93, report rates of profit as follows:

Year	Before Tax	After Tax
1948	15.6	7.9
1950	15.6	6.1
1955	14.5	6.4
1959	12.2	5.6
1965	15.9	9.1
1972	10.7	5.8
1977	9.5	4.9

environmental quality which increase the costs of production in manufacturing and services. On the other hand, the largest single cost for most industries—labor wages—has been falling in real terms in the 1970s, so that "vein" is becoming cheaper to mine. Why is this not revitalizing the economy?

Let's look at Thurow's argument a different way: if veins of ore are declining, the returns to investment (profits) in traditional industries should also decline. In fact, the *overall* profit rate did decline in America, but not in the 1970s, as this version of Thurow's analysis implies (see Table 4–5). Average profit rates rose in the early 1960s and then fell sharply in the late 1960s. Thurow's analysis may be right for this earlier period: in part profit rates increased in the expansion of the early 1960s because the spread between productivity and labor was so large, and declined later in the decade because that spread closed. But, surprisingly, the increased spread between wage and productivity increases in the 1970s (see Table 4-1, p. 63) did not raise profit rates significantly. The difference between wage and productivity growth was 1.1 percent per year from 1960 to 1966, fell to 0.3 percent between 1967 and 1973, and rose to 1.6 percent from 1974 to 1979, and to 2.7 percent in 1980–82. This means that despite wages falling drastically relative to productivity, the profit picture improved little. For Thurow, then, rising energy and other production costs would have had to offset falling real wages in the 1970s, holding profits down in traditionally dynamic industries.

Yet, although profits did recover somewhat after 1972 from their dive in the late 1960s, the business enthusiasm and higher investment per employee that should have followed such a recovery never appeared. Thus, the "declining vein" explanation of falling productivity is only part of the story. The other, and more important, part lies in the overall *slowdown* in business investment in the 1970s and the *type* of investment made during this period. Declining veins reflected in rising energy prices have something to do with both slowdown and investment shift. But even more crucial is the fact that business changed its strategy

from the postwar tradition of investment that raised labor productivity (accompanied by increasing wages). Instead, it began investing capital to lower labor costs and maximize short-run profits by
speculating in property and energy production.

Gross domestic private investment rose from about 9 percent of
GNP in the 1950s and early 1960s, to 10.5 to 11 percent in the late
1960s, and has stayed up there even in the 1970s despite falling
corporate profit rates in the preceding years. One reason for the
continued relatively high investment rate in the late 1960s was
that capital was readily available. The increasing wages during
that period produced a higher savings rate (see Table 4-1, p. 63).
People had a lot of money in their pockets and raised their savings
rate to the highest level since World War II. Not only that, but the
inflation that began in the late 1960s made the real cost of borrowing fall. For example, mortgage rates rose to about 7 to 8 percent,
but a 4 percent inflation made the real mortgage rate (the nominal
rate minus inflation) about 3 to 4 percent, lower than a decade
earlier. Ready availability of capital from increased savings and a
relatively low cost of capital kept investment high for at least a few
years despite falling profit rates.

But if we look at gross investment another way, we see that the
picture changed after 1972 to 1973. Although the investment *rate*
stayed about the same (11 percent of GNP) even after 1973, the
amount business was investing *per employee* dropped sharply.
Real non-residential gross private investment *per employed
worker* increased at a 0.7 percent annual rate in the 1950s, 5.4
percent in the early 1960s, 1.0 percent from 1966 to 1973, and an
average 0.2 percent annually from 1973 to 1979. So American
business invested the same percentage of GNP that it had since
the mid-1960s, but the absolute amount was not high enough in
the 1970s to keep up with an expanding labor force.

A direct measure of the change in capital per worker is the
growth of plant and equipment available for each worker in different industries. Net capital per worker in nonmanufacturing industries increased at 2.5 percent annually in 1948–59 when the wage
labor force in nonmanufacturing was only growing at a 1.8 per-

Table 4-6   A. Gross and Net Stock of Fixed Nonresidential Private Capital per Employee, 1948–79 (in 1972 dollars)

Year	Gross Stock of Capital/Employee		Net Stock of Capital/Employee	
	Manufacturing	Nonmanufacturing	Manufacturing	Nonmanufacturing
1948	11,530	17,980	6,430	8,910
1953	12,380	19,130	6,850	10,180
1955	13,780	19,980	7,520	10,850
1959	15,540	20,770	8,340	11,600
1966	16,210	24,010	9,310	14,350
1973	19,470	26,500	10,710	16,080
1979	23,340	26,790	13,340	15,580

Source: Gross and net capital stock from U.S. Department of Commerce, *Survey of Current Business,* Vol. 61, no. 2 (February, 1981), p. 59. Number of wage and salary workers from Table 4–3, above. Net stock of capital equal to gross stock minus depreciation.

B. Growth of Real Capital Stock per Employee and Productivity, 1948–79 (percent)

Year	Capital Stock per Employee				Productivity	
	Manufacturing		Nonmanufacturing		Manufacturing	Total
	Gross	Net	Gross	Net		
1948–59	2.7	2.6	1.3	2.5	2.5	2.6
1960–73	1.6	1.8	1.7	2.3	3.3	2.2
1974–79	3.1	3.7	0.2	−0.5	1.4	0.5

cent annual rate, decreased slightly to 2.3 percent annually in 1959 to 1973 when the labor force was growing at a higher 3.0 percent every year, but began decreasing at a 0.5 percent annual rate in 1974 to 1979 when the labor force was still growing as quickly as in the 1960s (3.5 percent). Like overall investment, growth of capital stock in nonmanufacturing failed to keep up with labor force growth after 1973 (see Table 4-6, p. 81).

There are several trends contained in these numbers, and we have to separate them out in order to understand what happened. First, total investment per employee slowed down sharply after 1973. This cannot be blamed on rapid labor force growth alone because labor had been increasing almost as quickly in the late 1960s.

Second, there were significant differences in investment patterns among different economic sectors after 1973: non-manufacturing slowed down its spending on new plant and equipment whereas manufacturing increased its spending. Even so, productivity growth also slowed in manufacturing. Thus the explanation of decline may be different in different types of industry.

Third, as we mentioned already, there were shifts of labor force from high productivity growth manufacturing to low growth wholesale/retail trade and services. Although these shifts had also been occurring in the 1960s, they were accentuated in the 1970s.

Outside of manufacturing, capital stock per employee stagnated in the 1970s and this halted the increase in capital per employed person that had characterized the postwar period. In non-farm, non-manufacturing business (dominated by wholesale/retail trade and services), the average real value of structures and equipment available per employed person had leveled off by the mid-1970s. Table 4–6 shows that in 1973 each employee in non-manufacturing business had about $16,000 of net capital stock (measured in 1972 dollars) to work with; by 1979, the figure had decreased. It appears, therefore, that productivity increases slowed down in non-manufacturing business partly because there was a significant slowdown in the amount of investment per employee.

But in the manufacturing sector, the relation between growth of capital per employee and productivity is more complex. Net capital stock per employee *increased* from $10,700 per worker in 1973 to $13,300 in 1979. Yet productivity measured by sector GNP per employed worker increased by only 1.4 percent annually in that six year period, compared to a 3.3 percent annual increase from 1959 to 1973 (3.8 percent between 1959 and 1966 and 2.8 percent from 1966 to 1973). Looking again at Table 4-6, we see that fixed plant and equipment per employee in manufacturing grew relatively quickly in the 1950s and so did productivity. But in 1960 to 1973, the net stock of capital per employee grew relatively slowly, while productivity increased rapidly. This productivity increase may have been the result of the large investment in the 1950s. Yet, in the 1970s, despite rapid growth of capital stock per employee in the late 1960s and 1970s, productivity growth slowed down drastically.

Low productivity growth in manufacturing in the 1970s may be explained if we assume that most of the increased stock of plant and equipment went (a) to replace high-energy consuming with low-energy consuming machinery, (b) for moves from high-cost to low-cost labor regions in the U.S., and/or (c) for production abroad.[2]

All three types of investment are designed to raise the return to capital by lowering costs rather than by increasing labor productivity. They are perfectly sensible investments—particularly those needed when the price of energy increased—but they do not necessarily raise productivity. Rather, they are profit-motivated, and in the case of building new plants in low labor-cost, non-unionized regions (domestically and abroad), also are designed to take advantage of lower wages and may even lower productivity. The important factor in such investment is the

2. Capital spending abroad by majority-owned affiliates of U.S. companies did, in fact, increase in 1972–80, especially in manufacturing and petroleum, but no more rapidly than in domestic manufacturing. Spending by manufacturing affiliates rose from $7–20 billion (current dollars) in this period as compared to an increase in total manufacturing spending on new plant and equipment of $35–116 billion in the same period (*Survey of Current Business,* September, 1981). Thus, it is least likely that low productivity growth is caused by spending abroad.

spread attained between wages and productivity, not productivity alone. The New Deal accords were built around higher profits combined with higher productivity. In this way both profits and real wages could rise. In the 1970s—even with an increasing real value of capital per worker in manufacturing—the investment was such that productivity increases slowed down and real wages per employee fell. Of course, the accords had been fraying all along. Manufacturing moves overseas and to the South and West did not begin in the 1970s. Yet it was during this last decade that the emphasis on investment in lowering costs became the norm rather than the exception.

In terms of investment, then, two kinds of changes took place in the 1970s that apparently reflected a new approach by business to the economy. On the one hand, something happened in the late 1960s and early 1970s that made business generally less bullish on America. The change in attitude toward long-term, productivity-increasing investment has left American business struggling to compete against aggressive foreign competition and has brought our economy about as close to its knees as any time since the Great Depression. This is observable even within the manufacturing sector, a sector where overall spending on new plant and equipment went up in the 1970s. Crucial industries like steel and autos simply held back on productivity-raising investments while the Japanese, Europeans, and some Third World countries such as Korea and Brazil were investing frantically in exactly those industries. Productivity growth slowed down in American manufacturing primarily because management was interested in lower labor costs and acquiring other firms (U.S. Steel's purchase of Marathon Oil, for example), rather than investing in rapid productivity increases. As a result, productivity growth fell as sharply in manufacturing as in services or wholesale/retail trade.

James Balanoff, a former director of District 31, United Steelworkers of America, writing in the weekly newspaper *In These Times* (January 20–26, 1982), noted bitterly: "Our steel industry has not remained competitive with foreign steel companies, but not for the reason they [steel executives] claim. Their game plan,

the outlines of which have been clear to any knowledgeable ob-
server for many years, has been to run a certain percentage of
their American plants into the ground, cutting wages wherever
possible, avoiding pollution controls as long as possible and bleed-
ing these plants and these communities as much as possible in
order to finance expansion elsewhere and diversification. . . .
American steel companies have been investing heavily in petro-
chemicals, natural gas and natural resources all over the world
since the mid-1960s. Much of their investment in steel has been
in foreign operations. Armco has built mills in Argentina; U.S.
Steel has built mills in Brazil and Colombia and supervised construction of an integrated steel works in Taiwan."

Why did business go bearish and shift from productivity-increasing to cost-reducing investment?

For one thing, profit rates fell and then did not rebound to the
high mid-1960s levels. The decline to an average 10 percent profit
rate began to look permanent. Business was not happy with the
new situation. Profits also shifted to oil and gas companies after
1973, so it was this highly concentrated industry that had a much
greater percentage of available private investable capital after
that year. Higher oil prices did not reduce the average profit rate;
they shifted absolute profits to oil and gas producers, processors,
and distributors from those industries that could not pass along
higher energy costs to the consumer. Services were not among
those high-energy-consuming industries, yet investment per
worker went down in that industry.

Business was also trying to turn around a government economic
policy that had unintentionally helped produce higher wages and
employee benefits at the expense of profit. Government policy
was also blamed for inflation, but popularized mythology about
inflation hurting business and causing it anxiety does not make
much sense: European investors have lived comfortably with relatively high rates of inflation for years. Yet, whatever government
policy had done or had not done, American business wanted a
better deal after 1973 and held back its productive investment.
This put a drag on business expansion and successfully pushed

down real wages in occupation after occupation.

An investment strategy that concentrates on lowering labor costs to increase profits obviously cannot be sustained indefinitely. It means lowering demand, and unless the United States intends to become increasingly an export economy, lower demand at home means lower growth. On the other hand, as a short- or medium-run approach to "rationalizing" the economy on "firmer ground," union-busting and real-wage reduction might mean higher profit rates for those companies that can survive the shaking-out period implied by such a strategy. Supply-side economics, as we have seen, claims that real wages can fall in the short run and demand be sustained by cutting personal income taxes. But as we have also seen, the whole idea is based on false premises. The real purpose of the policy is to allow blatantly pro-business government administrators to cover for business while business works through its attempt to raise profits at any social cost.

Can High Tech Save Us? At the same time, there has been a sharp increase of investment and employment in rapidly rising productivity electronics. But most Americans will continue to work in other industries. The real impact of high tech will be the degree to which it changes and expands service industries. *Business Week* is optimistic that these changes will be instrumental in turning around the productivity decline:

> In sharp contrast to much of manufacturing and agriculture as well as its own poor performance in the past, the service sector will shine during the 1980s, helping to offset the other weaknesses in the economy. Output and employment will rise steadily as demand for services burgeons both domestically and internationally. And productivity, long the most critical problem for service, will finally grow briskly as more advanced technology and modern management techniques are introduced. (June 1, 1981, p. 82).

The technology already exists to improve productivity in the service sector. However, *Business Week*'s projection of private-sector service expansion depends a great deal on a long-term increase in demand. There are certain trends, such as the aging of the population, that will contribute to this increase, particularly in health care. But there are other trends, such as the decline in workers' real income, which unless sharply reversed will dampen demand. It is also unclear just how much of the new technology will actually be adopted in the next ten years, and whether it will be adopted "efficiently." The *Business Week* analysis depends implicitly on higher productivity being passed on in lower prices of equivalent services or, possibly, in higher quality services for the same price.

However, technology adoption is a risky business and plenty of mistakes are made. There are winners and losers. Usually, in a transition process, the correct guessers pull ahead and the wrong guessers fall by the wayside. Sectors concentrate. If this process takes place in services, concentrated industries may not pass price reductions along; rather, profits may rise for those who survive in a market where demand increases slowly along with rising prices. Finally, there is no guarantee that capital will move into services as quickly as *Business Week*'s forecast implies.

In order to absorb all that labor force *and* raise productivity, capital investment per employee in services has to increase rapidly. Although profits in the service sector have remained high, investment growth per worker between 1973 and 1980 was negative. Why should this low investment rate change so radically in the next decade? And where is the capital to come from to finance increased investment in services? Finance capital would have to shift radically from speculation and high tech to even more risky service innovations. The fact is that the capital for the enormous investment required will have to come from outside the nonfinancial service enterprises. Service-sector productivity will therefore continue to grow slowly despite innovations that can increase productivity rapidly in some of its subsectors (for example, telecommunications) and in many individual service enterprises.

As children of the baby boom and married women began to work, the gap between the capital-accumulation and labor-employment sectors of the economy accentuated the impact on wages of large increases in the labor force. Increased energy prices certainly affected old-line industries, especially since their production processes were organized around cheap fuel. But the main effect of high energy prices was to concentrate capital in the energy sector. Much of this capital has gone to search for more energy, purchase other forms of energy, purchase other enterprises, and speculate in real estate. Little of it seems to have gone or to be going into renovating capital equipment in old-line industries or even into increasing productivity in the service sector.

But more important, the emphasis on high tech and other "sunrise" industries does not by itself address the last decade's general business-investment strategy and the implications of that strategy for employment, consumption, individual security, community life, and government revenues. Business has given up on the New Deal accords and is in the process of trying to raise profits through lower costs. What makes the technology fans believe that high tech will continue producing in America when threatened by Japanese competition? Or that high-tech industries will not move from state to state looking for better deals (as they already are doing), forcing labor to become nomadic in its search for work? And if other industries are pushing for lower labor costs, where is the increased demand to come from for these high-tech products? Will people substitute microcomputers for shelter and food? Will businesses invest in computers when the demand for their goods sputters along in a weak, crisis-ridden economy? And if investment in computers grows, the widespread adoption of computers in other sectors could add to the unemployment problem.

Regional Shifts. Moves to regions of the country that offer a better "business climate" leave other regions—first the Northeast and now the upper Midwest—stricken with much higher than average unemployment, declining cities, and a lesser tax base for public services. Economists Barry Bluestone and Bennett Harrison call this "corporate flight."[3] Not only the Northeast and Midwest have been affected, however. For example, the Georgia Pacific Company now ships Oregon logs to Georgia to be processed

3. Barry Bluestone, Bennett Harrison, and Lawrence Baker, *Corporate Flight* (Washington, D.C.: The Progressive Alliance, 1981).

into lumber, having closed down its Northwestern mills, thus helping destroy one of Oregon's most important industries. High-tech industries are moving from California to Texas (and to Oregon) in search of lower housing costs for its executives and engineers.

There are two distinct parts to the regional-shift problem. The first is the issue of capital shift from "sunset" to "sunrise" manufacturing industries and from manufacturing as a whole to oil/gas and financial corporations, which we have already discussed. Old-line manufacturing industries have declined partly because the management of these companies allowed them to become obsolete. Foreign competition took care of the rest. Some of these manufacturing industries—like textiles, lumber, and shoes—move south, but others like the steel and auto industries—just close down. On the other hand, growing industries such as gas and oil are located away from the traditional industrial centers. Their massive accumulation of profits have made the Southwest a particularly fast-growing area. Other industries have located around this new capital concentration. High-tech industries have produced a similar, though much smaller, phenomenon. And in some cases, high tech has located in previous growth areas like California (military, entertainment, agriculture, and tourism) or depressed areas like New England. Unemployment rates in New England during the 1981–82 recession have been distinctly lower than in 1974–75 because most old-line industries had already died in that first downturn.

The second part of the problem is the shift away from unionized labor and states where labor has local political power. Orthodox economic theory argues that investment decisions are based on management's meticulous examination of the relative costs of doing business in alternative locations, and choosing those sites which minimize costs (assuming that markets are available for the firm's products or service). It follows that those communities which offer the least-cost package of inputs will attract capital from higher-cost areas. There is evidence to support the least-cost notion, but Bluestone and Harrison argue persuasively that business tends to locate with other factors primarily in mind, particu-

larly "business climate." A good business climate is a more important part of the location decision than wages, energy costs, or
anything else.

As they look behind the business-climate theory, however, it
appears that what business is really interested in is escaping labor
unions and states where labor unions have powerful friends in
government. A great deal of evidence indicates that the Frostbelt-
to-Sunbelt shift is largely a response to unions and labor activity
in the North; second, in the world economy, multinational corporations are attempting to organize the international division of
labor in order to play off workers of one nation against those of
another. Therefore, some companies have fled the Northeast and
upper Midwest because of the traditionally more "organized,"
higher-wage, and higher-educated labor force in those regions.
Southern states offer a different tradition: no unions, labor docility,
and lower wages.

The result of such shifts in the 1970s have been dramatic: between 1969 and 1976, Frostbelt firms destroyed about 111 jobs
through plant closings for every 100 new jobs they created, while
companies in the South and West shut down 80 jobs while opening
100 (Bluestone, Harrison, and Baker, 1981, p. 26).

The epitome of "corporate flight," however, is the shift overseas
—over the long term—of old-line industrial capital (as well as
energy and financial capital). U.S. direct investment abroad in
current dollars rose from $12 billion in 1950 to $32 billion in 1960
to $75 billion in 1970 to $137 billion in 1976 to $188 billion in 1979
to $216 billion in 1980 and to $227 billion in 1981.[4] This investment represented 22 percent of gross private domestic investment in 1950, 43 percent in 1960, 54 percent in 1970, 53 percent
in 1976, down to 45 percent in 1979, up to 54 percent in 1980, and
down to 48 percent in 1981. While it appears that in the late 1970s
foreign investment was down from its relative highs in the early
part of the decade (1980 seems to have been an exceptional year

4. For the 1950 to 1976 figures, see U.S. Department of Commerce, *Survey of
Current Business*, February, 1981, p. 50. For the 1979 to 1981 figures, see *Survey
of Current Business*, August, 1982, p. 12.

because of unusually low GPDI), it still represents a significant flow of funds out of the domestic economy.

The shift in investment has been marked by an important change in what happens to the profits of capital going abroad. Until World War II, U.S. overseas investment was largely in extractive industries, with profits repatriated to the United States. Economist Paul Baran argued that although capital investments abroad did not create jobs at home, those investments brought home profits many times greater than the original capital outflow and ultimately helped raise wages in the United States relative to wages in less-developed countries.[5] After the war, there was a gradual shift in U.S. foreign investment to *industrial* production both for reexport back to the United States and for foreign markets themselves. In this new situation, American companies created in foreign countries branches that borrowed abroad, borrowed in the United States, used profits created in the United States to invest overseas, repatriated profits to the United States, and simultaneously invested in foreign securities, in U.S. Treasury notes, and wherever interest was highest. These enterprises, in other words, became *transnational* in their operations, and their profits no longer had a "home" in the old sense. For example, First National City Bank is a U.S. corporation but makes more than 50 percent of its profit abroad. Much of this profit is not only made overseas, it is reinvested there.

The other important shift that took place in the 1950s was from U.S. foreign investment in the Western Hemisphere to Europe and eventually Asia. For example, in 1950, about 70 percent of all U.S. direct foreign investment was in Canada and Latin America, but by 1970 this had fallen to about 45 percent, in 1976 to 42 percent, and by 1981 38 percent.[6] Meanwhile, the European share had risen from 15 percent in 1950 to 30 percent in 1970 to 40 percent in 1976 to 45 percent by 1980. From a negligible share in 1950, investment in Asia (excluding Australia and New Zealand)

5. Paul Baran, *The Political Economy of Growth* (New York: Monthly Review Press, 1957).
6. *Survey of Current Business,* op. cit.

rose to 7 percent of the total in 1976, where it stayed until 1980.

The European shift was correlated with the change to foreign investment for local market production. But an interesting development during the 1960s was the extension of this investment in local markets to Latin America (automobile production in Brazil and Mexico, for example). Further, more and more U.S. companies fled to low-cost labor zones to produce goods for export back to the United States. Hong Kong, Korea, Taiwan, Singapore, the Philippines, the Mexican border, and Brazil all became "platforms" for cheap U.S. exports to the home market. A high percentage of foreign trade in the world now consists of trade internal to transnationals (for example, petroleum shipped from Gulf Oil's wells in the Persian Gulf to refineries on the U.S. East Coast or from a high tech's printed circuit plant in Taiwan to its missile-component assembly plant in California) and industrial countries' plants overseas exporting to home markets (Zenith television sets produced in Asia but sold in the United States).

By 1973 nearly 80 percent of U.S. total direct investment involved U.S. ownership or control of foreign-based enterprise. The vast bulk of the investments are now in the form of wholly —or largely—owned foreign affiliates of U.S. corporations. And foreign investment is overwhelmingly the province of the giant, oligopolistic corporations. There is much greater domination of foreign investment than domestic by such large corporations.

It is difficult to tell what percentage of profits made by U.S. companies overseas is reinvested in the United States, but we do know that a higher and higher percentage of corporate pre-tax profits is made outside this country. Between 1960 and 1973, this figure rose from 6 to 13 percent, and between 1973 and 1980, the rise continued from 13 to 16 percent.[7] Given the investment trends of the 1960s and 1970s, it is likely that an *increasing* percentage of new investment in plant and equipment is being made

7. *Economic Report of the President, 1982*, Table B-83.

overseas. In 1967, capital expenditures by majority-owned foreign affiliates of U.S. companies were about $10 billion, or 12 percent of total nonfarm business spending on new plant and equipment, and 44 billion, or 14 percent of the total, in 1981.[8]

Profits are still coming back to the United States, but the net effect of overseas investment is increasingly one of lowering U.S. productivity and placing downward pressure on U.S. wages. No longer dominant is the old model of U.S. foreign investment exploiting agriculture and mine labor of low-income countries in order to ship profits back to the United States, increasing wages at home and producing industrial goods in the United States for our home market. Naturally, some U.S. foreign investment still does exactly that. Much of U.S. foreign production, however, is now *competitive* with American labor and/or is largely interested in developing foreign markets for its goods produced abroad.

The United States still exports, and export industries did well in the mid-1970s as the dollar weakened. But all in all, the transnationalization of capital has tended to accelerate the shift of American workers into lower productivity service industries and to cut down the incentive for innovating in U.S. manufacturing and services. This massive overseas investment is not just in automobiles, television sets, and tape recorders; it is in food, clothing, drugs, forest products, transportation—almost any industry found in the U.S.[9]

Big business apparently slowed down its transnationalization in the 1970s compared to the 1950s and 1960s. American business— particularly big business—still invests huge amounts overseas every year and increasingly views its investment market as the world, not just the United States. This means that a large U.S. corporation in the 1980s tends to open and close plants on the basis of arranging its *worldwide* production of goods and services,

---

8. U.S. Department of Commerce, *Survey of Current Business*, September, 1976, p. 22; September, 1982, p. 42; and March, 1982, p. 26.

9. For a detailed analysis, see Barry Bluestone and Bennett Harrison, *The Deindustrialization of America* (New York: Basic Books, 1982).

even though much of the market for those goods and services may be in the United States.

The Bottom Line

The U.S. economy has gone through a host of changes since the end of World War II. Until the early 1970s, these changes were based on the idea—developed during the New Deal—that profits and real wages could grow together. It was also assumed in the postwar period that U.S. capital flowing freely around the country and the world would work to *increase* the average American employee's consumption and well-being. Until the late 1960s, this idea worked, or at least seemed to work. At the same time, however, the social costs of a corporation-led development were being picked up by government in the form of increasing social security, expanding health care, unemployment insurance, direct employment, military spending to protect foreign investment, and by the public itself, in the form of polluted air and water, poor health and inadequate safety on the job, and the insecurity for communities engendered by capital moving to another part of the country or abroad.

In the late 1960s and early 1970s, many of these hens came home to roost. Blacks and women wanted a better deal in the midst of a war economy protecting American business' prerogatives abroad. Environmentalists and unions fought for legislation protecting people against pollution and unsafe, unhealthy working conditions. Consumers asked for protection against unscrupulous merchandising and false advertising. Profit rates fell.

On top of all this, oil producers came together and as a cartel raised prices rapidly from 1973 to 1979.

The reaction of American business to these events was to reject the New Deal accords that had "governed" labor-business-government relations for thirty-odd years. In place of an investment policy that had shifted capital to lower-cost foreign production and simultaneously invested in higher productivity at home, business concentrated increasingly on trying to lower costs through an anti-labor, anti-environmentalist policy at home. The anti-labor aspect of this investment policy was manifested through investing in states and regions that were especially anti-union and pro-business. In addition, businesses held back on investing as much per employee as they had in the past. And, finally, as capital became more concentrated in the hands of oil/gas producers and financial institutions, other businesses increasingly had to follow big oil companies and banks in making decisions on what to produce and where to produce it.

This process was inseparable from the role of government as manager and employer. At a minimum, government acted to soften the worst aspects of business practices and the worst inequities of the so-called free-market system. But post–World War II government involved much more, as we shall now discuss. Government spending directly employed a larger and larger share of the labor force, and this employment was not random: college graduates in general and female and black college graduates in particular found their way into government employment when the private sector would not give them professional jobs. Other spending subsidized private arms production with military contracts and all kinds of electronics and other hardware with a massive space program. Research and development boomed with federal spending in universities and research institutions. Hospitals and clinics expanded rapidly with the passage of Medicare. Private corporations came to rely on the President and the Federal Reserve Board for a fiscal and monetary policy that would promote steady economic growth and on the President and Congress to protect their growing investments abroad.

At some point, the roles of government as manager and employer of the public and government as manager of business had to clash. This it did in the late 1960s and throughout the 1970s. Indeed, the history of the 1970s, given the huge changes in the private sector and the abandonment of New Deal accords by business, can be analyzed largely in terms of this conflict. Ultimately, any economic-political policy has to come to grips with whose side government should be on. Reaganomics certainly did just that.

Alternatives to Reaganomics will not be excused from making that choice.

In the next chapter, we take a close look at the nature of the government-business conflict as it has played itself out in the last twenty years.

5 Government as Conflict Manager

The Great Depression brought government into the economy because employment and income decline on such a scale was and continues to be unacceptable to most Americans. But there were other factors in the rise of government spending and government intervention. Even before 1929, the market was being replaced by large corporations that planned expansion and worked increasingly with government to get subsidies and protective regulation from "cutthroat competition." Automobile companies wanted more roads built, as railroads had received free land fifty years earlier. Utilities wanted water rights and government-constructed dams. Airlines wanted mail contracts. Oil companies wanted depletion allowances to reduce their taxes.

With the Crash, traditional supply-side economics went into disfavor. Millions of people were ready to work in factories that were standing idle. There was no lack of production facilities or labor. Goods and services were not being produced, because there was no demand for them. Consumers did not have enough income to expand consumption. Acting more from political reflex than on a new economic theory, the Roosevelt Administration knew that government had to guarantee people's bank savings and put people back to work. Whether Roosevelt had to do more than that to stimulate demand is a moot point: politically, private corporations had failed to keep the economy afloat; government needed support from labor to maintain the capitalist system's legitimacy.

Roosevelt got that support by sponsoring legislation that recognized unions, social security, unemployment compensation, and government work programs.

Roosevelt, a C minus economics student at Harvard, was a Keynesian without having read Keynes (who did not publish *The General Theory of Employment, Interest and Money* until 1936). But though Keynes' work is generally associated with demand-side economics and the Roosevelt Administration is associated with increasing government payments to labor (increasing demand), the American brand of Keynesianism grew as much out of the pre-1929 tradition as from a pure form of demand-side economics. Economist Robert Lekachman comments:

> American Keynesians in their time of glory were not obsessed with demand, as the ruling caricature now proclaims. During the Kennedy years, Walter Heller and his Council of Economic Advisers colleagues persuaded their intelligent President to endorse a series of encouragements to supply . . . tax credits for new investments, job training designed to improve the skills of the unemployed, and wage-price guidelines addressed to the habit of major corporations and some unions to behave in an inflationary manner.[1]

Government intervention in the post–World War II years was therefore far from Left- or liberal-dominated. Spending was used to encourage investment as well as to support demand. And an important part of demand support was in the form of military purchases—direct subsidies to private enterprise. Both supply-side and demand-side intervention served the purposes of *managing* the economy for smooth and continuous economic growth; this management was designed to serve corporations as much as labor. Alan Wolfe, in *America's Impasse* (New York: Pantheon, 1981), argues that growth fetishism *substituted* for "real" Keynesian economics—an economics that at least in theory called for considerable socialization of investment and more equal distribution of income and wealth. Growth fetishism entailed government's promotion of investment even at the cost of relatively high

1. Robert Lekachman, *Greed Is Not Enough* (New York: Pantheon, 1982), p. 35.

Table 5-1 Distribution of Family Personal Income Before Taxes by Income Quintile, All Consumer Units, Selected Years (% of income)

Quintile	1929	1935/36	1941	1944	1947	1950	1956	1961	1964	1970	1971
				Old series					New series		
Lowest	3.5	4.1	4.1	4.9	5.0	4.8	4.8	4.6	4.2	4.6	4.8
Second	9.0	9.2	9.5	10.9	11.0	10.9	11.3	10.9	10.6	10.7	10.8
Third	13.8	14.1	15.3	16.2	16.0	16.1	16.3	16.3	16.4	16.4	16.4
Fourth	19.3	20.9	22.3	22.2	22.0	22.1	22.3	22.7	23.2	23.3	23.3
Highest	54.4	51.7	48.8	45.8	46.0	46.1	45.3	45.5	45.5	44.9	44.6
Total	100.0	100.0	100.0	100.0	100.0	100.0	100.0	100.0	100.0	100.0	100.0
Top 5%	30.0	26.5	24.0	20.7	20.9	21.4	20.2	19.6	20.0	19.2	19.1
Percentiles 81–95	24.4	25.2	24.8	25.1	25.1	24.7	25.1	25.9	25.5	25.6	25.6

Source: Mordecai Kurz, "Income Redistribution: Theory and Evidence," Institute for Mathematical Studies in the Social Sciences, Stanford University, Working Paper No. 80, February 1977 (mimeo), p. 14.

unemployment, lingering poverty, and continued concentration
of economic power in a relatively few private hands.

**Table 5-2 Estimated Shares of National Income After
Taxes, Transfers, and Government Expenditures (%)**

	1950	1961	1970
Lowest 20%	7.2	8.7	7.9
Middle 60%	54.8	56.3	55.5
Highest 20%	38.0	35.0	36.6

Source: Mordecai Kurz, "Income Redistribution: Theory and Evidence," Institute for Mathematical Studies in the Social
Sciences, Stanford University, Working Paper No. 80, February 1977 (mimeo), p. 16; original table taken from M. Reynolds and E. Smolensky, "Post-Fisc Distribution of Income:
1950, 1961, and 1970," University of Wisconsin, Madison,
May, 1975 (mimeo).

Wolfe's analysis of growth fetishism is supported by studies on
U.S. income distribution since 1929, and, in particular, during the
postwar period. Pre-tax income distribution, for example, did
change significantly between 1929 and 1944 because the Depression wiped out many high incomes and the war economy controlled those high incomes while providing full employment (see
Table 5-1). From 1944 to 1971, however, pre-tax, pregovernment
spending income distribution hardly changed at all. Yet, what
about *after* taxes and public social spending? Reynolds and Smolensky's 1975 study (see Table 5-2, below) indicates that the government does shift income from higher- to lower-income Americans
(see Table 5-2). Even though the data in Tables 5-1 and 5-2 are not
comparable, they do indicate that income is taken from the top 20
percent of family-income units, and that a high fraction of this
income is then redistributed to the bottom 20 percent of income
earners. However, the percentages shifted are not enormous, nor
did they change between 1950 and 1970. According to all indica-
tions, the 1970s were marked more than anything by an income
distribution that became more unequal, if for no other reasons than
the deterioration of real wages and rising unemployment.

In all likelihood, taxes and spending have had their greatest impact on the top and bottom 5 percent of income earners. Stanford economist Mordecai Kurz concludes: "During this period [1936 to 1971] the entire change in the distribution of income after taxes and transfers occurred in the two extreme tails, lowering the relative share of the top 5 percent, raising the share of the bottom 5–10 percent and leaving essentially unchanged the share of the 85–90 percent of the consuming units."[2]

So government intervention did serve to reduce income inequality from what it might have been in a 1920s-style market economy. Even more, government spending reduced the working American's *insecurity* in the market system. While economic growth continued to feature business cycles, these cycles no longer resulted in panics or crises. Increased government spending cushioned the shocks of financial failures, which in the past had triggered a sequence of unemployment, reduced investment, further unemployment, reduced demand, and depressions. Since government notes (money) were always acceptable, increased unemployment compensation and a higher percentage of the labor force employed by government reduced the impact of such private failures on the economy as a whole. The insecurity of old age and poor health were also reduced. Although neither the social security nor the health-care system could be compared with the kinds of benefits won by European workers in the post–World War II period, pensions and various forms of Medicare ensured that minimum protection was available.

Monetary policy also took on a distinctly countercyclical tendency after the Depression. The concept of lowering interest rates and increasing the money supply to combat downturns became legitimate, normal federal policy after 1933—at least until inflation became a primary concern in the late 1970s. This kind of monetary policy, along with increasing deficits due to continued (or even increased) government spending combined with lower tax receipts

2. Mordecai Kurz, "Income Redistribution: Theory and Evidence," Institute for Mathematical Studies in the Social Sciences, Stanford University, Working Paper No. 80, February 1977 (mimeo), p. 17.

during recessions, made government policy in the postwar period specifically countercyclical. Similarly, during the expansionary phase of the cycle, reduction of the deficit and rising interest rates were used to temper the boom. At the same time, however, interest-rate policy affected the housing and auto industries more than others and hit small business harder than large business, so using interest rates rather than fiscal instruments for countercyclical policy has had important sectoral-growth implications.

Despite the potential and actual power that government policies have over the growth of different industries and over the distribution of income—and the often inequitable use of that power—government management worked quite well economically and politically, at least for that first postwar generation. It worked because the economy was growing, real wages were rising, consumption was going up, and—most important—both labor and employers accepted the general conditions of the New Deal accords.

One main reason that the Keynesian solution functioned (making the New Deal accords acceptable) was the United States' position in world markets. We simply had no serious competitors in one manufacturing industry after another. We dominated both technology and management techniques. And significant government support of research and development through universities and the space program (begun in the early 1960s) allowed us to leap forward in electronics and communications when other countries had not even thought of the potential in these areas. A second reason was that government was very helpful to business, even though there were often serious conflicts between the two. The percent of gross national product going to wages and salaries, for example, stayed between 52 and 53 percent for the first twenty postwar years except for the last year of the Korean War (see Table 5-3). U.S. military spending on troops stationed abroad and on mobile-strike forces, plus U.S. government military and economic foreign aid, made it possible for American corporations to obtain favorable investment conditions in Europe and the Third World. A third reason was that government successfully acted as a cushion against the worst injustices of corporate capitalism, in its roles as both economic manager and employer. There seemed to be enough money and resources to take care of everyone.

Nevertheless, the primary assumption of the New Deal and Keynesian economics under the American format is that control over investment decisions is *supposed* to be in the hands of private corporations. While it has always been true in the postwar period that about 5 to 9 percent of GNP is spent by government for military purposes and that federal tax, subsidy, transfer payment, and monetary policy have important effects on almost every industry in one way or another, private corporations get the lion's share of total capital and can use it as they please. Government can create financial incentives and punishments but invariably has to depend on corporate responses to such carrots and sticks to achieve desired policy.

Table 5-3   Wages-Salaries and Employers' Supplements to Wages-Salaries as % of Gross National Product, 1948–1982

Year	Wages and salaries	Employers' supplements to wages and salaries
1948	52.2	2.3
1953	54.1	3.0
1959	53.1	4.2
1962	52.7	4.8
1965	52.3	5.0
1966	52.7	5.4
1967	53.4	5.5
1968	53.8	5.8
1969	54.6	6.0
1970	55.3	6.4
1972	53.6	7.0
1973	53.0	7.4
1975	52.0	8.1
1979	51.2	9.3
1980	51.5	9.6
1981	50.8	9.9
1982	51.0	9.7

Source: Economic Report of the President, 1983, Table B-21.

In the late 1960s and early 1970s, the business-government relationship began to deteriorate, spelling the end of the New Deal accords. Many big businesses were already transnationals, so their ties to domestic U.S. economy were as related to selling as they were to producing. Government fiscal policy during the Vietnam War produced the first sustained inflation since before the Depression. But most important, that same government policy was—it seemed from business' viewpoint—clearly and irrevocably tilted toward labor rather than corporations. The social upheavals of the 1960s seemed to business to have produced a permanent change in its relation to both government and labor—a change that had forced even the pro-business, Republican Nixon government to cave in to popular movements demanding greater government social spending without higher taxes. On top of that, conditions on the international front were also changing rapidly: Japanese cars and steel were invading U.S. markets; the dollar had lost its dominance in international trade and was falling rapidly against all other major currencies; and, in 1973, Third World oil producers began raising prices of crude to unheard-of levels.

The 1970s showed how much postwar government policy in America depends on the cooperation of business. Once big business began holding back productive investment, turning instead to short-term acquisitions, real estate, and plant shifts to anti-union regions; and once big business began trying to increase its profit rates by raising prices even during the major 1974–75 recession, traditional American Keynesian monetary and fiscal policies could no longer work.

Not only that, but business behavior wreaked havoc with government income distribution policy. As business slowed expansion of the high-wage domestic manufacturing sector, employment expansion in that sector ground to a halt, despite the emergence of a dynamic, rapidly growing high-technology industry. New employment flowed into low-wage, nonunionized services and wholesale/retail trade. Even new manufacturing investment went to regions where labor was relatively low-paid and local governments were extremely hostile toward union organizers. Real wages fell rapidly under these conditions, especially because workers were increasingly less able to protect themselves against inflation. More, not fewer, people were faced with poverty. The last resort was government, and government was called upon to increase its social welfare (particularly health) benefits to offset falling real wages, to raise payments to cover increased unemployment, and to increase social security benefits.

With declining real wages and inflation-pushed rising tax rates, middle-income earners became more and more reluctant to pay for social welfare spending. Part of the pressure came from elsewhere: corporate taxes began dropping as a percentage of total federal, state, and local taxes paid, and this decline was picked up by personal income taxes. In 1959, corporate income tax accounted for 17 percent of all taxes; in 1979, the figure was 10.7 percent, and in 1981, 7.9 percent. Personal income taxes, meanwhile, increased from 33.6 percent of all taxes paid in 1959 to 37.2 percent in 1981. Social security taxes rose from 12.9 to 22.5 percent in the same period. Sales taxes increased from 8 to 10 percent of the total. It is easy to see why wage-earning taxpayers feel that they are bearing the brunt of the tax burden. They are.

The reaction came about first in the form of initiatives like Proposition 13 in California, which cut property taxes and put a ceiling on the percentage rate that such a tax could levy. Unfortunately, most of the benefits of the tax cut went to corporations, the federal government (since property taxes are deductible from federal taxes), and apartment-house owners, while the cuts in services hit schools, medical services, and other local services used by individual homeowners.

But that was the tip of the iceberg. Convinced that government was the villain of the piece, the middle class turned for relief from taxes—above all, the inflation tax—to Reaganomics. Fiscal policy became the hottest issue in the country, on the assumption that it could be used successfully by a budget-cutting, tax-cutting, conservative President to halt inflation and promote economic growth. Two years later, inflation was down and taxes too. In a way, this New Deal-jaded constituency had what it wanted, but at the terrible price of losing real income to the rich and to large corporations, increasing unemployment, and, worst of all, turning the poor out into the cold. Price stability had meant, in Reagan's terms, transferring national product away from those who most needed it; raising unemployment; increasing the profitability of business and short-term investment by the rich; making wage earners and consumers increasingly vulnerable to unsafe, unjust business practices; and expanding military spending to frightening proportions. Had government inefficiency justified voters asking for such policies? Or had taxpayers been seduced by a business community smelling gold in them Reaganite hills?

Government Spending and Private Investment

As long as profits and wages went up while government expanded, New Deal liberalism was a popular solution to the worst aspects of "boom and bust" capitalist development. But the situation definitely changed in the late 1960s. The *interaction* among government, capital owners, and labor underwent a subtle alteration that has had important repercussions on economic growth and public policy.

On one hand, the change resulted largely from what were viewed as *positive* effects of the New Deal, since rapid post–World War II population growth and the increasing longevity of the population was related to increased affluence, and the New Deal did promote economic growth and increased affluence. More important, post–World War II *pro-business* government intervention allowed American management to find favorable investment conditions in foreign countries, though this made management less innovative at home. Competition from abroad, particularly from Japan, found U.S. managers unable to meet its challenge. They blamed government's labor and welfare policy, but much of the blame has to be placed on management itself. The decline of manufacturing as the principal source of capital accumulation and employment had already begun in the second half of the 1960s, even before the oil crisis.

Government policy in the late 1960s had a different kind of impact on the U.S. economy. The war in Vietnam combined with the simultaneous War on Poverty to expand demand for labor so rapidly that wages and salaries ate into profits. An aging labor force and an uprising of the poor increased government spending on social security and welfare, including a sharp rise in medical care. The average rate of profit fell. The 1970s, therefore, were marked by business' efforts to restore the conditions under which it could invest profitably again, and most of these efforts were aimed at making government policy more "pro-profits" and less "pro-labor/pro-poor," on the assumption that only through such a policy could the economy grow rapidly again, productivity increase, and U.S. business be competitive in world markets. Government was and is seen by business as the key factor in achieving higher profits. And business could exacerbate the crisis by investing less in productive activities until conditions were "right," meanwhile exerting all kinds of pressures in the economy to make conditions as right as possible even under unfavorable government policy. This was not a conspiracy but large American corporations acting in their own individual interests—interests that generally and in broad terms coincide, especially when it comes to overall government action on taxes, regulation, inflation/unemployment, labor unions, and wages.[3]

Profits and Wages. We have shown how nonfinancial corporate before-tax profit rates fell in the United States from an average 15 to 16 percent in the mid-1960s to 10 to 11 percent in the 1970s. After tax-profit rates also declined from a high of about 9 percent in 1965 to about 6 to 7 percent by the late 1970s and 5.6 percent in the early 1980s. (Table 4-5, p. 78). Correcting this significant drop is the central theme of Reaganomics' solution to the crisis. The most important assumption of Reaganomics is the direct causality between declining profits and government intervention. Government consumer protection and occupational health and safety, for example, allegedly reduce *pre-tax* profits since compa-

3. Anyone who doubts that the managers of various corporations communicate with each other regularly, that there are shared values among these managers, and that they try to implement shared values through government policies, should see sociologist William Domhoff's extensive research (e.g., *The Higher Circles* [New York: Random House, 1970]) into the various levels of managerial connections. A useful report on corporate leaders' views on the 1970s is *Ethics and Profits* by Leonard Silk and David Vogel (New York: Simon and Schuster, 1978).

nies have to spend valuable resources on pollution control, waste treatment, protecting workers, and so forth. These measures increase costs of production, making American companies less able to meet foreign competition if they pass on these costs in higher prices, or less profitable if they do not. Minimum-wage laws further restrict the ability of enterprises in particularly competitive industries to lower wage costs. The Reagan plan began with the idea that corporate profits were too low; raising them would increase investment in plant and equipment. For conservative Republicans, then, New Deal liberalism's main sin was that the growth of the public sector cut into investment profitability.

Superficially, the conservative assertion that government expansion reduced profit rates is correct, if we assume that government intervention always takes place *as it occurred in the late 1960s*. That the effect was unintended by government policy is rarely discussed, but also probably true. The Vietnam War could not be construed as a measure designed to favor labor at the expense of profits. Ironically, however, that is what it became, primarily because the economy was already at capacity when the Vietnam buildup began.

Business was good, but labor's wages and salaries increased from 52.5 percent of GNP in 1965–66 to 55.3 percent in 1970. And supplements to wages and salaries, consisting mainly of employers' contributions to social security, rose from 5 percent of GNP in 1965 to more than 6 percent in 1970. In those five years, then, total employee compensation rose about 4 percentage points, mostly as a result of the increase in the total wages and salaries paid out by business and government. Wages and employers' contributions to employee benefits increased sharply from 1966 to 1970, reaching a combined high of 61.7 percent of GNP in 1970, a high that has never been exceeded (Table 5-3, p. 103). Wages and salaries as a percentage of gross national product rose not so much because real wages per employed person went up rapidly but because average pay continued to rise modestly while the labor force increased by almost 2 million annually (see Tables 4–1, p. 63, and 4-3, p. 70).

Labor was able to win wage increases *and* increased employment in the late 1960s because government spending was increased at a time of already relatively low unemployment. Employers bid workers away from each other and brought in new workers at relatively high wages as demand for their products increased. In addition, government welfare benefits increased for those working, those retired, those unable to work, and those unwilling to work. But most of the taxes to pay for these increased benefits came not from capital but from labor itself. Thus, increased government spending allowed labor to make gains at the expense of profits, but then the government turned around and taxed the larger labor force's higher income to pay for the war and increased benefits.

Personal taxes plus one-half of social insurance taxes (assuming that employees and employers split the social insurance bill) accounted for 53.5 percent of federal revenues in 1965, 61.3 percent in 1970, and 61.4 percent in 1972. Corporate taxes plus one-half of social insurance taxes accounted for 43.2 percent of federal revenues in 1965, 28.8 percent in 1970, and 29.9 in 1972. Indirect business (excise) taxes accounted for the rest, but even these were largely passed on to consumers in the form of higher prices. There was thus a significant increase in the taxes paid by consumers (labor) and a decrease in taxes paid by capital. Social welfare spending increases in the 1960s and early seventies were mostly financed by increased taxes paid by labor.

Capital's share fell because labor and government got their hands on resources that would otherwise have gone to private businessmen for profits and reinvestment. Government then turned over an increasing fraction of those resources to labor in the form of higher benefits. Profit rates fell not because of any direct intervention of government in business but because labor was able to bargain well in a period of rapidly expanding demand. The effect of government spending was *indirect:* the very Keynesian logic that brought about recovery from recessions and made government a partner in economic stabilization created—in this case—an "excessive" demand that enabled labor to gain higher consumption and savings at the expense of profits. The Johnson Administration attempted to wage war in Asia and mediate do-

Table 5-4 Labor and Capital Share of Total Output, 1948–80 as % of Gross National Product

Year	Consumption by labor financed by wages and salaries	Social welfare spending	Capital's gross share	Capital depreciation	Nonsocial welfare spending	Capital's net share
1948	58	8	34	7	11	16
1950	58	8	34	7	12	14
1955	55	8	37	9	15	13
1959	55	10	35	9	15	9
1965	54	11	35	8	15	12
1972	52	19	29	9	14	6
1977	50	19	31	10	14	6
1979	50	18	32	10	14	8
1980	51	19	30	11	14	5

Sources: 1948–72: Samuel Bowles and Herbert Gintis, "The Crisis of Liberal Democratic Capitalism: The Case of the United States," *Politics and Society,* Vol. II, no. 1 (1982), Tables 5 and 6; 1977–80: calculations based on Bowles and Gintis' method, using more recent data.

Note: The total labor consumption share equals column 1 plus column 2; capital's gross share equals 100 minus the total labor consumption share. Capital's net share equals capital's gross share minus capital depreciation minus nonsocial welfare spending. The net share represents that part of GNP available for net domestic and foreign investment and capitalists' consumption.

mestic strife in a period of relatively full employment. Labor gained and capital (as a whole) lost from this policy, even though a similar policy had had positive economic effects for both only thirteen years before, when the United States fought in Korea.

But directly or indirectly, there is little question that the increase in labor's consumption power was won at the expense of profits. And private investors lost additional control over investable capital to government spending intended to benefit them rather than labor. Although this part of government spending declined as a percentage of GNP between 1955 and 1979, it remained high enough (14 percent) to reduce private capital's net share of GNP (see Table 5-4, p. 110).

Business as a whole was worse off in this last decade than it was in the 1950s and early 1960s. The postwar period until 1965-66 was generally a good time for investors and corporations in terms of controlling directly a relatively high fraction of gross national product. Most of this control resulted from the relatively lower share of workers' consumption in gross national product, but capital after the Korean War until 1965 was also getting a relatively higher fraction of government spending on capital-supporting projects like road building, military, and space. From business' point of view, reducing social welfare spending is crucial to increasing the capital share of gross national product. But in terms of increasing private control of investable funds, decreasing nonsocial welfare spending is also important. So the Reagan Administration's insistence on keeping military expenditures increasing rapidly relative to social welfare spending benefits business by increasing overall capital share, yet may decrease private business' control over investable funds by shifting those funds to the federal government. This is why the business sector is ambivalent about defense spending financed by budget deficits.

This is not the end of the story, however. The American version of Keynesian policies did not fail simply because government spending in an already tight labor market allowed the labor share of GNP to rise relative to profits. As Table 5-3 shows, the wage/salary share of GNP retreated to a mid-1960s level by 1973, and has since fallen further. The real saga of liberalism's demise lies in the attempts of business to reestablish high profit conditions in the economy and the resistance to these attempts by groups that had benefited from the rise in wages and social welfare spending in the late 1960s and early 1970s.

Business pushed for "normal" profit rates in three ways: first, by trying to push wages down, at least relative to prices; second, by raising prices even in periods of severe downturn like 1974–75; and third, by trying to get government to lower business taxes and simultaneously to reduce social welfare spending. All these measures tend to increase the capital share at the expense of labor. Business was apparently reluctant to invest in new plant and equipment until the overall profit picture changed significantly.

The investment rate per employee declined sharply because business did not like the "conditions" under which it had to invest,[4] and one of the most powerful pressures on government that large corporations exerted in this period was holding back on major increases in domestic investment per employee and concentrating investments in new plant and equipment on saving energy or moving to less unionized, more anti-union regions. Government responded to business' disenchantment by inducing the recessions of 1970–71, 1974–75, 1980, and 1981–82. These were all government attempts to "correct" labor's victories of the late 1960s that increased real wages and real welfare spending.

The slowdown in business investment relative to employment increases in the 1970s was a reversal of business behavior in the period between 1948 and 1972, and even in the years of rapidly declining profits between 1966 and 1970. In those years, private investment more than kept up with a rapidly expanding labor force.

Although wage increases slowed down in the late 1960s, the large expansion in the labor force combined with higher average

4. James O'Connor ("The Fiscal Crisis of the State Revisited," *Kapitalistate*, No. 9, 1981, pp. 41–61) also argues that capital was on a not so subtle strike in the 1970s, holding back capital investment because it did not like the structural conditions under which it was forced to invest.

real wages and increased social benefits to increase the wage share: demand for goods and services was rising as the average American received higher average wages and benefits. Second, savings as a percentage of disposable income were rising rapidly in this period—from 6 to 8.6 percent between 1966 and 1973— so capital was available for investment. The real cost of borrowing, measured by nominal interest rates minus the inflation rate, therefore stayed relatively low. There was certainly no capital shortage in the late 1960s. Thus, despite declining profit rates of nonfinancial corporations, investment and growth continued, producing relatively full employment, rising real wages, and the continued rapid incorporation of higher-educated minorities and women into public-sector jobs.

By the early 1970s, however, the business community—under the banner of anti-inflation—was putting pressure on government to end the Vietnam War, cut spending on social welfare, and reduce wage growth. This pressure was generally successful. American troops were all but withdrawn from Vietnam by 1973; real social welfare spending per capita had grown at 6.5 percent annually from 1959 to 1973, but only increased at 2.8 percent annually between 1973 and 1979; and real wages slowed their increase in 1973, fell precipitously in the 1974–75 recession, and never recovered, dropping sharply again in the 1980 recession, and yet again in 1981. Yet all these pressures failed to return the capital share back to the 1960s level by 1980.

At the same time, business tried to return to "normal" profit *rates* by more direct means. Mordecai Kurz shows that from 1971 to 1977 the "lower than normal" profits contributed about 2 to 2.5 percentage points to the inflation rate as business raised prices in an attempt to raise profit rates. This contribution to inflation was *in addition to* any price increases that reflected higher costs of production.[5]

These moves by business and government were resisted by

5. Mordecai Kurz, "A Strategic Theory of Inflation," Stanford University, Institute for Mathematical Studies in the Social Sciences, Technical Report no. 283, April 1979.

labor. The resistance primarily took the form of pressure on government for increased social welfare spending to maintain the consumption levels achieved in the late 1960s and early 1970s. Labor also resisted permanently higher unemployment rates. Thus, Gerald Ford's government lost the 1976 election largely because of the severity of the 1974–75 recession and its effect on unemployment and real wages. Labor resistance helped create a massive amount of government debt in the 1970s, a debt needed to finance social welfare spending during the frequent recessions being used to drive down wages and attempt to reduce inflation. The federal government ran large budget deficits in fiscal years 1971, 1972, 1975, 1976, 1980, and 1981. Interest rates were driven up sharply by budget deficits combined with reduced savings rates on the part of consumers trying to maintain their standard of living in the face of declining real wages, which created a real investment crisis rather than merely a mid-1970s business slowdown in investment.

Thus business attempted to raise profits in the early and mid-1970s by holding back on increasing investment, pushing government to pursue policies that reduced wages relative to prices and social welfare spending, and raising prices even during the severe 1974–75 recession. Labor resisted these moves by pushing government to increase social welfare spending, in order to keep unemployment rates at historically "normal" levels and by keeping real wages increasing by reducing inflation. The result of this "zero-sum game," as Lester Thurow calls it, was an economy in which almost everybody loses. The struggle over conditions of investment *in a democracy* cannot be resolved by asking those who work in a society to be permanently worse off so that a small minority of citizens—those who own capital—can be much better off. In the United States of the 1970s, business' attempt to raise profits through "corrective" corporate price increases and pressures on government to reduce wages and social welfare spending produced a predictable resistance, and that resistance, in turn, produced besieged government—federal, state, and local—caught among business, labor, and consumers, all acting out their roles as income earners and taxpayers.

American business' attempts to correct the high wage share / reduced profits of the 1960s allowed Europeans and the Japanese to take over many traditionally U.S. markets, even much of the U.S. domestic market itself. If business really had national interests in mind, it would have worried less about its profit rates in the 1970s and worried much more about sales, markets, and productivity. U.S. corporations have therefore been relatively successful in reducing real wages and social welfare spending but have also lost markets and driven up the cost of capital.

So the problems for New Deal growth policies began in the late 1960s, not in 1973 as neoclassical economists argue. OPEC price increases contributed to the inflation and to important structural changes already taking place in the economy, but they did not cause the fundamental problems already undermining the post–World War II expansion. The inflation of the 1970s also began in the 1960s; if anything, it was the result of a particular set of responses, by both the private and public sector, to the changes that were taking place after 1965–66.

The remarkable aspect of the years after 1973 is that real demand for goods and services has risen only because of the greatly increased number of people working. Real wages per person have fallen rapidly. Americans have to work more and save less to stay even. Average profits have stopped their decline but have not risen significantly. Capital has become increasingly scarce, and with this scarcity those sectors of the economy that are accumulating capital through high profits—like energy and high-tech producers, and real-estate companies—are able to dominate investments in the economy. Only a surge of demand for consumer goods and services will push capital toward the production of those products, and that surge is unlikely. At the same time, foreign competition, both from U.S. companies overseas and foreign producers, eats into the consumption of U.S.-produced products, hurting traditional sources of job expansion and rising wages.

Was government to blame for what happened in the 1960s and the resulting crisis of the 1970s?

The superficial argument is that the government's policy from 1966 to 1969, in trying to pursue a war and mediate social conflict at home, bit off more than it could chew and betrayed the successful "fine-tuning" of the Kennedy and early Johnson years. Liberal economists like Walter Heller and the late Arthur Okun have made precisely this case. But blaming government alone for these policies assumes that the President and Congress are totally independent of forces that make the American economy and government what it is and push it toward the policies that it takes.

The Vietnam War was not illogical in the context of the worldwide post–World War II expansion of American capital and its virulent anticommunism. The only mistakes the government made on that score were underestimating the tenacity of its opponents in Vietnam and losing the American public's support for the war. And the War on Poverty emerged from riots in Watts and threats of riots in other urban black ghettos. Blacks were vocal and well organized in the 1960s. They also constituted a relatively high percentage of those who actually did the fighting in Vietnam. In addition, most Americans—especially American business—did believe in the 1960s that through government spending the United States could simultaneously put a man on the moon, contain communism, and keep things cool at home. That they were wrong is certainly the fault of a government leadership that did nothing to correct this belief, but it is just as much the fault of those who wanted the belief to be true even when a careful analysis of the facts made the outcome of such a policy very tenuous. We could even argue that given U.S. foreign policy after 1945, the Johnson Administration was intractably biased toward intervention in Asia just as it had to respond as it did to urban riots and the demand of minorities for full economic participation.

Yet what would have happened if the United States had not spent those billions on Vietnam?

Heller and Okun are probably correct in claiming that the inflation could have been avoided, at least for a few more years. But profits would also have declined from their 1965–66 peaks, and the growth rate in the late 1960s may have been lower. The increased foreign competition from Japanese and Third World produced manufactures would have been no less, and the size of the U.S. labor force to be absorbed in the late 1960s and 1970s the same. U.S. defense expenditures would probably have increased substantially through the entire period in order to show the world that despite the loss of Indochina, the United States could still defend its interests everywhere. Real wages would have leveled off once large labor-force increases combined with slower economic growth. Labor and capital would have begun to struggle over GNP and its government component. The population would have grown older and social security taxes would have become a problem even without Vietnam. Since OPEC was supported by U.S. oil producers, its formation may have occurred altogether independently of the Vietnam War. Although these are speculations, the point of them is to show that the economic and social forces at work in the world and in the United States were not totally altered because the United States decided to make war in Vietnam. The war accentuated and may have speeded up historically the advent of the crisis. Whenever that crisis would have come, the "zero-sum society" would have replaced the New Deal accords.

The crisis might have occurred for other apparent reasons, but its fundamental underlying dynamic would have been the same: wage claims on the private-production sector plus social claims on the government would have exceeded the capability or willingness of capital to pay for those claims. Sooner or later, this problem, fundamental to U.S. economic development since the 1930s, would have undermined economic growth. "Good" versus "bad" government policies could only have forestalled the crisis under present conditions.

Social demands were increasing the costs of production in the 1960s regardless of the war. And these demands were not excessive, nor are they today. Why should there be so much poverty and urban blight alongside incredible wealth? Why should there be a "normal" 5 to 6 percent unemployment rate? Shouldn't an advanced industrial society be able to sustain its aged, either through employment or income subsidies? Shouldn't all Americans have guaranteed, preventive health care? Shouldn't all workplaces be organized for health, safety, democratic participation, and high productivity? Shouldn't the environment be sustained for future generations and for the health and enjoyment of present ones? Shouldn't all members of our society have the same opportunity to have decent work and living standards no matter what their color, sex, or ethnic group? These are legitimate issues for citizens to raise in a democracy. The failure to make good these claims lies as much in the profit motive and the inefficiency of American enterprise as in the government spending increases needed to meet social demands—if not more so.

What happened in the 1970s has been blamed on inadequate or faulty government policy and on greedy labor unions. However, the unions did no more than business was and is doing now: trying to get the best conditions possible to make the highest possible incomes (profits). Government was and is caught in the middle, necessarily trying to keep business happy since government depends on economic growth for its own revenues, yet necessarily having to keep labor and consumers happy in order to get re-elected. And most big business, unwilling to invest aggressively in the new equipment and technology necessary to meet foreign competition, allowed that foreign competition to surpass U.S. producers. Private corporations, while claiming leadership in the U.S. economy, have been unable to guarantee steady economic growth, will not take responsibility for full employment, will not guarantee citizens affordable health care, have not provided for people in their old age, and have not taken the responsibility for educating and training the young. Neither have they fought against sex and race discrimination nor for better safety and health conditions in work. Instead, in the 1970s, big business brought its guns to bear on wages that were "too high" and on social welfare benefits. It held back on investing more capital in an expanding labor force apparently because the climate for such investment was not "favorable enough." It concentrated the investments it did make on seeking a better "investment climate" abroad and within the United States. In short, labor apparently became "too powerful" economically and politically in the late 1960s, and business held back investment, meanwhile pushing for higher profits and an unabashedly pro-business, anti-organized-labor/anti-environmentalist government policy. Predictably, the economy floundered, and other factors like Japanese and European competition, high energy prices, and a rapidly growing labor force led to important economic restructurings.

What, then, can we say about the failure of New Deal–style government management, and what does this failure teach us about future public policy?

The crisis which began in the late 1960s had to be resolved in the context of a rapidly growing U.S. labor force, the result of an earlier baby boom. The U.S. population had also become older, so that many employees not only retired but lived longer on social security. These older Americans also required more medical care. And the crisis had to be resolved in the context of a much more competitive world market than the United States faced for its industrial products in the 1950s or early 1960s. We were about to lose the lead in steel, automobiles, electronics, and other important industrial products unless industrialists incorporated the latest technology and were innovative in the products they produced and in quality control. When profits fell because of the particular situation in the late 1960s, business reacted exactly the opposite of what was required to meet the international challenge, at the same time blaming government and labor for the loss of competitive edge. Government, faced by the structural changes in the labor force and population, could not satisfy business and laborers/consumers at the same time. Growth and productivity declined, inflation increased, and real wages dropped precipitously. A succession of governments was unwilling to take business by the horns and force it to the line.

Instead, a political ideology came to the fore that would give concessions to business in the hope that the corporations would be willing to invest more, increase output, and save the day. This is exactly what the corporations wanted. Government management failed because once big business saw that liberal governments could and would give in to wage earners, the poor, and the old at the expense of profits, it gradually made the New Deal solutions unworkable. An important fraction of the business community was and is willing to do whatever is necessary—including bringing on a series of severe recessions, as occurred in the 1970s and early 1980s—to get the new and satisfactory conditions of low wages, low welfare spending, low corporate taxes, minimal regulations, and weak unions consistent with high profit margins and control over capital formation. Far from wanting government off people's backs, business in the 1970s was pushing for *government interven- tion in its favor.*

New Deal ideology, fostering an economic development based on a historical compromise among labor, business, and govern- ment, could not abandon its labor-consumer political base to achieve what business wanted. Neither was it willing to abandon its business ally to strike out in new, imaginative pro-community, pro-labor, pro-consumer directions. It thus collapsed as a viable political ideology.

Collapse does not mean that important elements of that ideol- ogy cannot be preserved in alternatives to an even more disas- trous neoconservativism. Government management has had *two* sides: The first and more significant has been to promote growth by subsidizing business and—through government taxation, spending, and monetary policy—smoothing the ups and downs of total goods and services demanded. The use of Keynesian ideas and government resources promoted the expansion of large corporate, now transnational, enterprises. On the other hand, government management also represents attempts to le- gitimize corporate-led expansion by giving in to popular de- mands for greater economic and social participation. This is the response to pressures for greater democracy. The pressures take a special form because they are "defensive," but they still re- spect human needs, such as economic security, the right to a healthy body and environment, the right to knowledge, and the right to equal social and economic treatment. If an alternative to New Deal economics is to extend democracy rather than restrict it, it must preserve these democratic claims.

Reaganomics argues that these claims *restrict* democracy by causing increased government intervention. Anything that interferes with the market reduces individual liberty. But government management made possible increased economic participation for the unemployed, minorities, women, and the aged. It increased the role of workers in shaping their workplace and involved them in collective bargaining over wages and working conditions. The way this was achieved was not as democratic as it might have been, however, because it had to fit into the more general purpose of government management to assure corporate growth. Thus, income distribution after World War II did not become more equal, the role of unions was limited to prewar gains, social welfare spending increased but was largely paid for by workers themselves and was carried out in the context of increasing levels of unemployment and racial/sexual discrimination.

Of all the government programs, the most productive in easing the ill effects of corporate capitalism has been government employment. Through public-sector employment, minorities and women have been able to achieve social mobility closed to them in the private sector. Historically (even in the nineteenth century), the public sector led in labor reform. Through public-sector employment many of the most important demands of social movements in this century have begun to be met. So when conservatives demand the reduction of the public sector, they are effectively increasing income inequality, reducing the possibilities for full employment, and hitting particularly hard at the social mobility of women and minorities. Any alternative to Reaganomics has to resolve the need for increased austerity with the social needs met by public instead of private jobs. Can we design an effective, efficient government sector to respond to both these conditions? Before turning to that task, we have to understand the nature of direct and indirect government employment as it now exists.

6 Government as Employer

Government not only serves as a manager of the economy but acts as a major employer. The government sector currently employs one-sixth of the U.S. work force and has generated one-quarter of all new jobs in the economy during the last two decades.[1] In the last twenty years, its role as employer has grown rapidly.

The *type* of jobs created by government is as important as the *number* of jobs created. The proportion of professional-level jobs in government is twice as large as the private sector, while the proportion of low-level jobs is half as large. Government employs one-third of all college graduates. And it has generated one-third of all new, professional jobs and one-third of all new jobs for college graduates during the last two decades.

Government employment has benefited women and minorities particularly. The public sector has always employed a lower proportion of white males and a higher proportion of women than the private sector. This is largely due to the nature of the jobs in the two sectors. Most women work in few occupational areas—for example, teaching, clerical work, and nursing. Government provides most of the teaching jobs and a large number of clerical jobs. The growth of the public sector has meant an increasing number of job opportunities for women. By 1980 over one-third of all high-level jobs held by white and Hispanic women and over one-

1. The figures cited in the introduction are based on the detailed analysis that follows in the remainder of the chapter.

half of all high-level jobs held by black women were in government. The government has also served as an important source of high-level jobs for Hispanic and black males.

Since the government has more high-level and fewer low-level jobs than the private sector, average earnings in the public sector are higher. Yet only workers in low-level jobs receive a premium from being employed in the public sector. And this wage advantage has eroded over the last twenty years to less than 10 percent.

Average figures belie group differences, however. Women and minorities gain a clear advantage from working for the government. Earnings discrimination exists in both the private and government sectors—women and minorities earn less than white males at similar occupational levels. Even with similar qualifications—education and experience—they earn less. But these groups are relatively better off working for government: the gap between their earnings and the earnings of white males is smaller in government than in private firms. In fact, minority males with similar qualifications actually earn as much as white males in the government sector, at least in high-level occupations.

Some progress has been made in reducing earnings discrimination since 1960 in both private and government jobs. But this progress has mostly benefited minority males in high-level occupations. Little change has occurred in middle and low-level occupations, where most workers are concentrated. And the relative economic position of women has also changed little over this period. They continue to earn substantially less than white or minority males, even with the same qualifications.

These characteristics of government employment are similar at the local, state, and federal levels. State and local governments provide a greater proportion of high-level job opportunities than the federal government, whereas federal workers receive higher salaries. The federal government has provided relatively more employment opportunities for black men and women than for other groups. Women have found a large number of jobs at the local government level, partly because the teaching profession mostly employs women.

Not only does the government employ workers directly but it also generates employment indirectly, through the purchase of goods and services in the private sector. In fact, the government spends more money on purchases in the private sector than it does on compensating its own employees. Most of these purchases at the federal level are for defense programs. A third of all defense spending went to two defense industries in 1972, ordnance and aircraft. These industries depend on the government for the majority of their sales. Several other industries depend on defense spending for much of their support as well.

State and local governments together outspend the federal government. Half of their private-sector spending in 1972 went for new construction and maintenance. All told, the government supports almost one-third of the construction industry.

Government spending in the private sector generates about 8 million jobs. But whereas direct government employment provides relatively more job opportunities for women and minorities, indirect government employment favors white males. Those industries in which a large portion of government spending ends up—defense industries and construction—employ more white males and fewer women and minorities than many other private-sector firms. So government spending in the private sector mainly benefits a few industries and provides jobs for white males.

Altogether, government purchases of goods and services generate one-quarter of all jobs in the U.S. economy. More important, it generates a third of all high-level, professional jobs. While many Americans may feel that government has grown too big, few seem to realize that their livelihood depends on its existence.

Government transfer payments to individuals—social security, unemployment compensation, Medicaid, and the like—also generate jobs in the private sector. Transfer payments primarily benefit the poor and elderly, supplementing their income and increasing their expenditures in the private sector. The money is used to buy food, clothing, and shelter and to purchase medical and other social services. Thus it generates jobs in those industries.

But unlike defense and construction, industries that benefit from social welfare purchases do not depend on government funds for most of their support. They have much less interest, therefore, in preserving these programs.

Of course, while government expenditures for transfer programs increase the spending of some groups and create jobs, taxes used to support those programs reduce the private spending of other groups and eliminate jobs. It is unclear whether more jobs are created by this process than are eliminated, and our analysis leaves this question unanswered. But changing the patterns of government spending clearly has an impact on employment.

The Reagan Administration and many of its supporters believe that the recent reductions in federal spending will benefit the economy and create more jobs. Our own estimates reveal that recent and proposed cuts in nondefense spending—for transfer programs and aid to state and local government—will eliminate more jobs than increases in defense spending will generate. And more jobs will be eliminated in the private sector than in government. In all, cuts in government spending will reduce the number of jobs in the economy.

Will the tax cuts and reduced government regulation create more jobs in the private sector to make up for the ones lost from government cuts? Only time will tell. We do know the loss of public-sector jobs will hurt women and minorities particularly. They will lose an important source of jobs, particularly at the high end of the job hierarchy. They will benefit much less from increased defense spending and a larger private sector.

The government's role as an employer is sizable. The government employs millions of people, in both the public and private sectors. Changing the spending patterns of government will modify its role as employer. It will benefit some and hurt others.

This impact is not often discussed explicitly. But it should be. And it should be an integral part of any discussion of the government's role in the economy.

Private and Government Jobs

A century ago, most people worked as independent, self-employed farmers, artisans, merchants, and professionals. Today most jobs are in large organizations, which is as true for the private sector as for the government. Many Americans correctly see government as a large bureaucratic organization with complex rules and hierarchical decision-making. Yet much of the private sector is organized in exactly the same way—in huge corporations with a small number of supervisory positions at the top of the organizational pyramid and many middle-level and low-level jobs at the bottom. The creative, small private firms where initiative is rewarded may still exist in America, but they are the exception rather than the rule.

The government employs a much higher percentage of white-collar workers in its labor force than does the private sector, because government provides services that employ clerical and professional workers. About one-fifth of the jobs in the private sector are still in manufacturing, and many of those are blue-collar or production jobs. The U.S. Census defines jobs as white-collar or blue-collar; so according to their definition, the average government job is different from the average private-sector job.

But Census occupational categories are merely titles. They indicate very little about the content of jobs, what tasks are performed, or how complex they are. To say that the government employs a high percentage of white-collar or professional workers does not reveal much about the nature of their jobs. For example, clerical work, while labeled a white-collar occupation, may be no more stimulating or rewarding than many blue-collar jobs in the private sector.

To make a more meaningful comparison, we divide occupations into three types: high-level, middle-level, and low-level. High-level jobs are generally the most desirable. They offer the highest salaries, carry the most decision-making responsibility, and require the most skill. Middle-level jobs comprise the bulk of the jobs in the economy: they offer moderate salaries, require some education and training, and carry little decision-making responsibility. Low-level jobs are the least desirable: workers in these jobs are paid near or even below the minimum wage, the jobs require little or no skill, and they offer little stability.

How do jobs in the government and private sectors compare based on this classification?

Most jobs in the economy fall in the middle level, with correspondingly fewer jobs in the upper and lower ends of the distribution. The government sector has twice the proportion of high-level jobs and half the proportion of low-level jobs as the private sector. Roughly half of the jobs in each sector fall in the middle category. These differences have remained pretty much unchanged over the last two decades. The proportion of high-level jobs in both the government and private sectors increased somewhat over this period, while the proportion of middle-level jobs decreased.

Government not only employed 17 percent of the work force in 1980 but also 25 percent of all professionals (high-level jobs) in the economy. And it employed 33 percent of all college graduates. Between 1960 and 1980 it accounted for almost one-third of all new high-level jobs and new jobs for college graduates (Table 6-1).

Government employment is also much more secure than private employment. During economic downturns, the private sector is likely to lay off part of its work force, while government can tolerate and even encourage deficit spending in order to keep its programs and activities going. The most severe government cutbacks usually entail hiring freezes, rarely layoffs. Thus, over the last two decades, government workers had an unemployment rate that was just half the rate of private-sector employees.

Race and Sex Differences. There are widespread differences in *who* works in the public and private sectors. Minorities and women have benefited much more from the growth in public-sector employment than have white males.

Government has attempted to improve the economic status of minorities and women not only as an employer. Many of the social welfare programs started in the 1960s, beginning with the War on Poverty, were aimed at the poor and disadvantaged. Since minorities and women make up a disproportionate share of this group, they have been the primary beneficiaries of such spending. Yet while poverty rates overall have declined, minority families and those headed by females (both white and minority) are much *more* likely than white, male-headed families to lie below the poverty line now than ten years ago.[2] Government education and training programs have also had little impact on improving the wages and employment opportunities of minorities and the poor.

Minorities and women have sought to improve their economic status through legislative reform. The civil rights movement pushed for legal reforms as well as social welfare programs. The Civil Rights Act of 1964 was the most important piece of legislation that resulted. It prohibited employers, unions, and employment agencies from discriminating on the basis of race, color, sex, or national origin. The Act was extended to state and local government employment in 1972. Discrimination in hiring, discharge, compensation, training, promotion, and terms and conditions or privileges of employment was prohibited. Racial and sexual discrimination became illegal but did not end.

Women also sought to eliminate legal discrimination through legislation. The Equal Pay Act of 1963 ended separate pay scales for men and women of similar skills working under the same working conditions. It did not mandate equal employment opportunity, however. The Civil Rights Act did (although the inclusion of gender in the legislation was intended to ensure the bill's defeat). Yet it has taken a series of amendments, guidelines, and legal challenges to even approach equality of opportunity for women under the law.

Equality is much easier to define and achieve where women and men hold the same jobs. But most women work at jobs in which few men are employed. In fact, three-quarters of all women em-

2. U.S. Bureau of the Census, *Characteristics of the Population Below the Poverty Level: 1980,* Current Population Reports, Series P-60, No. 133 (Washington, D.C.: U.S. Government Printing Office, 1982), Table 5.

Table 6-1 Employment in Private and Government Jobs, 1960, 1970, 1980 (in millions)

| | All Jobs | | High-level Jobs | | College Graduates | |
---	Private	Government	Private	Government	Private	Government
1960	47.9	7.9	6.8	2.9	3.2	2.0
1970	56.5	12.5	9.6	5.1	4.9	3.9
1980	71.6	15.9	16.2	6.7	10.6	6.0

Source: Calculated from the 1960 and 1970 Public Use Samples and the March 1980 Current Population Survey.

ployed in 1980 were working in occupations filled predominantly by females—a larger percentage than in 1900.[3] Only in 1981 did the U.S. Supreme Court rule that sex-based discrimination charges under Title VII of the Civil Rights Act are not limited to "equal pay for equal work." Nevertheless, the Court did not endorse comparable worth—equal pay for comparable work. True equality of opportunity for women remains much more difficult to achieve, even under the law.

Legislative reforms not only promoted equality of opportunity but also affirmative action. The Equal Employment Opportunity Commission (EEOC) was established to enforce federal antidiscrimination policy. This role included monitoring discrimination, issuing guidelines, and even bringing civil action suits against private firms engaged in discriminatory practices. Court settlements required employers to pay back-wages and to undertake major efforts to redress past discriminatory practices, including hiring, training, and promoting minorities and women. The $33 million settlement to women employees of the American Telephone and Telegraph Company in 1973 was the largest and most publicized of these so-called consent decrees. Such actions by government have undoubtedly spurred affirmative-action programs among other private employers, programs where women and minorities have been sought out for jobs in which they are underrepresented.

A variety of indicators compiled by the U.S. Commission on Civil Rights show that the economic position of minorities and women relative to white males has generally *not* improved over the last two decades, and by some criteria, it has worsened.[4] For example, the relative unemployment rate increased between 1960 and 1976 for nearly all minority and female groups, and for teen-agers. Black and Mexican American teen-agers now have unemployment rates that are four to eight times the white teen-age unemployment rate.

3. Linda J. Waite, *U.S. Women at Work* (Santa Monica, Calif.: The RAND Corporation, 1981), p. 24.
4. U.S. Commission on Civil Rights, *Social Indicators of Equality for Minorities and Women* (Washington, D.C.: U.S. Government Printing Office, 1978).

Earnings remain far from equal. Black males earned 52 percent of what white males earned in 1959, and after more than a decade of civil rights activity, their relative earnings only increased to 65 percent by 1975. Of course, earnings differences not only result from discrimination but also arise because of differences in education and training. Yet even adjusting for those differences, as well as differences in the amount of time worked, black males still received only 85 percent of white male salaries in 1975. Although black males have shown some economic improvement (their relative "adjusted" salaries rose from 71 percent in 1959 to 85 percent in 1975) and black females are also doing somewhat better, the relative earnings of white and Hispanic women have not improved in the last two decades. They continue to earn roughly 50 percent of what is earned by white males with similar education and experience. Overall, minorities and women have not made many inroads into white male domination of higher wages over the last two decades, despite the growth in government expenditures directed at minority and low-income populations and the vast legislative reforms that have attempted to end race and sex discrimination.

Even so, government as an employer has contributed to minority and female equality in the labor market. Not that government doesn't discriminate. It does, but not nearly as much as the private sector. More important, since the government has been responsible for an increasing share of high-level, high-paying jobs in the economy and since an increasing share of those jobs has gone to minorities and women, the growth in government employment alone has accounted for some if not all of the economic improvement for blacks, and has prevented further economic deterioration for other groups, particularly white women.

Differences in Employment Opportunities. The Great Society begun by Lyndon Johnson was not simply aimed at the black poor; it greatly benefited the black middle class. Government spending, particularly at the federal level, funneled billions of dollars into social welfare programs. This spending generated jobs. The Great Society alone generated 2 million jobs, over one-quarter of all government employment between 1960 and 1976.[5] A large proportion of these went to blacks. Over 50 percent of the growth in black employment between 1960 and 1976 was in government, which also generated more than half of the professional, administrative, and technical employment for blacks in this period—most due to social welfare spending.

Why were blacks able to make these employment gains in the government?

It was not due to the benevolence of elected officials or to government affirmative-action programs; rather, political demands by the black community and the civil unrest in many cities during this time made government respond with Great Society programs. Growing government employment in many cities compensated for declining employment opportunities in the private sector. Yet despite the apparent economic gains by at least some blacks in public agencies, their political gains may have been much less.

Women made similar gains from the growth of the public sector. Of course the government has long provided a larger proportion of the jobs for blacks and white women than for white men (Table 6-2). They continued to make gains during the rapid expansion of the public sector in the 1960s. By 1970 almost one-quarter of all black females and nearly one-fifth of all black males and white females worked in the government sector, compared with less than one-seventh of all white males. Employment in the public sector stabilized during the 1970s. By 1980 the proportion of black males and white females had dropped slightly, but the proportion of black females approached 30 percent. Hispanic females also found increasing employment opportunities in the government sector during this decade. Hispanic males did not, however.

Generally, in the American economy, minorities and women are less likely to hold high-level jobs than white males. This is true in government as well as the private sector. At the federal level, for example, minorities and women are concentrated in the lowest-level jobs. A recent Congressional report showed that

5. Michael K. Brown and Steven P. Erie, "Blacks and the Legacy of the Great Society," *Public Policy*, Summer 1981, p. 304.

Table 6-2 Percentage of the Labor Force Employed in the Government Sector, by Race, Sex, and Types of Jobs, 1960, 1970, 1980

	Males			Females			
	White	Black	Hispanic*	White	Black	Hispanic*	TOTAL
All Jobs							
1960	10.5	12.9	8.3	16.0	13.5	8.0	12.3
1970	13.7	19.4	11.0	19.8	24.6	12.9	16.4
1980	13.9	17.9	10.8	19.0	29.4	17.7	16.6
High-Level Jobs							
1960	11.5	18.2	12.5	39.9	57.9	27.3	18.9
1970	18.7	37.1	21.0	44.4	63.3	39.5	27.2
1980	17.7	29.3	21.6	34.5	56.7	37.3	24.6
College Graduates							
1960	21.5	50.8	†	57.7	74.8	†	33.1
1970	27.5	57.1	30.2	61.7	79.3	34.0	39.3
1980	24.8	38.8	31.3	43.7	64.4	41.5	32.5

Sources: Calculated from the 1960 and 1970 Public Use Samples and the March 1980 Current Population Survey.
*The number of Hispanics was undercounted in the 1960 decennial census because they were only identified in five Southwestern states.
†Insufficient number of cases to provide reliable estimates.

70 percent of all minorities held jobs in the lowest 8 levels (out of eighteen levels).[6] And while minorities represented 21 percent of all workers in those agencies surveyed, they held less than 7 percent of all high-level jobs. Women held nearly 50 percent of the jobs in these agencies, but also 80 percent of all jobs in the lowest four levels and only 6 percent of the jobs in the top six levels.

Nonetheless, government has provided more professional opportunities for women and minorities than the private sector. In 1960 only 11 percent of white males in the labor force holding high-level jobs were employed in the public sector. In contrast, the proportion was 18 percent for black males, 40 percent for

6. U.S. House of Representatives, Committee on Education and Labor, "Comparison of Employment Trends for Women and Minorities in Forty-Five Selected Agencies," July 1980, p. 2.

white females, 27 percent for Hispanic females, and 58 percent for black females. During the 1960s the government sector became an even more important source of high-level employment for minorities and women. For minority males particularly, the increase was dramatic: the proportion of black males holding high-level occupations in the government sector more than doubled in the ten-year period! Hispanic males benefited almost as much. During the 1970s, when government employment remained stable, these proportions changed very little. Only white females were able to find an increasing share of high-level employment opportunities outside the government sector. During this decade, the exodus of women from the teaching profession alone could account for that change.

Government also provided a larger proportion of jobs for minority and female college graduates than for white male college graduates during this period. Even in 1960, over half of all black and white female college graduates were employed in government. These proportions increased during the 1960s. During the 1970s government employment opportunities for college graduates slowed considerably, except for Hispanics. But government still remains an important source of jobs for degree holders, particularly for minorities and women.

Differences in Earnings. Earnings vary widely within the public sector just as they do in the private sector. But differences in earnings between high-level and low-level jobs are generally less in the public sector than the private sector. There are also differences in average earnings between the public and private sectors, although those differences have declined over the last two decades and now amount to only about 4 percent. Differences in earnings between race and sex groups, however, remain large in both sectors.

Men are more likely than women, and whites are more likely than minorities, to hold high-level jobs, both in the private and government sectors. These differences contribute to inequalities in earnings. But they don't account for all the observed differences in these earnings.

Table 6-3 Relative Earnings of Persons Employed in High-level Private and Government Jobs, by Race and Sex, 1960, 1970, 1980

	Males			Females		
	White	Black	Hispanic*	White	Black	Hispanic*
Private						
1960	100	52	85	43	32	†
1970	100	67	85	50	42	43
1980	100	74	87	51	53	50
Government						
1960	100	78	†	71	63	†
1970	100	88	95	69	68	69
1980	100	103	101	68	75	69

Sources: Calculated from the 1960 and 1970 Public Use Samples and the March 1980 Current Population Survey.

*The number of Hispanics was undercounted in the 1960 decennial census because they were identified in only five Southwestern states.

†Insufficient number of cases to provide reliable estimates.

Note: Relative earnings are ratios of adjusted annual earnings for women and minorities to earnings of white males. Adjusted earnings calculated from estimated earnings coefficients (education, experience, and annual hours worked) for each group in each category and mean values of independent variables for white males employed in the private sector.

Women and minorities also get paid less than white males when they hold the same jobs. But even when they hold the same jobs, minorities and women may have less education and experience than white males, so they may be less productive and thus receive less pay. Only when comparisons between groups are adjusted for education and training differences as well as differences in the types of jobs can earnings discrimination be detected.

Such comparisons have been done. And they reveal that discrimination exists in the government sector as well as in the private sector, although the level of discrimination is generally less severe. In 1980, for workers employed in middle-level jobs, the relative adjusted earnings for black males to white males was 90 percent in the government sector, compared with 83 percent in the private sector. Relative earnings for Hispanic males were somewhat lower in the government sector (90 percent as opposed to 92 percent in the private sector).[7] The relative earnings of all female groups were higher in the government sector, although not much higher.

Differences in levels of discrimination between the government and private sectors are greatest among high-level jobs and lowest among low-level jobs. In 1980, black males employed in high-level jobs within the private sector earned 67 percent as much as white males, 74 percent after adjusting for differences in individual education and other characteristics (Table 6-3). Yet among those with similar characteristics, black males actually earned more (3 percent) in the government sector than white males. Hispanic males with similar characteristics also earned the same as white males in the government sector, but not in the private sector. So among males, there is little evidence of discrimination within the government's highest levels of occupation. The government does discriminate, however, within most lower-level and middle-level jobs.

Among black men discrimination appeared less severe in 1980 than twenty years earlier. The relative earnings (adjusted) of black males employed in middle-level jobs improved from 70 percent in 1960 to 83 percent in 1980 within the private sector, and from 82 percent to 90 percent in government.[8] There was also some improvement for black males employed in low-level jobs. But for Hispanic males and all females, levels of discrimination changed very little between 1960 and 1980, at least for those employed in low-level and middle-level jobs.

More substantial improvements occurred among workers employed in high-level, professional, and managerial positions. Hispanic males and women registered modest gains but by 1980 still earned substantially less than even those white males with similar characteristics. Black males registered the most impressive gains; their relative adjusted earnings increased from 52 percent in 1960

7. Russell W. Rumberger, "Social Mobility and Public Sector Employment," Stanford University, Institute for Research on Educational Finance and Governance, January 1983, Table 3.
8. Rumberger, op. cit.

to 74 percent in 1980 in the private sector, and from 78 percent to 103 percent in the government sector (Table 6-3).

Except for a relatively small group of blacks and Hispanics in high-level jobs, discrimination remains widespread in the government. Yet government employment offers a more valuable and rewarding place to work for minorities and women. Average earnings for all workers—whites and nonwhites, men and women—are higher in the government sector than in the private sector, at least at the federal level. When differences in vacation and other benefits are included, the public sector becomes even more attractive. Women especially benefit. Minorities and women also do better working for state governments than they do in the private sector.

Differences Within the Private Sector. Although employment and wage patterns vary somewhat among the federal, state, and local levels of government, there are much bigger variations in the private sector. These variations are especially pronounced between industries that are characterized by many small competitive firms (for example, construction, food processing, textiles, and apparel manufacturing) and those that are dominated by a few large corporations (for example, steel, electrical machinery, automobile, and business machines).

Competitive industries generally pay lower average wages than noncompetitive industries to all race and sex groups for low-, middle-, and high-level jobs. The greatest differentials occur in low-level jobs, the least in high-level jobs (Table 6-4). Both competitive and noncompetitive industries discriminate against minorities and especially against women. The greatest differences between male and female earnings occur in middle-level and high-level jobs in competitive industries. For males, on the other hand, the greatest differentials occur in noncompetitive industries.

But only about 20 percent of all women and blacks working in the private sector are employed in noncompetitive industries. Women and minority males are forced to find work in the low-paying, more discriminatory competitive industries because apparently higher-paying, large corporation-dominated industries

Table 6-4   Average Annual Earnings, by Type of Job, Type of Industry, Race, and Sex, 1980

	Type of Job		
	Low-level	Middle-level	High-level
White Males			
Private Competitive	$ 7504	$13,749	$22,262
Private Noncompetitive	$13,177	$17,429	$26,390
Public	$ 8653	$15,156	$20,803
White Females			
Private Competitive	$ 4028	$ 6500	$10,475
Private Noncompetitive	$ 6852	$ 8396	$12,883
Public	$ 4022	$ 7449	$11,809
Black Males			
Private Competitive	$ 6381	$ 9989	$15,026
Private Noncompetitive	$10,996	$14,121	$17,278
Public	$ 7151	$12,478	$17,568
Black Females			
Private Competitive	$ 3719	$ 5915	$10,270
Private Noncompetitive	$ 7246	$ 8484	$13,836
Public	$ 5189	$ 7894	$13,471
Hispanic Males			
Private Competitive	$ 7276	$11,084	$18,545
Private Noncompetitive	$ 9996	$14,397	$21,148
Public	$ 7123	$12,217	$18,485
Hispanic Females			
Private Competitive	$ 4193	$ 6383	$ 9117
Private Noncompetitive	$ 6771	$ 7572	$12,652
Public	$ 3856	$ 6319	$11,445

Source: Calculated from the March 1980 Current Population Survey.

will employ very few. The vast majority of minorities and women in low- and middle-level jobs therefore work for low wages in the most unstable part of the private sector, while a substantial portion (or a majority, in the case of black women) of them in high-level jobs work in government, with most of the rest in competitive industries. *Private enterprise in the noncompetitive industries— including the defense industry—is still the domain of white males.*

All these dimensions of government employment illustrate the increased importance of the public sector as a source of jobs during the last twenty years. More than one-fourth of all new jobs and one-third of all professional jobs in the labor force between 1960 and 1980 were due to government expansion. College graduates, minorities, and women benefited most from these increases. And while it can be argued that if government had not expanded, the taxes used to pay for that expansion would have increased personal consumption—and hence increased private-sector jobs—it is highly unlikely that the jobs created would have been as predominantly professional or employed as high a percentage of women and minorities as resulted from government spending. Furthermore, since government discriminates less in earnings, especially in high-level positions going to minorities and women, expansion not only made it possible for many more college graduates to find suitable jobs but provided higher (less discriminatory) salaries for women and minority graduates.

And when we divide the private sector into competitive industries and those dominated by a few large corporations, we see that these large corporations have been particularly unwilling to hire professional women and minorities, although when they do hire them, salaries are more comparable with government jobs. Since competitive industries pay low wages and the bulk of women and minority college graduates working in private enterprise end up in such industries, the average income of white male college graduates is much higher than that of other groups. The greatest opportunity offered to minorities and women for increasing their salary is through government jobs. Otherwise, they are likely to work in low-paying competitive industries that tend to have the most wage discrimination. By hiring minority and female college graduates into well-paying jobs, government therefore helps large corporations avoid facing the issues of affirmative action and comparable worth.

Indirect Government Employment

Government spending not only employs people directly, it also generates employment both through purchases of goods and services in the private sector and through individual consumption supported by government transfer payments.

Most government spending creates jobs in the economy. When the government builds new buildings, private firms do the work and hire labor. When the government buys paper and fighter bombers, it helps support the industries that produce those products. Even more jobs are created when these private firms purchase materials and services from still other firms—another form of indirect employment initiated by government spending.

Government transfer payments also create jobs. Welfare and social security payments go to individuals who, in turn, use that money to purchase goods and services in the private sector. This spending creates jobs. And, as in the case of direct government purchases, there is additional employment generated as the firms who sell these products purchase other goods and services in the market.

Estimates have been made of the amount of employment generated by the government's purchases of goods and services in the private sector: the U.S. Bureau of Economic Analysis calculated that in 1980, 8 million private-enterprise jobs—about 11 percent of all jobs in the private sector—were created by government spending in the private sector (excluding transfer payments). Our own estimates show further that direct and indirect government employment accounted for one-third of all high-level jobs in 1980 (Table 6-5).

Table 6-5   Direct and Indirect Government Employment, by Type of Job, 1980 (% Distribution)

	Type of Job			
	High-level	Middle-level	Low-level	Total
Direct Government	24.7	14.6	9.7	16.6
Federal	4.8	4.8	2.1	4.3
State	5.7	3.0	1.8	3.6
Local	14.2	6.8	5.8	8.7
Indirect Government	7.8	9.0	6.6	8.3
Federal	3.5	3.9	3.1	3.7
Defense	2.4	2.8	2.5	2.6
Nondefense	1.1	1.1	.6	1.1
State/Local	4.3	5.1	3.5	4.6
Private Sector	51.3	70.0	80.7	66.5
Self-employed	16.3	6.4	3.0	8.6
Total	100.0	100.0	100.0	100.0

Sources: Calculated from the March 1980 Current Population Survey and the 1972 I-O tables for the U.S. Economy; Paula C. Young and Philip M. Ritz, *Updated Input-Output Table of the U.S. Economy: 1972* (Washington, D.C.: U.S. Government Printing Office, 1979), p. 20.

Yet rarely is employment impact a concern of or rationale for government spending. The only exception is public-employment programs, such as the Emergency Employment Act (EEA), signed by President Nixon in 1971, and its successor, the Comprehensive Employment and Training Act (CETA), signed by President Ford in 1973. But most government spending goes into procurement, providing services, or transfer payments—programs that have other goals, not particularly employment. Even so, such spending has enormous implications for employment, and shifts in spending can affect jobs significantly.

The Reagan Administration has reduced transfer payments and cut nondefense spending. It has cut federal employment. These actions will reduce direct and indirect government employment. At the same time, the Administration wants to increase defense spending, which will increase direct and indirect employment. What will be the overall effect of these actions on employment? Will they increase or decrease it?

We are not only interested in the *amount* of employment generated by government spending but also the *type* of employment and *who* gets employed. Direct government employment favors high-level jobs, jobs for college graduates, and opportunities for women and minorities.

How does indirect government employment compare? What kinds of jobs are created and who holds those jobs?

Employment from Government Purchases. A large portion of government spending is used to purchase goods and services in the private sector. In 1980 the federal government pumped $117 billion, 19 percent of its total budget, into the private sector.[9] Of that total, $79 billion was for defense programs and $38 billion was for nondefense programs. State and local governments pumped in another $148 billion, 42 percent of their total budgets. This spending accounted for over 10 percent of all private-sector sales of goods and services. Obviously the government is an important customer for private enterprise in America. While many business leaders complain about the taxes they pay and the regulations they must follow, they rarely acknowledge how important the government is for much of their livelihood.

Most federal spending in the private sector is for defense programs, which are concentrated within a few industries. The ordnance and aircraft industries alone received one-third of all defense spending in 1972. Another 12 percent was spent in communications. Nondefense federal spending was somewhat more diffused, with one-quarter going to construction and 10 percent to medical and educational services. State and local spending outweighs federal spending, and over half was spent on construction and another 10 percent on business services in 1972. The

9. U.S. Bureau of Economic Analysis, *Survey of Current Business*, March 1982, p. 11.

remainder was spread over many other industries.[10]

A number of industries depend heavily on government purchases, which in 1972 accounted for a sizable portion of the total demand in construction (29 percent), ordnance (86 percent), chemicals (30 percent), communications (39 percent), aircraft and parts (61 percent), and business services (44 percent). Most spending for ordnance, chemicals, communications, and aircraft comes from defense spending, while spending on construction and business services comes from nondefense spending. A shift in spending policy from nondefense to defense spending, as the Reagan Administration is pursuing, will obviously benefit some industries at the expense of others. It will also affect employment.

As we have noted, direct government employment favors women and minorities—it provides proportionally more and better employment opportunities than they can find in the private sector. But the same is not true of indirect government employment.

While government spending is spread over many industries in the private sector, defense spending is more concentrated. Much of it is spent on weapons systems. These employ proportionally more white males than other groups. A large fraction of state and local government outlays in the private sector was spent in the construction industry (almost 50 percent in 1972), which also employs proportionally more white males than women or minorities. So while government spending generates a substantial number of jobs in the private sector, these jobs benefit white males more than other race or sex groups.

Employment from Transfer Payments. Transfer payments represent an increasing share of government budgets in recent years, especially at the federal level. The federal government spent $245 billion dollars, or 41 percent of its budget, on transfer

10. Paul C. Young and Philip M. Ritz, *Updated Input-Output Table of the U.S. Economy: 1972* (Washington, D.C.: U.S. Government Printing Office, 1979), p. 20. These data are the latest available.

payments in 1980.[11] State and local governments spent another $39 billion—11 percent of their budgets.

Transfer payments to individuals supplement personal income. They increase personal consumption expenditures. And they generate jobs. Most transfer payments originate from social welfare and retirement programs, such as unemployment insurance, aid to families with dependent children, Medicaid, civilian and military pensions. They are used primarily to purchase food, clothing, housing, and medical services.

Consumption generated from transfer payments is concentrated in a few private-sector industries. The major part of each dollar spent on transfer payments in 1972 went to four industries —food products (14 cents), wholesale and retail trade (19 cents), real estate and rental (14 cents), and medical and educational services (17 cents).[12] Yet none of these industries depended on these expenditures for a large portion of their sales. This situation contrasts sharply with some of the recipients of government purchases, especially defense industries, who do depend heavily on government support.

The magnitude of transfer programs suggests that an additional portion of private-sector employment in this country results from increased private consumption by the poor and elderly due to transfer payments. This consumption creates jobs, primarily in human-service industries, half of which are in the private sector. This segment of the economy accounted for one-fifth of all employment in 1980 and one-quarter of all new jobs between 1960 and 1980. Six million of these jobs—one-third of the total—were generated by federal social programs.[13]

Employment growth in human-service industries have particularly benefited women. A third of all women—who comprise a majority of human-service workers—are employed there. Be-

11. U.S. Bureau of Economic Analysis, op. cit.
12. Young and Ritz, op. cit.
13. Michael K. Brown and Steven P. Erie, "Women, Blacks and Reagan's Assault on the Great Society," paper presented at the annual meeting of the Conference Group on the Political Economy of Advanced Industrial Societies, Denver, Colorado, September 2–5, 1981, p. 16.

tween 1960 and 1980, human services created over one-third of all new jobs for white women and over half of all new jobs for black women. Over half of all professional, technical, and managerial job gains for white and black women took place in this sector during the same period. So government spending on transfer programs definitely produced employment gains for women.

Of course, the taxes used to support transfer programs reduce the personal consumption of other people, mainly those with higher incomes. In the absence of taxes, the wealthy would no doubt increase their consumption of luxury goods, creating more jobs in those industries. It is difficult to estimate whether more jobs are created or lost from the redistribution of income. But our calculations suggest that transfer payments generate *more* employment than other types of private spending, including fixed investments (see Table 6-6).

The Employment Impact of Shifting Government Spending. Government spending has a tremendous employment impact on both the public and private sectors of the economy. The Reagan Administration's changes in the pattern of this spending have profoundly altered job opportunities for various groups in society.

While the current administration has been unable to actually reduce the total federal budget, it has shifted spending patterns. Defense spending has increased; nondefense spending, grants to state and local governments, and transfer payments to individuals have been cut. At the same time, private spending has increased, largely due to the tax cuts stemming from the Economic Recovery Tax Act of 1981. The Administration believes that these actions will create more jobs in the private sector than will be lost in the public sector. We disagree.

The U.S. Bureau of Labor Statistics (1975) made demand projections of the U.S. economy in 1980 and 1985. In Table 6-6 we use them to estimate the average amount of employment generated by $1 billion (in 1963 dollars) in demand. Estimates are shown for separate demand components—government (federal and state/local) and private (personal consumption expenditures, fixed investment, and gross exports). Since these figures are based on projec-

Table 6-6   Estimated Employment Impact of Changing Government Expenditures

Budget Categories (Demand Categories)	Jobs created per $1 billion (1963 dollars) of demand in 1980*	Proposed budget changes, 1983 (in billions of dollars)	Employment impact of budget changes†
	(1)	(2)	(3)
Purchases of goods and services (federal government demand)			
Defense	96,690	16.2	463,425
Government jobs	54,351		260,499
Private sector jobs	42,339		202,926
Nondefense	86,476	−3.7	−94,633
Government jobs	40,050		−43,842
Private sector jobs	46,426		−50,821
Grants-in-aid to state/ local government (state and local government demand)	126,487	−9.4	−351,769
Government jobs	87,865		−244,358
Private sector jobs	38,622		−107,411
Transfer payments to persons (personal consumption expenditures)	74,151	−10.3	−255,963
Government jobs	1503		−4580
Private sector jobs	72,648		−221,383
Total change		−12.0	−208,970
Government jobs			−32,281
Private sector jobs			176,689

Sources: U.S. Bureau of Labor Statistics, *The Structure of the U.S. Economy in 1980 and 1985* (Washington, D.C.: U.S. Government Printing Office, 1979), p. 108; Charles A. Waite and Joseph C. Wakefield, "Federal Fiscal Programs," *Survey of Current Business* (March 1982), p. 23.

*Components of state and local government demand and personal consumption expenditures aggregated based on distribution of demand in 1980.

†1983 dollars (column 2) converted to 1963 dollars, then multiplied by column (1).

tions, the exact figures may be inaccurate. Moreover, the figures represent the *average* amount of employment associated with each $1 billion of demand, not the incremental number of jobs created with a $1 billion increase in demand. But the estimates can still be used to make relative comparisons between the number of jobs generated by government spending and the number of jobs generated by private spending. We have used them to assess the employment impact of Reagan's 1983 government budget, as he first proposed it in February 1982.

One billion dollars of government spending, particularly at the state and local levels, generates *more* total jobs than $1 billion of private spending: Federal spending on defense produces 96,690 jobs per $1 billion, while spending on nondefense programs generates 86,476 jobs. These jobs are about evenly divided between the public and private sectors. State and local government spending generates 126,487 jobs, most of those in the public sector (many in teaching). In contrast, $1 billion in personal consumption expenditures generates 74,151 jobs, while a similar amount spent on fixed investments is associated with 67,726 jobs.[14]

In its original 1983 budget, the Reagan Administration proposed increasing defense spending $16.2 billion over 1982 levels and decreasing all other spending—$3.7 billion in nondefense spending, $10.3 billion in transfer payments to individuals, and $9.4 billion in aid to state and local governments. Total federal expenditures were to be cut by $12 billion.

Each of these changes will affect employment, in both the private and government sectors. Their net effect is to eliminate over 200,000 jobs, most of them in the private sector (see Table 6-6). The President also wants to cut other federal-level jobs. Reductions in the federal work force have already begun, with women and blacks suffering the highest layoff rates (at least in managerial positions). Will new private-sector jobs be created to replace the jobs that are lost from federal expenditure cuts? That is impossible to predict, but this evidence suggests that the fiscal policies of the

14. U.S. Bureau of Labor Statistics, cited in Table 6-6.

current administration will *reduce* the number of jobs in the economy, not increase them.

Since a relatively high percentage of government jobs go to professionals and college graduates—especially minority and women college graduates—cuts in government employment will have a particularly big impact on these groups. Despite the more rapid growth of private-sector employment among these groups in the 1970s, most of it was in competitive private firms at much lower wages than they would have received in government. The Reagan cuts practically spell the end of social mobility for higher-educated women, blacks, and Hispanics.

The expansion of government spending is more than the provision of social welfare. It is a social investment policy. As we have noted, one-third of all U.S. college graduates are now employed by government (this figure reached almost 40 percent in 1970). A much higher percentage of the skills of highly trained women and minorities would not have been utilized and rewarded if it had not been for government.

And it isn't as if government employed these skills and produced nothing with them. For the most part, government employees deliver educational, health, and other services that are demanded by the public. When government employment is cut, it means that these services are reduced. And it means a corresponding decrease in the human capital formation—through formal schooling, training, and health care—that has been instrumental to our rapid, scientifically oriented economic development. Further, government employment has helped reduce inequality in our society by paying more equal wages to women and minorities than they get in the private sector.

We therefore see expanded government employment as a crucial element in our overall alternative to present economic and social policies. Full employment cannot be achieved without it; greater income equality and social mobility are impossible without it; and greater economic democracy is integral to sound and equitable employment policies. Our crime, welfare, and social security policies also hinge on the government's function as employer. The last fifty years should have provided enough convincing evidence that "trickle-down" employment and income are illusory—not only for the poor, but for many of the nation's professionals and college-educated.

7 The Democratic Alternative: Neoliberals vs. Economic Democrats

Reaganomics as an alternative to exhausted New Deal liberalism has public appeal because it promises simple solutions: the more we can get government—especially taxes—out of the economy, the better things will be. Reaganomics is also backed by American business, which has not enjoyed such a profit-oriented administration since the 1920s. But the blatantly pro-business, pro-high-income policies of supply-side economics have an important drawback: by taking away hard-won entitlements and shifting national income to profits and the rich, the policies create serious resistance among the vast majority of voters.

Apparently set adrift by the disintegration of New Deal accords, Democrats have been slow to develop or embrace sensible alternatives for actual and potential victims of supply-side policies. One widely discussed solution to the present crisis comes from neoliberal economist Lester Thurow and financier Felix Rohatyn. That solution calls for the creation of a Reconstruction Finance Corporation that would use tax monies to fund America's reindustrialization. In other words, the RFC would be a kind of national bank in the business of promoting capital investment in U.S. industry.

There is not total agreement among neoliberals about what kind of industry would be supported by the RFC. Thurow thinks that unprofitable, sunset industries should be allowed to die and sunrise industries like high-tech computer firms should be promoted. Rohatyn feels that the RFC should save America's sunset heavy-industry base through renovating its machinery and equipment (robotizing the automobile industry, for example), even though such industries may have difficulty competing in international markets. Nevertheless, a national public financial institution investing directly in American business—as the Japanese government invests in Japanese business—is central to the neoliberal approach. Who will run the RFC is less clear, but it seems likely that financiers and corporate managers are the kind of people Thurow and Rohatyn have in mind, perhaps with a few labor leaders included for show.[1]

Thurow's brand of neoliberal economics includes many of our views: He believes that full employment is the only real answer to poverty and the welfare spending problem. He argues for a more equal income distribution for Americans, close to the income distribution of the white male 40 percent of the labor force. He wants fairer taxation rather than higher tax rates. He agrees that government is not only here to stay but that it can play an active and creative role in making America a better place for everyone to work and live in. He believes that Americans' innovativeness is a source of continued economic renewal and that high technology and increased education and research can provide solutions to productivity and production.

However, with all this agreement there is also profound disagreement. We are firmly convinced that Thurow and other neoliberals make crucial errors at several levels.

They place all their confidence in the very same big-business community that contributed and is continuing to contribute so actively to the present crisis. Indeed, they share with Reaganomics the erroneous assumptions of private business' social conscience and managerial efficiency.

1. The original RFC was run by big businessmen and used public funds to subsidize America's largest corporations throughout the 1930s and 1940s. For an excellent discussion of the RFC experience and corporate influence over public agencies, see Kim McQuaid, *Big Business and Presidential Power from FDR to Reagan* (New York: Morrow, 1982). On the need for a new RFC, see Felix Rohatyn, "Why the Biggest Problems Are the Biggest Opportunities," *The Economist*, September 19, 1981, and Lester Thurow, "Thurow's Third Way," *The Economist*, March 31, 1982.

They focus so heavily on the emergence of high-tech industry that they ignore the tremendous concentration of profits in oil/gas companies and the financial sector. The structure of the economy has changed drastically and with it control of investments. How will neoliberals deal with these new concentrations of private capital, if at all?

The neoliberals' fondness for a high-tech future ignores a number of less than pleasant realities about the electronics industry. The employment structure of microchip production is highly segmented between high-paying good jobs for engineers or trained specialists and jobs for the chip producers and circuit assemblers. Production and assembly work in what has been dubbed "Silicon Valley"—the home of hundreds of computer firms in California's Santa Clara Valley—is carried out almost entirely by women and minorities, increasingly by women immigrants from Korea, Thailand, the Philippines, and Vietnam. The work is low-paying, employing nonunion labor, and frequently being done under arduous and hazardous conditions—for example, the acids and solvents used in the production of microchips pose a number of health hazards.[2]

Economists Barry Bluestone and Bennett Harrison, in their study of unemployed manufacturing workers in the Northeast, find that a middle-aged machinist who loses his job in basic industry almost never finds a job with high-tech firms. In Oregon, high-tech industries coming into the Willamette Valley hired newly arrived workers from out of state and local women but did not pick up the unemployed from the wood and timber industry. The growth of the high-tech computer industry will not provide jobs for the unionized blue-collar workers who lose jobs as plants in heavy industry continue to shut down. Where will the jobs for these skilled workers come from?[3]

2. For a description of working conditions in the microchip industry and other related problems, see Robert Howard, "Second Class in Silicon Valley," *Working Papers,* September/October 1981.

3. The Bureau of Labor Statistics estimates that high-tech industries will employ only 5 percent of the work force in 1990, the same proportion as in 1980 ("Current Employment and Projected Growth in High Technology Occupations and Indus-

Another social effect of making computer high tech into *the* growth industry of the future is that the increased use of computers and robotics will, in many other sectors of the economy, actually cause greater unemployment. It might make sense to introduce robots into a new auto plant or to computerize office services to increase productivity, but both will certainly put workers out on the street. Little thought is given by the neoliberals to the management of this transition.[4]

There is also the sticky problem of *already* worldwide overcapacity in the microchip industry. Every country cannot be a winner in the world high-tech sweepstakes. To rely mainly on computers to win back international economic strength is to gamble the nation's future on a single horse.

Neoliberals view high tech as a breeding ground for entrepreneurs—a hotbed of opportunities for small businesses to appear, grow, create jobs, and prosper. While it is true that many successful computer firms have been started in garages or spare rooms by a few engineers or software geniuses, the staying power of these new firms is often weak. For example, Bowmar Instrument Corporation—the firm that produced one of the first handheld calculators, the Bowmar Brain, in the early 1970s. Large corporations soon produced cheaper copies, undersold Bowmar, and it went out of business. As the technology matures, large corporations with tremendous capital resources and marketing/

---

tries," submitted to the Joint Economic Committee, August 1982). High-tech firms may provide even fewer jobs if they follow the lead of Atari, which announced in March 1983 that it was dismissing 1700 employees and moving production to Hong Kong and Taiwan (*The New York Times,* March 19, 1983).

For a critical discussion of employment prospects for high tech, see Henry M. Levin and Russell W. Rumberger, "The Educational Implications of High Technology," Stanford University, Institute for Research on Educational Finance and Governance, February 1983 (forthcoming in *Technology Review*); "America Rushes to High Technology for Growth," *Business Week,* March 28, 1983, pp. 84–98; and "High Technology Industries and the Future of Employment," edited by Ann Markusen and Marc Weiss, University of California at Berkeley, Institute of Urban and Regional Development, 1983.

4. Robots alone could displace up to 8 million workers—currently 8 percent of the employed work force—by the year 2025 (Robert Ayres and Steve Miller, "Industrial Robots on the Line," *Technology Review,* May/June 1982, p. 42.)

advertising capabilities come to dominate industries.

Finally, much of the other high-tech production being touted as the growth engine of the future—particularly bio-engineering and robotics—is heavily capital intensive and will generate relatively few jobs. Bio-engineering plants, for example, are similar to breweries in that the processing of the organic product is highly mechanized and computer-controlled.[5]

The neoliberal solution also counts heavily on wage accords that make and supposedly keep American industry competitive in world markets. Yet these wage accords seem primarily to promote higher profits. What does labor get in return? A full-employment policy? Legislation to promote union organizing? More control over the work process? Equal representation on boards of directors? Open books? Participation in investment decisions? Neoliberals do not discuss these crucial matters.

Neoliberals stress the need to compete in world markets. They support "free trade" and deplore union attempts to save jobs through protective legislation. The problem with simply being pro–world trade without considering the power of multinational corporations is that such a narrow perspective takes the increasing worldwide division of labor as a given. The working conditions of "cheap labor" in many Third World countries raise questions about how human beings should be treated. Some neoliberals argue that the shift of low-wage manufacturing to these countries will help them develop economically, but all too frequently economic growth occurs with little sustained economic development for the mass of the population. Puerto Rico is just one case in point. In the 1950s and 1960s, many American firms located manufacturing plants on the island, attracted by low wages and special tax breaks. In the 1970s, however, industry left the island for areas with even cheaper labor. Unemployment in Puerto Rico soared. Seventy percent of the population remains below the poverty line; 60 percent are on food stamps. The firms took their profits and invested elsewhere. For a time there was economic growth, but

5. For the challenge posed by increasing mechanization see the special issue of *Scientific American,* September 1982, on the mechanization of work.

not balanced, indigenous economic development.[6]

And what about national self-sufficiency in basic industry like steel and automobiles? Should the United States shut down its steel and auto plants and rely on Brazil or Taiwan or Japan for these products? What is the optimal way of producing steel if we think it should continue to be produced? How much are we willing to pay to have a national auto industry? What has to happen to wages if these industries are to keep producing without large deficits? Who should manage them? These are matters for national debate, but neoliberals tend to downplay such questions by focusing so heavily on high tech and free trade.

Finally, the neoliberals are fundamentally elitist. They believe that in this technology-oriented world, "experts" should make decisions for the mass of nonexperts. It is no accident that Gary Hart—product of the JFK era—should embrace the neoliberal technocracy. The early 1960s were the zenith of belief in technical solutions to social problems, including solving guerrilla wars in Vietnam and poverty in Watts and Detroit. The point is that "experts" like those economists who thought they could fine-tune the American economy and the bankers who now sit on the Federal Reserve Board (and those who would undoubtedly run the neoliberal RFC) ultimately make *political* decisions that benefit some at the expense of others. For Thurow, this is the very reason to have experts rather than representatives of constituencies like labor or consumers on the RFC board. But experts have a way of making serious errors because of their distance from the political and economic consequences of their acts.

Democracy and Economics: The Crucial Link

What both Reaganomics and the neoliberals propose has the great appeal of leaving to others the responsibility for our lives. The conservative philosophy—based on Adam Smith's "invisible

6. For an excellent discussion of the elements of a progressive trade policy for the U.S., see Bob Kuttner, "The Free Trade Fallacy," *The New Republic*, March 28, 1983, pp. 16–21.

hand"—tells us straightforwardly that if each of us pursues individual goals and tries to maximize income, the total benefits to the *whole society* are maximized. No one has to be concerned with the collective welfare because it is mysteriously taken care of by all of us doing the best we can individually. In fact, any interference by a collective institution like government can only reduce the chances of achieving that maximum collective welfare. How convenient. The only public function we as individuals have to be concerned about is to elect governments that will consistently ensure private enterprise and minimum government interference in our economic and social lives. Other than that, we should concentrate—as individuals—on succeeding economically (or not succeeding, if that's our thing).

Unfortunately, the leap of faith that allowed Adam Smith and later generations of utilitarians and conservatives to invoke laissez-faire never had any empirical or even theoretical basis: there is absolutely no evidence that individuals pursuing their own greedy ambitions produce maximum collective good.[7] On the contrary, we have seen under laissez-faire the development of huge fortunes, the concentration of industry, and the influence of giant, unaccountable corporations on allegedly "laissez-faire" government to further their interests. And what might Adam Smith say about a conservative administration's huge expansion of military expenditures in the name of defense (one of the "legitimate" functions of a laissez-faire government)? And what about the "invisible hand" of nuclear armaments destructive enough to end all economic systems? Must not the public be ever vigilant and participative to ensure that the collective good is maximized?

Neoliberals reject Adam Smith's philosophy. The collective good can only be assured and improved on through government intervention in what is a corporate system dominated by large, noncompetitive institutions. But neoliberals—like conservatives—

7. Albert Hirschman in *The Passion and the Interest* (Princeton, N.J.: Princeton University Press, 1978) and Lucio Colletti in *From Rousseau to Lenin* (New York: Monthly Review Press, 1970) are the best sources for understanding the flaws in Smith's argument.

also let the public off the hook. Elect us, they say, and we shall turn over the economy and government to experts who know the ropes. Experts will solve our economic and social problems, problems too complex to be left either to the marketplace or public participation. Again, the proposal is appealing politically. The public often wants to avoid getting involved—wants to avoid the anxiety and tediousness of political participation.

Economic democracy's emphasis on greater and wider participation, therefore, goes against the grain of recent American political history. For us, neither the Big Daddy of the "invisible hand" nor that of government "expertise" will work in the public interest. For democracy to work, each citizen must *increase* his or her responsibility for the collective good rather than give that responsibility away. Democracy is participation and struggle, not something that was signed into being at a Constitutional Convention two hundred years ago and then signed away to others.

The set of reform policies that we propose here are necessarily short-term, although they indicate a long-term direction for the economy. They speak most immediately to the next five to ten years. They are not revolutionary; they will not lead to a perfect society. But they can bring about a substantially more decent and democratic form of a mixed economy. Whether this is labeled a more humane capitalism or a step toward democratic socialism, we leave to theorists. We are interested in what will work to promote balanced economic growth, greater equity, and, above all, more democracy.

While taking a pragmatic view of the economy, we are not technocrats. We do not believe that simply having better managers at the heads of the major corporations or smarter economists in Washington is the answer to the nation's economic problems. Unlike some neoliberal politicians, we do not naïvely endorse reliance on high-tech or export-oriented industries as a magic solution. Science has certainly produced many miracles in the last century, but it has not and cannot solve the world's social problems. The social advances that have been made are the result of greater participation in governing science and the development of the uses of that science.

The reform policies that we advocate are *inseparable* from the democratic means of carrying them out. Raising wages and productivity, creating new enterprises, rebuilding inner cities—these and other vital economic tasks can only be carried out with the fullest cooperation and participation of a majority of citizens who are allowed and encouraged to take part—as citizens, workers, and consumers—in economic decision-making. This is, in simple form, the idea of economic democracy. If short-run sacrifices such as wage restraint or cuts in social benefits are required of some Americans to revive the economy—and they may well be necessary—then the sacrifices should be shared and the decisions about the nature of the sacrifices and trade-offs should be made as democratically as possible and include those affected by the results of the decision-making process. Closing a large plant in a community, for example, affects the workers at the plant and the community's small businesses, its schools and other services, and, in some cases, its very existence. The citizens of the community should therefore be represented in a company's decision to shut down or move.

Our analysis leads inescapably to the conclusion that, ineffective as it may be presently, the public sector has fulfilled the democratic mandate much more successfully than the corporations could ever hope or want to. While we believe in democratizing private corporations, it would be naïve to count on such a reform as the sole basis of economic democracy. Historically, it has been government that has recognized the demands of working Americans for collective bargaining representation and the demands of minorities and women for upward mobility. It has been government that has protected Americans' health and safety on the job and the right to guaranteed health care off the job. Wherever the issue of economic and social security and equality has arisen, we have turned to the public sector, exercising our democratic prerogatives to attain these goals. Our task, then, is to make our existing public institutions more democratic, to create new, democratic public institutions where necessary, and to use those institutions to make the private sector more responsive to public needs. The private sector can and probably should continue to play an important role in production, but if economic democracy is to be achieved, corporations' autonomy in investment and social decisions must be severely reduced at the same time that efforts are made to democratize these corporations.

Economic democracy can produce steady, equitable growth without inflation and with far less unemployment. While monetarists have associated inflation solely with expansion of the money supply, and thus with government overintervention, we have argued that much of the inflation during the seventies was due to attempts by large corporations to recover so-called "normal" profits and by labor's reaction to falling real wage rates. American business abandoned investment policies that raise worker productivity, opting instead for speculating in real estate and for wage-reducing moves to "better business climates." A program for growth that returns to investing in workers and adds increased participation could raise productivity sharply and increase employment with increased real wages and without inflation. And a more concerted attack on the structural components of inflation through fuel conservation and rationalization of the health-care system, food production, and housing would also help move us toward full employment and equity without rapid price increases.

The winning of these new reform policies will require a mass-based, democratic movement which supports political leaders who believe in economic democracy. The movement and its leaders must be willing to confront the established, corporate-supported, economic reasoning that has led us into our present impasse. They must be willing to move beyond many of the traditional views of the relation between government and economy. We discuss the possibilities for such a movement later, but before doing that, we address the movement's need for a clearly spelled out and relatively simple set of new national economic policies that it can advocate, and outline how to make our present public institutions more democratic.

Elements of a National Economic Policy

Greater Public Investment: Jobs and Balanced Growth. The path to economic recovery should be led by increased investment in nonmilitary goods and services. The case for cutting back ever-higher military spending has been made persuasively by other experts (see particularly the Boston Study Group's report),[8] and we will not repeat it here. What we argue for is a well-planned expansion of the public sector in nonmilitary areas. The goal is not only jobs per se, but the production of socially desirable goods and services to meet unmet needs, and the shift from jobs that are primarily filled by already skilled white male workers already in great demand and earning high wages (see our analysis in Chapter 6) to more jobs for minorities and women, especially high-unemployed, low-wage minorities and women. These goals point to fuller employment and the economic/social mobility of the least incorporated groups in the labor force, as well as to improving the quality of American life.

Some unmet needs are becoming obvious even to business publications. For example, the public infrastructure of many American cities is decaying. Both *Business Week* and *Newsweek* devoted cover stories to this situation in 1982. A detailed report, *America In Ruins,* commissioned by the Council of State Planning Agencies, noted that "the maintenance of public facilities essential to national economic renewal has been deferred." Greater public spending for roads, bridges, urban water systems, and mass-transit lines will create jobs and stimulate suppliers of goods in the private sector. Increased spending for public arts and public television and radio provides both jobs and easily accessible public goods at low cost. Increased investment in education not only provides some chance for minority-group and blue-collar economic and social mobility but is a long-term investment in human capital vital

8. Boston Study Group, *The Price of Defense* (New York: Times Books, 1979), and the useful summary by Philip Morison and Paul Walker, "A New Strategy for Military Spending," *Scientific American,* October 1978.

to our society's economic and cultural health.

Government cuts in this kind of public spending in the name of halting inflation are consistent with the private-sector investment attitudes we analyzed in Chapter 5. Rather than investing in higher worker productivity, private firms have concentrated their spending on lowering costs, particularly labor costs, even if this also means lower productivity. Cost-effectiveness and profitability in the short-term now dominate corporate thinking. Influenced by this trend, government, particularly under the Reagan Administration, has reduced human services without taking into account the effects of those reductions on productivity, especially in the long-term. The maintenance and renewal of our urban centers, the expansion of public education and health care, and the maintenance and development of transportation systems are all crucial to the quality of life, people's well-being, and labor's productivity. Beyond these obvious needs, we should be thinking about ways to improve American life in the coming decades, including new ways of looking at health care, the use of increased leisure time in more active and self-educational ways (rather than simply an increase in television viewing), and the relationship between the educational system and the workplace.

The case for decreasing the role of government in the economy is based on the relative inefficiency of public spending. We not only question the validity of that idea but argue that when "employment efficiency" and "equality efficiency" are included in social performance criteria, government has done much better than private enterprise. Private enterprise is either unwilling or unable to achieve full employment at wages that are socially acceptable to the American people. Government has provided jobs and social mobility to minorities, women, and the growing percentage of college graduates in the labor force. It is inconceivable that America can significantly reduce unemployment and equalize opportunity for minorities and women (thus reducing poverty) without increased public investment and public intervention.

In addition, production of goods and services for improving the quality of American life rather than jeopardizing it through an

Table 7-1   Illustrative New Programs or Major Expansions of Existing Federal Civilian Programs, Fiscal Year 1972

Program	Hypothetical expenditures (billions of dollars)
Total expenditures	39.7
Education	7.0
Preschool	1.0
Elementary and secondary	2.5
Higher	3.0
Vocational	.5
Health	3.8
Kiddie-care	.5
Medicare for disabled	1.8
Comprehensive health centers	1.0
Hospital construction and modernization	.5
Nutrition	1.0
Community service programs	.8
Jobs and manpower	2.5
Public jobs	1.8
Manpower Development Training Act	.5
Employment service	.2
Social security and income support	9.5
Unemployment insurance	2.0
Public assistance	4.0
Social security improvements	3.5
Veterans	.3
Economic, area, and other special development programs	2.2
Entrepreneurial aid	.5
Area redevelopment	.5
Rural development	1.0
Indian assistance	.2
Crime, delinquency, and riots	1.0
Violence and riot prevention	.1
Safe streets programs	.3
Rehabilitation of offenders and delinquents	.3

Source: "Report to the President" from the Cabinet Coordinating Committee on Economic Planning for the End of Vietnam Hostilities, in Economic Report of the President, transmitted to the Congress January 1969. The Report includes an explanation of the content of the program categories. Taken from: Seymour Melman, The Permanent War Economy (New York: Simon & Schuster, 1974), pp. 192–193. Copyright © 1974 by Seymour Melman. Reprinted by permission of Simon & Schuster, a division of Gulf & Western Corporation.

Program	Hypothetical expenditures (billions of dollars)
Prevention of delinquency and crime by special measures for delinquency-prone youth	.3
Quality of environment	1.7
Air pollution prevention and control	.1
Public water supply construction programs	.3
Water pollution control and sewage treatment	1.0
Solid waste disposal	.1
Natural beautification, environmental protection, and recreational development	.2
Natural resource development and utilization	1.4
Land and forest conservation	.2
Water resources and related programs	.5
Mineral and energy (excluding hydroelectric) development	.2
Natural environmental development	.5
Urban development	5.5
New cities	.5
Land acquisition and financial planning (suburban)	.5
Urban mass transportation	.5
Model cities	2.0
Other urban facilities and renewal	2.0
Transportation	1.0
Airway and airport modernization	.4
Rapid interurban ground transit	.1
Modernization of merchant marine	.2
Motor vehicle and transportation safety research and safety grants	.3
Science and space exploration	1.0
Post-Apollo space program	.5
Scientific research in oceanography communications, social and behavioral sciences, and natural sciences	.5
Foreign economic aid	1.0

arms race requires a shift in federal spending from military to nonmilitary purposes. Various economists have drawn up plans for nonmilitary spending. Columbia University professor Seymour Melman, an expert on alternative uses of military production facilities, proposes—in *The Permanent War Economy*—alternative budgets showing what present military spending could buy in transportation and human services, as well as adequate defense (see Table 7-1). Economists Barry Bluestone and Bennett Harrison advocate a program of investment in mass transit, freight rail transport, housing, energy, and health care.[9] The Urban League has called for a massive Marshall Plan for the cities. The Mid-Peninsula Conversion Project, a northern California–based organization, is working with unions, engineers, and activists in military-dependent communities and with the defense industries to develop alternative production projects.

Table 7-2   Jobs Generated by $1 billion (in 1970 dollars) in Public Spending

Job Corps	151,000
Teachers	100,000
Nurses	77,000
Public Housing	76,000
Sewer Construction	76,000
School Construction	50,000
Defense (civilian)	55,000

Source: Congressional Record, May 23, 1972, H, 4917

We are not arguing for the specifics of one plan or another, just for the idea of increased public spending for needed social production. Public investment in tangible goods and services provides results because it can be *targeted* to areas and sectors of social need; in the process, jobs are created in numerous private concerns— frequently in small businesses—that supply local and state government programs with materials and services. Our analysis in Chapter 6 showed how Reaganomics' shift of government spending from social welfare to the military would cost the economy private-sector jobs: jobs generated by nonmilitary spending outnumber military-related jobs because aircraft and ordnance industries are generally high technology and capital-intensive. In addition, the figures below give some further indication of the differences.

9. Barry Bluestone and Bennett Harrison, "Economic Development, the Public Sector, and Full Employment," in Marcus Raskin, editor, *The Federal Budget and Social Reconstruction*, Washington, D.C.: Institute for Policy Studies, 1978.

We showed in Chapter 6 that the higher number of total jobs created by nonmilitary spending is only part of the effect such a shift would have on employment. Military contract jobs are filled —perhaps more than in any other sector of the economy—by skilled white males in the prime of their work lives. This is precisely the group that least needs increased job opportunity. Increasing nonmilitary spending will provide jobs for the groups with the highest *unemployment* rates and the groups that are most in need of opportunities for upward mobility. But to repeat: military spending tends to reduce the total number of jobs for *everyone,* not just minorities and women. White male steelworkers are also indirectly affected by spending tax dollars for missiles instead of helping steel or bringing new industries to Pittsburgh and Youngstown.

The process of identifying the kinds of nonmilitary spending most needed can be democratized by asking city councils and local planning commissions to draw up an inventory of unmet public infrastructure needs. The Congress, each year, would establish a National Capital Budget to identify public infrastructure investments and to allocate public funds to decentralized grants programs in cities and states. A new vehicle might be created—a National Development Bank—to provide federal front-end financing for major regional and local economic development projects. (There are a number of legislative proposals for such a bank now in Congress.)

Democratization of Investment. The economy needs more than just greater public investment and greater accountability for that investment to workers and consumers. The private investment process itself must be democratized. Investment decisions by large banks and insurance companies and by the managers of large pension funds have played a significant role in creating the current economic crisis. The large banks have rushed to finance mergers and real-estate speculations and to loan billions overseas. The largest insurance companies have financed suburban malls and high-rise office buildings and helped to dehumanize America's urban landscape, force reliance on the private automobile, and to isolate minorities in the inner city. Manufacturers have moved operations away from the Northeast and Midwest to the union-free South and Southwest, destroying communities and forcing labor to follow capital to areas of "better business climate."

Large-scale investment decisions need to include the perspective of a longer-run Public Balance Sheet. It is not simply a question of an investment's profitability but also of the social costs of different investments—costs that are usually borne by the taxpayer. A decision not to modernize a plant and instead to invest abroad or to purchase a company in another industry or to move to a low-wage, unionized area in the United States has effects on workers and communities that private investment bodies ignore.

In many European countries, the largest banks and insurance companies are publicly owned. We believe that the federal government must take stock ownership in and give direct investment guidance to some major banks and insurance companies. During the Franklin National Bank crisis in the late 1970s, Congressman Henry Reuss proposed that instead of bailing out the troubled bank, the government should purchase it and run it as a model of how a bank ought to operate. Working through an investment holding company similar to Canada's Canadian Development Corporation, the federal government should purchase a controlling interest in at least three major banks and three major insurance companies, and place representatives of the government, labor, and small business on the boards of these financial institutions.

The operation of these institutions would obviously not change overnight, and they would not be required to invest in unprofitable schemes requiring subsidies; that would be the responsibility of other programs. They would, however, be required to take into account the nation's need for a balanced economic growth that creates jobs at home and does not destroy either the environment or the nation's cities. Such banks and insurance companies would invest in public-private partnerships that would assume a longer-time horizon and would be willing to broaden their concept of profitability to include social costs of production.[10]

Pension funds are another major source of investment. Pension funds collectively own over 25 percent of the stock on the New York and American stock exchanges. During the 1970s, pension funds accounted for half of all new common-stock purchases. Efforts are now under way in the labor movement to exercise greater employee control over pension-fund investments. The AFL-CIO recently commissioned two studies on pension-fund operations, and in 1980, the executive board of the AFL-CIO called for pension-fund investments to increase employment through reindustrialization, to advance socially desirable spending, such as on housing, and to increase the ability of workers to exercise stockholder rights. Unions are now working for at least joint administration of their pension funds—a right that is already exercised by unions in most European countries—and for the establishment of a labor data exchange on corporate performance, anti-union activities, and investment in undemocratic countries such as South Africa.

One serious argument against controls on credit and investment is that the largest corporations will ignore or get around them by tapping the free-floating and largely unregulated international money market and by exporting even more capital abroad. In recognition of this likelihood, we propose direct government involvement in investment decisions through public ownership of some financial institutions. It is also certain that export controls on capital will be needed. The major European countries and Japan already have such controls, and the United States should also have them, with stiff penalties for major violations.

Democratizing the Federal Reserve. Simpleminded monetarism helped plunge the economy into deep recession between 1980 and 1982. Reviving real economic growth requires not only a rejection of this doctrine but a reform in the basic institutions

10. The National Council for Urban Economic Development has compiled a number of case studies of successful coordinated public-private economic development projects in a report, "Coordinated Urban Economic Development," Washington, D.C., March, 1978.

that allow for monetarist domination of credit: the banker-controlled Federal Reserve system.

As the late populist congressman Wright Patman argued, the Federal Reserve was not meant to be a privately-controlled banking system.[11] It is a public entity and should be held directly accountable to publicly elected officials. The head of the Federal Reserve should hold a four-year Cabinet term or a Treasury post appointed by each incoming President. The terms of the Federal Reserve Board members should be reduced from fourteen to five years and seats on the board should go to representatives of labor, consumer organizations, and small business. This broader representation should also be required of all regional Federal Reserve banks.

The activities of the Reserve's Open Market Committee (which buys and sells government securities and thereby affects the overall money supply) should be more open, with the committee's decisions made public immediately after meetings. The Federal Reserve's budget should be subject to audit by the Government Accounting Office and receive annual appropriations from Congress like other government departments. This would cut down the directors' present high life-style, a life-style that helps insulate them from the effects of their decisions, and would also reduce some of the Fed's elitism and separateness.

The policy of a more accountable and open Federal Reserve should be to restrict credit available for nonproductive activity such as real estate and commodity speculation or corporate mergers. Member banks should be required to hold higher reserves to back up such loans. On the other hand, credit should be expanded, in a targeted fashion, for housing, small business, and urban revitalization projects. In the past, the Federal Reserve, particularly under chairman Arthur Burns, used the system to bail out such large corporations as W. T. Grants, Pan Am, and Chrysler. The system under current chairman Paul Volcker has

11. See *The Federal Reserve System,* a study for the Joint Economic Committee of the United States Congress (Washington, D.C.: Government Printing Office, January 3, 1977).

made no effort to stem the tide of corporate mergers. Intervention is therefore selective and questionable regarding its public interest.

The reforms that we propose are hardly unprecedented. Central banks in most industrialized countries designate sectors of the economy that are to receive greater availability of credit and, in some cases, at below-market rates of interest. In some instances, this is done to aid particular industries and offset the uneven operation of private credit markets. For example, the Riksbank in Sweden targets credit for housing and export-oriented growth industries. Japan's Central Bank (Nihon Ginko) has indirectly financed Japan's economic growth through loans to commercial banks that were reloaned to expanding industries. In France, the central bank carries out credit policies in line with national economic development plans drawn up by a national planning agency. All of these banks engage in direct credit creation using quantity restraints on credit, limitations on borrowing from the central bank, and direct limits on commercial bank credit. They also directly allocate credit at subsidized rates for special purposes targeted by national development plans.[12]

Similar credit allocation plans have been endorsed by Congressman Henry Reuss, an expert in banking and urban development, and by the late Wright Patman. The goal of these reforms is to reduce, *de facto,* allocation of credit to the largest corporations and richest individuals who least need it while other sectors are credit-starved. Furthermore, credit allocation assures that funds are available for productive economic enterprises and socially needed products and services.

Industrial Policy. Ira Magaziner and Robert Reich amply demonstrate in their study, *Minding America's Business* (New York: Harcourt Brace Jovanovich, 1982), that the United States has the worst possible industrial policy. Inefficient, dying industries are protected with a variety of subsidies; large corporations are show-

12. *Activities by Various Central Banks to Promote Economic and Social Welfare,* Washington, D.C.: Committee on Banking, United States House of Representatives, December, 1970.

ered with unneeded tax breaks and subsidies; the consequences of corporate disinvestment in America for workers and communities are left untreated—disinvestment's social costs fall to the public; opportunities for new economic growth, particularly in the export market, are not encouraged; and public spending is not consciously used to stimulate new industries or to create needed jobs.

A rational, fair, and democratic industrial policy would have the following elements:

1. Plant Closing Legislation and Worker Retraining. As is common practice in Europe, corporations should be required by law to provide advance notice of major plant closings. Advanced notice allows communities and workers time to plan for alternative sources of employment. Corporations should also be required to contribute to a government-administered worker retraining fund that would underwrite local efforts to retrain displaced employees for new jobs.[13]

2. Worker Ownership and Participation in Management. Worker purchase of branch plants is an alternative to plant shutdowns, but it is an approach that needs to be taken with care. There is danger that workers will be pressured into buying losers —firms that stand no real chance of making it economically—and that departing corporations will be let off the hook under the guise of promoting economic democracy. Each situation must be evaluated on its merits.

In Clark, New Jersey, for example, workers agreed to take a pay cut and purchase a General Motors ball-bearing plant using an Employee Stock Ownership plan (ESOP). GM guaranteed three years of orders, and the ESOP was structured to allow each employee equal shares and immediate pass-through of voting rights so that workers will be able to elect directors of the new firm. At Ford Motor Company's aluminum casting plant in Sheffield, Alabama, however, UAW members refused to accept a package that included a 50 percent cut combined with plant ownership. Ford

13. A comprehensive worker-retraining program geared to economic renewal is proposed by Pat Choate in *Retooling the American Work Force*, Washington, D.C.: Northeast-Midwest Institute, July 1982.

subsequently closed the plant. Many workers blamed the closure on Ford's management decisions. These allegedly resulted in deliberately running down the plant, while trying to use high wages as the reason for the shutdown. Workers viewed the sale offer as part of Ford's attack on UAW workers' wages across the country.

When Firestone announced the planned closure of its Dayton Tire plant, the United Rubber Workers local led a fight to keep the plant open. The union commissioned a feasibility study of continued plant operation under worker ownership but dropped the idea when the study concluded that the plant could not be run economically. Members of the Food and Commercial Workers Union, faced with store closings by A&P, agreed to shorter vacations and lower wages in exchange for keeping the stores open under worker ownership.

Workers at the Rath meat-packing plant in Waterloo, Iowa, purchased the plant to keep it open. They learned, however, that worker ownership is no panacea. Market conditions in the industry made it rough going. The attitudes of Rath's managers did not change overnight with the change of ownership, and many worker-owners expressed dissatisfaction with the management of their own firm. As Jim O'Toole, professor of management at the University of Southern California, has noted, new, more flexible management attitudes are required of supervisory personnel in worker-owned firms.

Where feasible, the government should support efforts at worker ownership. This support should include government funding for market studies and government assistance in management after conversion to worker ownership.[14]

In the short run, relatively few workers can be affected by conversion of ownership, given the special circumstances of almost every situation in which such opportunities arise (usually in the tension-charged atmosphere of a threatened shutdown). Advance

14. The most helpful work on employee ownership is *Worker Participation and Ownership* by William Whyte, T. H. Hammer, C. Meek, R. Nelson, and R. N. Stern (Ithaca, N.Y.: ILR Press, Institute of Industrial Relations, Cornell University, 1983). This book includes case studies of successful transitions to employee ownership, as well as a useful bibliography and list of technical resources.

notice of plant closings will certainly help in the consideration of worker buy-outs. However, more workers can be represented in corporate decision-making by requiring through national legislation that they be represented on the boards of all major corporations, as is the practice in Sweden and West Germany. Studies of worker representation on boards in these countries show that it is precisely on such issues as plant closings and shifts in economic activity that worker representatives play the greatest role. Workers should legally have the right to this representation. If they are going to be asked to take wage cuts to keep a plant open of if they are asked to leave long-standing jobs in a firm, they should be a party to those decisions, with access to the corporate accounting that justifies such actions.

Once workers are represented on corporate boards, they can play a role in designing new plant-level programs in participatory management. There is now considerable evidence from experiments in a few U.S. firms and from abroad that greater worker participation at the plant level does raise productivity and simultaneously improves the quality of employees' working life.[15] Many unions have steered clear of advocating worker participation in quality-of-working-life programs because they are seen as anti-union measures (and they frequently are), but with worker representatives on corporate boards, union fear of the programs should lessen.

3. Government Purchasing and Production as Stimulant. U.S. government purchase of computers and airplanes in the 1950s provided the market demand that allowed American manufacturers to develop a low-cost, high-quality product. In both cases, American firms—stimulated by government purchases—went on to dominate world markets in these products for decades.

Similar government purchase stimulation should be carried out in selected sectors, particularly in renewable energy (most notably photovoltaics) and mass transit (high-speed rail and inner-city

15. See our *Economic Democracy: The Challenge of the 1980s* (Armonk, N.Y.: M.E. Sharpe, 1980), Chapter 4. Also useful is the journalistic report *Working Together* by John Simmons and William Mares (New York: Alfred A. Knopf, 1983).

mass transit). And in some cases, the government could directly engage in production through public enterprise. In this regard, the United States could learn from France. In the 1950s, the French government decided to modernize the Paris Métro. They chose to accomplish the task by creating a public company, the Société Française d'Études et des Réalisations de Transports Urbains. The firm is now one of the world's leading designers of subway cars and systems and exports to many other countries. In 1982, French exports of subway cars and designs brought in more than $150 million of foreign exchange. Customers included San Francisco's BART and New York's MTA.

In the aircraft industry, France's public firm, Aerospatiale, helped to develop the European Airbus that is challenging Boeing in the midsize jet market. France's government-owned auto company, Renault, has successfully competed in the world market. These French public enterprises are efficiently run, produce useful products at competitive prices in domestic and world markets, and provide jobs for French workers.

The government should also provide research and development grants for new technology through a Department of Technology. These might be in the form of matching funds or joint ventures through a government investment firm. The department should pay particular attention to firms producing products for potential export.

4. Policy Coordination and Economic Data. Noble Prize Economist Wassily Leontief points out that the United States relies too much for its economic policies on abstract theories and wishful thinking (supply-side economics, for example) and not enough on the actual facts of economic operations. Some data-gathering is necessary to develop a rational industrial policy. One agency of the government—either the Council of Economic Advisors or a section of the Commerce Department—must build up its capability as a national planning agency similar to France's Plan Commission or Japan's Ministry of International Trade and Industry (MITI). This planning body would bring together all of the existing government programs that affect industry, analyze them, and

spell out a more rational industrial policy for the Administration and for Congress. The agency would also increase data collection on the economy using input-output tables. As Leontief notes, "Creating and maintaining a comprehensive supply of data would permit a drastic reduction in the amount of guesswork and idle theorizing that goes into our policy-making now."[16]

Collection of data by one agency is not a substitute for other policies, but it is a necessary support system for analyzing the effects of long-range investment decisions, both public and private.

5. Wage Policy and Collective Bargaining. Will increased participation in corporate policy (including open books) alter the collective bargaining process? For some industries, like autos and steel, where mismanagement and rapid wage increases in the 1960s and early 1970s have put them on the brink of extinction at the hands of foreign competitors, wage givebacks and high unemployment are already the order of the day. Wage restraint (although not necessarily givebacks) may and probably should continue even under a more effective management in which workers and consumers participate: it is likely that the steel industry, for example, can only be competitive domestically if wages are restrained and productivity increased, at least in the short run. And, as University of California labor economist Claire Vickrey Brown has argued, in the 1970s wages of steel, auto, and some other groups of workers were much better than those of labor as a whole. She believes that, with a different social contract, such unions would voluntarily allow wages to equalize with those of less well-paid labor by holding down wage demands. Right now these workers and even those who have not done as well are forced into taking wage reductions only through fear of unemployment—with little recourse. The corporations can still close plants if they, not the union, deem them unprofitable.

But under an economic democracy model, labor will get something in return for wage restraint: a national full-employment

16. Wassily Leontief, "What Hope for the Economy," *New York Review of Books*, August 12, 1982, pp. 31–34.

policy, participation in deciding investment and management directives for the industry and economy, and legislation that would make it easier for unions to organize in nonunionized regions and industries. And rather than practically unenforceable agreements calling for the lowering of prices if profits rise, as in the UAW–General Motors contract, labor will have access to the books and some direct control over pricing policy. Further, plants will not be able to close by management's directive alone.

A "solidarity wage policy" which raises the wages of lower-paid workers relative to higher wages has to be matched by concurrent policies to raise output per worker in the low-productivity industries if fuller employment without inflation is to be achieved. Productivity should go up with unionization and increased participation,[17] but investment per worker also has to rise, and to maximize the impact of productivity, labor should have a lot to say about how that investment takes place.

The use of rising real wages and rising labor productivity to increase employment is still the essential element of a growth economy. Unless the United States intends to live off the export sector—with all the implications that has for depending on other countries' growth and wage policies—demand for U.S. output will continue to come largely from U.S. workers. The decisions about how rapidly the economy should grow and how that growth should be distributed are also part of a democratic wage policy, but the fundamental facts of demand-pull growth mean that real wages and full employment are unavoidably important components of any industrial rehabilitation.

Corporations and Planning Agreements. "More than class," writes Yale political scientist Charles E. Lindblom in *Politics and Markets* (New York: Basic Books, 1977), "the major specific institutional barrier to fuller democracy may . . . be the autonomy of the private corporation."

Lindblom concludes his book with the following:

17. See interview with Harvard economists James Medoff and Richard Freeman, *Fortune*, December 1, 1980, pp. 149–152.

Enormously large, rich in resources, the big corporations . . . command more resources than do most government units. They can also, over a broad range, insist that government meets their demands, even if these demands run contrary to those of citizens. . . . Moreover, they do not disqualify themselves from playing the partisan role of a citizen—for the corporation is legally a person. And they exercise unusual veto powers. They are on all these counts disproportionately powerful. . . . The large private corporation fits oddly into democratic theory and vision. Indeed, it does not fit (p. 356).

One necessary reform measure, proposed by Ralph Nader, is to require that all large corporations be chartered by the federal government.[18] Now companies can shop around the states to find the one—usually Delaware—with the fewest requirements. Federal chartering, in contrast, would impose a uniform set of rules and regulations on all large American corporations. The draft of Nader's chartering bill includes these major provisions:

• Corporate democracy: the board of the corporation would include mandatory consumer and worker representatives.

• Stricter merger standards: corporations would not be allowed to grow in conglomerate fashion.

• Corporate disclosure: firms would be required to produce a social balance sheet that includes the environmental impact of the firm's activities, hiring practices, and other related data, including criminal violations.

• Rights of employees: the Bill of Rights would apply within corporations, so employees could not be fired simply for criticizing the company or exercising other constitutional rights.

These chartering standards would be embodied in the legislation. In addition, and most important, all nationally chartered firms would be required to file long-term investment plans with the government. In these planning agreements firms would provide detailed information on their future corporate activity, including major investments, plant locations, managerial salaries,

18. This proposal is discussed in Ralph Nader, Mark Green, and Joel Seligman, *Taming the Giant Corporation* (New York: W.W. Norton, 1976).

and exports. The government would evaluate, using input-output methods, how these plans fit into the overall growth needs of the economy.

There would also be a core of major firms that would be highly responsive to signals from the government, because the government—through a public holding company—would own shares and have public representatives on the board. These would include firms in steel, automobiles, oil and gas, chemicals, and computers. Some new public or public/private mixed corporations should also be created—similar to TVA—to carry out particular purposes: the development of high-speed rail transit or the production and distribution of energy, both renewable and nonrenewable.[19]

Environmental and Worker Protection. The arguments against government regulation of unsafe products, protection of the environment, and concern for worker health and safety are largely specious. This short-run, fast-buck mentality ignores the long-run needs of a healthy society. Regulation is often attacked to blackmail workers or communities into risking their health or physical environment in return for jobs or taxes.

Staff researchers at Environmentalists for Full Employment in their 1977 study "Jobs and the Environment," conclude that hundreds of thousands of jobs can be created through environmental protection. A 1981 study done for the President's Council on Environmental Quality predicted a net gain of more than 500,000 jobs by 1987 as a result of pollution controls alone.[20]

Economic activity is supposed to increase our standard of living. The economy exists for people, rather than vice versa. Public investment in environmental protection produces jobs and balanced economic growth. Both Japan and West Germany have tough environmental protection laws *and* highly productive economies. A study by economist Ruth Ruttenberg found that tough consumer and environmental protection laws actually en-

19. See *Economic Democracy,* Chapter 2, for a full discussion of our public-enterprise strategy.
20. See Richard Kazis and Richard Grossman, *Fear at Work: Job Blackmail, Labor and the Environment* (New York: Pilgrim Press, 1982).

courage industrial innovations as firms compete to improve products and production processes.[21]

One out of four American workers faces health hazards on the job and as many as one-third of all cancer deaths may be related to exposure to dangerous workplace substances. Even at its higher level of activity in the Carter Administration, the Occupational Health and Safety Administration (OHSA) had only enough inspectors to visit each workplace an average of once every eighty years. Now OHSA has been severely cut back by the Reagan Administration.

Sweden has far fewer work-related injuries per hour worked each year than the United States. A 1974 Swedish law requires that every workplace with five or more employees have at least one elected safety steward. Firms with more than fifty employees must have a labor-management health-and-safety committee. More than one-half the committee must be elected by nonsupervisory personnel. The committee has the legal right to know what substances are used in the plant, the right to participate in setting safety standards, and the right to refuse to work under unsafe conditions. The committee must review and can veto plans for new machines or materials or work processes. The committee approves the selection of company doctors and nurses and safety engineers, and reviews all medical records. The committee can also call for the shutdown of operations it deems unsafe, and the company must demonstrate that the conditions have been remedied for work to start again.

Training for workers on the committee is paid for by a national Work Environment Fund financed by a 0.1 percent payroll tax on all employers. Training is conducted by unions using materials developed by the health-and-safety committees. The fund also conducts research into the workplace environment and publishes a magazine, *Work Environment,* that is sent to the more than 100,000 local union safety committee members.[22]

21. Ruth Ruttenberg, "Regulation Is the Mother of Invention," *Working Papers,* May/June, 1981.
22. Discussed in Matt Witt and Steve Early, "The Worker as Safety Inspector," *Working Papers,* September/October, 1980.

These are the types of reforms that should take place in a society that places people at the center of economic development. Firms can still make profits under such participatory regulation of the workplace environment, as evidenced by the performance of Swedish firms themselves. The advantage of this kind of regulation is its decentralization and that it gives the power over regulation to employees working in each plant rather than to a federal bureaucracy.

New Enterprise Development: Is Small Beautiful? In the 1970s one-half of all new jobs created in the economy came from small business. This fact, documented by David Birch at MIT and other researchers such as Emma Rothschild, has been interpreted by some politicians to mean that promotion of small business should be the country's new economic policy.[23] It is ironic that the allegedly pro-small-business Reagan Administration's monetarist policies, which keep up interest rates, have led to the highest level of bankruptcies—generally among small businesses—since the Depression.

Small businesses do have some valuable attributes. They tend to be market responsive. If the local dry-cleaner does a bad job on your suit, you can shift your business to another firm. Small businesses are often locally- and frequently family-owned. They can treat customers in a friendly, personal fashion that engenders a sense of community. In many small businesses, the owner is present as manager and/or worker. Communication between employees and owners can be face-to-face with little or no interven-

23. Birch's study, *The Job Generation Process* (Cambridge, Mass.: M.I.T. Department of Economics, 1982), while highlighting the job-producing role of small business in the 1970s, ignores the *linkages* between many small businesses and large-scale private and public investment decisions. For example, small businesses may locate in a new shopping center, but the decision to invest in the shopping-center facility is usually made by a large insurance company or pension fund, and it approves the investment only after a large corporate department store agrees to "anchor" the shopping center. Similarly, the opening or closing of a large corporate manufacturing facility affects the fortunes of local small businesses, both as suppliers directly to the plant and as purveyors of services consumed by plant employees. For detailed criticism of Birch's study, see Barry Bluestone and Bennett Harrison, *The Deindustrialization of America* (New York: Basic Books, 1982), pp. 220–224; and for analysis of job creation in the 1970s, see Emma Rothschild, "Reagan and the Real America," *New York Review of Books*, February 5, 1981, pp. 12–18.

ing bureaucracy. And small businesses provide millions of Americans the chance to be their own boss.

However, the life of many small businesses can be short (nine out of ten will disappear over a ten-year period). Job security for employees is less than in a large firm and wages are usually lower. Few small businesses are unionized and benefits such as health insurance are frequently lacking. Owner-managers can be authoritarian, unpleasant, and treat employees in a discriminatory fashion. The productivity of many smaller firms suffers from a lack of investment in new technology, a lack that springs from short-term decision horizons and the difficulty such firms have getting relevant information. Many of the small businesses started in the 1970s were in such areas as fast foods, bars, and restaurants. Much of the new employment was for women in dead-end jobs that lead neither to career advancement nor substantial seniority wage increases.

A uniform pro-small-business policy is a shotgun approach that makes little sense. There is a world of difference between a small firm engaged in computer technology and another branch of McDonald's.

Small manufacturing firms in the high-technology industry need government assistance in penetrating foreign markets. The government can engage in aggressive export assistance for small firms, including the provision of insurance and market studies. The Small Business Administration should focus its efforts on providing technical assistance and management consulting to small businesses, particularly in manufacturing.

Contrary to conservative rhetoric, shortage of capital is not a significant problem for small business entrepreneurs, particularly in high-tech industries. The business press reports that there is more venture capital than there are projects to invest in. "Indeed, the venture capital industry is awash in money," reported the *New York Times* (June 17, 1981). The amount of money disbursed to small businesses by venture-capital companies rose from $250 million in 1975 to $1 billion in 1980.

The government should not simply encourage traditional small businesses that try to hit the jackpot by making a splash with a new product and then sell out to a corporate giant. There is plenty of venture capital available for such entrepreneurs. The government's focus should be on nontraditional, community-based small businesses that are employee-owned, consumer-owned, or community-owned. Thousands of such "alternative" businesses sprang up in the 1970s as co-ops, collectives, partnerships, and projects of nonprofit community development corporations. They have important goals in addition to profit-making. Of course, they must sell their products or services and make enough surplus to run the business and keep it running, but they are usually also concerned with maximizing worker participation, selling healthy or safe products to consumers, and/or providing jobs for community residents.

One quasi-federal agency, the National Consumer Cooperative Bank, was established by Congress during the Carter Administration with a mandate to provide loans and technical assistance to consumer- and worker-owned enterprises. The Reagan Administration tried to abolish the bank, but its effort was defeated in Congress. The Administration compromised, letting the bank go off the federal budget by converting the government's equity into a long-term loan. The bank has developed the staff expertise to assist nontraditional small businesses. One of its innovative programs helps retiring small business owners sell their firms to the employees; another assists community groups in studying the feasibility of entering new economic ventures. However, the bank is small—it disbursed only $50 million in loans in 1981. A new administration could provide additional funds for the bank to loan and new grant funds for increased technical assistance and below-market, high-risk loans for community enterprises in poorer communities and areas of high unemployment.

Democratic Tax Reform. The current tax code, with the supply-side additions, virtually eliminates the corporate income tax. While the 1982 tax bill somewhat revised the huge 1981 corporate tax cuts, the trend of declining corporate contributions to the overall tax burden will continue. The 1981 cuts further shifted the federal tax burden to the working and middle classes. Since many states and counties collect an important part of their revenues from sales taxes, local taxes tend to be regressive rather than progressive. The tax code contains numerous incentives for unproductive activity, including speculation in real estate and other commodities, and encourages corporate mergers. The tax investment credits do little to stimulate new, productive, job-creating activities. Instead, they are gifts to the largest, most capital-intensive corporations, many of whom have chosen to disinvest in American communities and are being rewarded for the move. The tax system is failing in its original purpose of simultaneously raising revenue and equalizing the economic condition of America's rich and poor.

The latest fad in tax "reform" is the idea of a flat-rate tax (i.e., a tax rate that is a fixed percentage of income) with no deductions. The premise of this proposal rests on the belief that the rich will *always* escape from paying taxes under a progressive system, so why not junk whatever semblance of progressivity (an ability-to-pay criterion) remains in the federal tax system? Variants of the flat tax that keep some progressivity and limited deductions, such as those for home ownership, have been introduced by moderate Democrats (for example, Senator Bill Bradley of New Jersey and Representative Richard Gephardt of Missouri), who propose a flat 14 percent for most taxpayers, with a maximum rate of 28 percent.

Some neoliberals like Senator Gary Hart and Lester Thurow advocate taxing consumption rather than income. This would supposedly provide more savings for productive investment since only consumption, not savings, would be taxed. But because low-income earners consume a greater percentage of income than higher earners, such a tax would have to be much more progressive than an income tax in order to avoid hitting the poor and middle class harder than the rich. Thurow also proposes to eliminate corporate taxes altogether and, apparently, either tax the increased personal-consumption spending stock and bond holders would undertake as they became wealthier, or tax the annual increases or decreases in the value of their stocks and bonds as income.

Associates of Ralph Nader have developed a simplified, reformed tax system which has been drafted into legislation titled the Tax Justice Act. It embodies a simplified code with lower but still progressive rates. Among the many loopholes the Tax Justice Act would close are: the oil-depletion allowance and other tax breaks for industry; accelerated depreciation provisions for business machinery and real estate; foreign-investment loopholes; the tax-exempt status of state and municipal bonds; the investment tax credit; tax-loss farming; and schemes to avoid inheritance tax.[24]

The purpose of a tax system in a democratic society is to raise revenues needed for public purposes in as fair a manner as possible with as little socio-economic distortion as possible. Obviously such an ideal is difficult to achieve; however, it should not be abandoned as a goal. Whether tax is on income or consumption, the progressive nature of taxation is crucial to this goal, and so is the elimination of deductions or subsidies.

Tax preferences cost the Treasury billions of dollars every year, dollars that are made up by higher tax rates for wage earners. The argument of the tax reformers is that loopholes—"tax expenditures," Harvard professor Stanley Surrey has labeled them— should not be used to make economic policy. If the government wants to encourage a particular set of activities (for example, home ownership or new investment), it should allocate grants or subsidies to the private sector as part of a regular budgetary process, not covertly as part of the tax system. Alternatively, the government itself could invest directly in such activities through development banks or by subsidizing community corporations. In both cases, appropriations and programs would be subject to normal Congressional scrutiny, and the tax system would levy an equitable burden on all.

The argument for maintaining progressivity while closing loopholes is that it is both fair and just. Those who benefit more from

24. The Tax Justice Act is described in Robert Brandon, Jonathan Rowe, and Thomas H. Stanton, *Tax Politics* (New York: Pantheon, 1976).

the economic system, and who have a greater ability to pay without cutting into necessities such as food and shelter, should contribute relatively more than those who benefit less. Or, put another way: since the society values the extra food that a working mother can buy for her children more than the executive's extra drink at the country club, that woman's income should be taxed at a lower rate than the much higher income of the executive.

Energy. The next Democratic administration should adopt an overall energy policy that gradually moves the economy away from reliance on fossil fuels (coal, oil, and natural gas) and, at the same time, begins to take control of energy policy away from the large, private-energy corporations.

At home, conservation in residential and commercial use should have first priority. Other advanced economies do a far better job at energy-efficient production. West German industry, for example, uses 38 percent less energy per unit of output than American industry, and Sweden 40 percent less than the United States for each dollar of GNP. Using existing methods and technology, the United States could save between 20 and 30 percent of energy used in manufacturing. A national residential-energy conservation program could provide home-energy audits and low-interest energy conservation loans to home and apartment owners.[25]

But even with the present "oil glut" and falling gas prices, in the longer run (assuming the current recession ends), gasoline consumption also has to be reduced through conservation. To its credit, the Carter conservation effort made the United States the first industrial country to reduce its absolute fuel consumption. This helped cut U.S. petroleum imports. During the 1980 Presidential campaign, both Edward Kennedy and John Anderson pushed for further reductions either through rationing or placing an additional fifty-cent tax on gas at the pump. Such measures would go far in changing fuel-consumption habits. Gas prices might initially rise by the full amount of a tax, but reduced consumption would eventually bring down the price. In any case, the

25. Steven A. Schneider, "Common Sense About Energy," Two Parts, *Working Papers*, January/February and March/April, 1978.

effect of reducing consumption would be exactly what it has been until now—significantly reduced imports, downward pressure on the wholesale petroleum price, and decreasing prices for industrial uses of petroleum—hence downward pressure on the prices of industrial and agricultural goods.

So even though there would be a once-and-for-all increase in gas prices due to a tax or some form of "white-card" rationing (where people could sell their gas allotment on the open market), reduced petroleum consumption would eventually have a deflationary effect. Such a policy would allow the Fed to lower interest rates because the price of one of the most important cost items in production would be stable even when there is economic expansion. In stark contrast to monetarism, which can only reduce inflation through severe recession and unemployment, conservation would be anti-inflationary and *promote* production and jobs. Finally, reduced petroleum consumption would decrease imports into the United States significantly, could create a balance-of-payments surplus on the commodity side, strengthen the dollar without high interest rates, and help non-oil producers by lowering the price that they pay for petroleum.

There are three political problems with white-card rationing or a high gasoline tax: First, it might be initially unpopular with consumers even though its positive effects would quickly become evident once it was implemented. A gas tax would also hurt the poor much more than the rich, so some provision would have to be made for low-income groups to get part or all of such a tax back. Both these problems could be overcome. The third opposition group—private American oil producers and distributors—will be much more intractable. It may be necessary in the short run to sweeten the pie for domestic producers by offsetting some of their "losses" as a result of a conservation policy.

The government should also actively promote the development of solar, wind, geothermal, and other renewable energy sources. This could be funded out of the enormous additional excise taxes on gasoline that would be part of a petroleum-conservation program. The government could provide hundreds of thousands of jobs through such a renewable-energy development program, as well as investments of excise taxes in maintaining our road system and the building of light rail and other alternatives to automobile transportation.

New federal agencies are needed to shift control of energy policy into public hands. First, the government should create a Federal Oil Purchasing Agency that would control the importation of all foreign oil. The agency would buy oil on a nation-to-nation basis and would wield greater strength in the foreign market than individual companies. Once the agency purchased oil, it would sell it to various customers in the United States.

More than 50 percent of America's domestic fuel lies on federal land, most of it unexploited. Reagan's Secretary of the Interior, James Watt, attempted to auction off these natural resources at bargain-basement prices with little regard for the environment. This public resource should, alternatively, be developed by a public body—a Federal Oil and Gas Corporation—as proposed by senators Kennedy, Mondale, and others in 1973. The corporation would be mandated to develop oil and gas resources on such federal land. It would be similar to the public-energy companies that exist in most European countries.

In addition to developing public-energy resources in a responsible way, the corporation would give the government direct and dependable data on the drilling, pumping, refining, and marketing of oil and gas.

Social Policy: Welfare, Crime, and Health. Numerous studies document the relationship between the state of the economy and such social problems as crime, welfare, and health.[26] Again, it is ironic that the Reagan Administration can mouth pro-family rhetoric but carries out economic policies that destroy families' health

26. See, for example, the comprehensive study "Estimating the Social Costs of National Economic Policy: Implications for Mental and Physical Health, and Criminal Aggression," by Professor Harvey Brenner at the School of Public Health, The Johns Hopkins University, published as a study by the Joint Economic Committee, October 26, 1976. Brenner found that a 1.4 percent increase in unemployment costs society nearly $7 billion in lost income due to illness, mortality, and added prison and mental-health spending.

and drive people to criminal acts or onto welfare rolls. The Administration's attack on the existing welfare system—food stamps, aid to families with dependent children, general assistance, supplemented security income, and Medicaid—is based on the social Darwinist view that welfare traps the poor in a permanent condition of poverty and dependence.

There is little evidence to support this position. In fact, Notre Dame economist Richard D. Coe, who analyzed the experience of five thousand families receiving welfare between 1969 and 1978, found that although the percentage of welfare recipients was a steady 10 percent of the population, 25 percent of all American households received some welfare assistance during the decade. Over half were on welfare for no more than one or two years. Coe found that only 7.7 percent of all recipients were dependent on welfare for their basic support in eight or more years of the decade. Coe concluded:

> For the majority of these people, the welfare system serves as a stepping-stone to a more normal standard of living. Despite its numerous shortcomings, [it seems to fulfill] the role that most people probably believe it should fulfill—that of an insurance system against unforeseen and largely uncontrollable adverse circumstances.[27]

So, the existing welfare system—even with its flaws and limitations (and minuscule percentage of "cheaters")—is a real benefit to the working poor. It is part of the overall social wage that has come under attack by Reagan and his corporate allies. The attack on welfare, as Frances Fox Piven and Richard A. Cloward point out in *The New Class War* (New York: Pantheon, 1982), is part of the attempt by business to discipline labor and bend it to business' purposes.

Of course, we would prefer that fewer of the poor and near-poor had to avail themselves of welfare. We believe firmly that a national policy of community-based full employment would take care of many of the nation's social problems.

27. Richard Coe, "Welfare Dependency: Fact or Myth," *Challenge*, September-October, 1982, p. 43.

• Increased employment would add funds to social security and decrease funds spent on welfare. Social security solvency problems come largely from burned-out workers retiring from the labor force at age sixty-two rather than at sixty-five. Fuller employment and retraining such workers into other interesting jobs would gradually raise the retirement age and take the pressure off social security payouts.

• The current panoply of welfare programs should be replaced by a decent, guaranteed family income and the opportunity for everyone who can work to get a job.

• National spending on health could be reduced through a combination of national health insurance delivered through consumer-controlled health-maintenance organizations oriented toward community-employment and operating at the community level, cost-control measures, and greater emphasis on preventive medicine.

The Reagan Administration's answer to crime is expensive and ineffective: increasing spending on prisons and police reduces the crime rate insignificantly compared with the cost of such programs. The National Academy of Sciences estimates that to achieve a 10 percent reduction in serious crimes, California would have to increase its prison population by 157 percent, New York by 263 percent, and Massachusetts by 310 percent. Criminologist Elliot Currie, writing in *Working Papers* (May/June and July/August 1982), argues that such a strategy of "incapacitation" will not only do little to change the dimensions of America's crime problem, it ignores or downplays many things we might do to reduce crime.

In place of the neoconservative policy of increasing the number of prisons or the liberal tendency to deny the seriousness of crime and to avoid intervention into the lives of offenders, Currie suggests a crime-reduction program with three main themes. First, it should wholeheartedly support criminal-justice agencies trying to do their job by allocating enough resources to police and prosecutors, and making sure that prison conditions are safe and decent.

Second, innovative interventions in the lives of people involved in crime should be part of any community crime-fighting program. Third, Currie points out that every advanced society with a lower level of violent crime than ours has also had a much more effective and humane employment policy, providing a better cushion against the disintegrative effects of the market. The main element of such employment programs is not just jobs, but jobs at decent wages. A RAND Corporation study of "repeaters" shows that those with jobs earning $100 per week have a crime rate one-fourth that of inmates who earned less. Job quality and stability are therefore crucial in an anticrime employment policy.

But even well-run employment programs are not enough. They are a necessary, but not a sufficient, condition for reducing crime. Supporting individuals and families economically is within the reach of an alternative economic policy designed to integrate people more effectively into the society; however, employment alone does not create "community," and community is a crucial factor in reducing alienation and hence crime. Combined with fuller employment in decent, steady jobs, community crime-prevention programs could provide a low-cost, participative way to help reduce serious crime. Alone, such programs as Citizens' Local Alliance for a Safer Philadelphia, New York's Guardian Angels, People for Change in the South Bronx, Santa Monica's community crime-prevention programs, and Detroit's Neighborhood Watch, or a parallel justice system like the Community Boards Program in San Francisco, cannot work, but when police and community cooperate, and larger social programs help eliminate the main causes of crime, the combination goes far to create safer towns and cities.

America in the World Economy. The United States is still the largest, most productive economy, the strongest military force, and the greatest cultural influence in the world. While we are still number one and will be for many years to come, we are no longer an imperial power that can dominate the world economy and dictate terms to the industrial countries and Third World nations. The Reagan Administration's yearning for Empire is hopelessly nostalgic and out of touch with reality. Worse, its policies do not deal adequately with the deteriorating competitive position of U.S. industries. And administration monetarism and militarism have alienated our European allies and threatened millions in the developing countries.

Most proposed solutions to the present economic crisis concentrate on making the United States more competitive with Japanese imports. Should the United States pursue a free-trade or a "fair-trade" (quotas and tariffs to match Japanese import restrictions) policy on imported goods? We think that the democratization and public planning of America's business would go far toward increasing its competitiveness in world markets. The United States could achieve fuller employment, produce those goods in which we are competitive with less costly transitions, and secure a more rational, long-term investment policy in physical and human capital—investment that would keep us at the forefront of developing new products that meet our own and the world population's real needs.

The issue of free versus fair trade in the context of a policy of full-employment and democratization cannot be decided just in terms of imports and exports. Many imports do not come from Japan but from U.S.-based transnational firms producing abroad and exporting to the U.S. market. What stance should U.S. policy take toward these "runaway shops"? What goods do we want to produce domestically regardless of our competitiveness in world markets? What meaning does "free trade" have in the context of a world economy where most trade is between huge transnational enterprises? Should the United States have a domestic steel industry even if it requires protection? Right now, if we wanted to revitalize rail transport by building high-speed inter-city train systems, we would have to import passenger railroad cars, since no U.S. producer makes them. Should we produce passenger rail cars ourselves? These are just some of the questions regarding free-trade policies, and the choice of free versus fair trade hinges as much on what kind of economy we would like to have as on what goods we can produce cheaply.

Even as the United States revitalizes domestic production to meet real domestic needs and full employment, our international economic policy has to help stimulate other countries' economic development. Any democratic alternative must simultaneously recognize the dominant position of the United States in the world economy and promote increased economic participation by lower-income countries and groups presently excluded in those countries. Just as democracy should be extended within our own society through greater economic and political participation, so American economic power should be used to promote similar trends in other countries.

Our present foreign policy is precisely the opposite: the Reagan Administration supports dictatorships as long as they are favorable to American foreign investment and are staunchly anti-Communist. Often, by supporting such dictatorships and trying to undermine genuinely populist (but Leftist) governments in other Third World countries, the United States pushes those governments to much less populist, more dictatorial positions. When, for example, the Nicaraguan or Angolan government has to face economic pressures and U.S.-financed military operations on and within its borders, the government itself becomes more militaristic and less populist.

These policies are based on the myth that all Left-populist governments are Soviet stooges and therefore must be opposed as part of the geopolitical struggle against Soviet hegemony. Nothing could be farther from the truth. In fact, if the United States stood for and supported popular social change, almost all Third World countries would much rather turn to us for technical assistance and trade than to the Soviets. We have the products and technology that—adapted to their conditions by them—are much more relevant and up-to-date than those made in the Eastern bloc.

But this mythology is not just plucked out of thin air. It does serve to support the "business climate" that American corporations prefer to have for their investments, the same business climate that they are looking for within the United States—nonunionized, unpoliticized labor; governments that will do anything necessary to bring investments into their country or county; low taxes; and no regulation. The largest U.S. corporations—oil/gas, manufacturing, financial, heavy construction, mineral extraction —dictate our foreign economic policies in the Third World and even Europe. And they push for the support of governments and policies in the Third World that would be totally unacceptable to voters if they existed in the United States. Imagine the National Guard shooting striking miners in West Virginia. But that is exactly what some of the Reagan Administration's favorite governments have done (in South Africa, for example, and in Bolivia).

The first axiom of an alternative international economic policy should therefore be to promote *participative development policies* around the world. Although such policies may not produce the appearance of luxury goods in the stores of Third World–country capitals, they will assure that the fruits of development will reach the large majority rather than a small minority. This corresponds precisely to the kinds of changes we are calling for within the United States. Those countries that do engage in such development policies should receive our economic and technological support, in accord with the way they define their needs.

Dollars and technology now get from us to the Third World primarily through U.S. transnational corporations. And while these corporations would like to pretend that they are independent of the U.S. government, they in fact depend in various ways on U.S. government bilateral and multilateral pressures (even military intervention) for the business climate in which they invest. A crucial element in international economic policy, therefore, is our government's policy toward U.S. transnationals. The real issues are the conditions under which they have to operate and whether they will choose to invest under less favorable conditions. The first depends in part on U.S. foreign policy: if the U.S. government makes clear that it will not intervene to support U.S. companies' commercial interests in those countries with dictatorial, repressive governments of either Right or Left (essentially Carter's Human Rights Policy), transnationals operating there are forewarned that they are there at their own risk. The second issue can only be influenced if transnationals have public and worker participation in their investment decision-making. If our suggested domestic reforms are implemented, investment decisions of large corporations will, in fact, be subject to public and worker influence, and the foreign investments of these corporations would be part of an overall social investment strategy. This strategy should include U.S. political-economic objectives in a world system, not just island America.

Government monetary and fiscal policies should also be changed to promote a different set of worldwide growth strategies. The Reagan Administration firmly believes that returning to market capitalism in the United States, the Third World, and in Europe will promote more rapid growth nationally and internationally if inflation is first cured through deflationary monetary policies. This strategy has had an incredible negative impact worldwide. Rather than the present "Beggar-Thy-Neighbor" deflationary policies, the next Democratic administration should launch a "Better-Thy-Neighbor" international development program that concentrates on increased productivity, fuller employment, the production of useful, needed products instead of military hardware, appropriate technology transfers to Third World countries, and the conservation of nonrenewable resources.

As part of this strategy, the activities of American-owned transnational banks would have to be more closely regulated. In search of greater profits, these banks have extended billions in loans to some "newly industrializing" Third World countries, such as Mexico, Brazil, and South Korea, while turning away from other, poorer countries. What is needed is a targeted, global, U.S.-led Marshall Plan that channels development funds through a multinational development authority—in concert with other industrial countries. Economic development in the Third World can provide markets for products of the United States and other industrial countries, but these development projects must be carefully designed, not left to unregulated transnational banks to finance by themselves.[28]

28. On the expansion of transnational bank activities in the Third World and its dangers to international economic stability, see Anthony Sampson, *The Money Lenders* (London: Hodder and Stoughton, 1981).

The second part of an international macroeconomic policy would be to cut energy consumption in the United States, putting increased downward pressure on petroleum prices. While this would lower oil-company profits and some countries' rates of growth, it would make expansion of most of the world's agricultural and industrial production less expensive, especially in terms of foreign exchange.

Finally, an alternative international economic policy would have to deal with U.S. agricultural exports and the role they play in world food policy. It is likely that in the next ten years there will be massive food shortages in many countries. Since the United States is the world's largest food and fertilizer producer, it is essential that some U.S.-led coordinated efforts are begun to develop a food production and distribution policy on a world scale.

The Nixon Administration's emphasis on promoting farm-product exports has been continued by all administrations that have followed. But this orientation is exactly the opposite of what we should do to lower inflation and solve world food problems. Instead we should be looking down the road a few years to the time when we cannot meet world demand for food without huge increases in farm and food prices. We are now very close to the limit of our productive capacity, and if food supplies are not increased in the United States, then they can only be increased in those regions that now underutilize their production potential— mainly in the Third World.

Traditionally the United States has not seriously supported agricultural development in the Third World, because U.S. farmers do not want competition in world markets. Nevertheless, agricultural policy expert E. Phillip LeVeen argues, every dollar invested in developing Third World agriculture has a potential payoff much greater than the same dollar invested in the United States. If we could promote the revitalization of agricultural development in these nations, we would be serving the immediate interests of consumers in the U.S., whose food costs will otherwise rise to yet new rounds of inflation. More important, if U.S. policy continues to insist that we can feed the world, and if we do not take steps immediately to increase food production where food is being consumed, we will contribute to the impoverishment of Third World countries and to a potentially disastrous Malthusian crisis.[29]

As in the case of oil, a rational long-term U.S. agricultural policy in a world economy will be opposed by powerful vested domestic interests. Even with conservation and Third World agricultural development, however, U.S. oil producers and farmers will survive and should do well. The upward pressure on oil and grain prices will continue in the long run. The United States will also remain a food exporter. The more relevant issue is whether we in an economically democratic United States can implement reasonable fuel- and agricultural-conservation programs that will increase the economic viability of Third World countries. Ultimately, this would increase the demand for a host of other U.S. goods, increase world trade, and help make the world a better, healthier place to live.

Most of the policies we recommend in this chapter require implementation or at least significant support at the national level by an economic democracy–minded President and a cooperative Congress. But we also believe that the reform policies we advocate are inseparable from the democratic means of carrying them out. Real local and state planning and implementation—not just a rhetorical New Federalism—are crucial elements of the New Social Contract.

29. For an excellent discussion of these issues, see Joseph Collins and Francis Moore Lappé, *Food First* (New York: Ballantine Books, 1981).

8 Local Control and Democratic Planning

Ronald Reagan—like Jimmy Carter before him—campaigned against the allegedly excessive power of the federal government while ignoring the excessive power of large corporations. Besides cutting social programs and government environmental and health and safety standards, Reagan's proposed remedy for an oversized Washington bureaucracy is a vague concept called the New Federalism. Based on the dubious legal and historical doctrine of states' rights and cloaked in antibureaucratic rhetoric, the New Federalism is primarily a smokescreen for cutting social welfare and regulatory programs: it puts the responsibility for their funding and administration onto state and local governments, which have neither the financial resources nor administrative staffs to maintain these programs at current levels.

The Reagan Administration's talk of local power is essentially a call for reducing overall *democratic* control over the nation's resources. In Reaganomics, local control means that "dynamic," "efficient" private enterprise and the market should decide how communities can best develop and how to provide education and health care, even if those decisions may be inequitable, against the public interest, and interfere with the adequate delivery of human services. In practice, the New Federalism gives less, not more, power to workers and consumers at the local level.

The Reagan philosophy *assumes* that citizens exert the greatest influence over resource allocation and distribution when they act as individual consumers and producers. So local control is interpreted to mean private production and consumption. But historically, it is precisely that kind of "local control" that has led to sharp differences in the quality of services delivered to different income groups in the community and state, to the unfettered development and underdevelopment of urban areas, and to the pollution of our air and water. The New Federalism is, in fact, designed to undercut local democratic control by putting the development of municipal and state physical and human resources even more completely into the hands of private business.

For example, administration-promoted tuition-tax credits for private schools would hasten the decline of public education, now locally controlled by elected school boards. Republican proposals for penalizing cities with locally enacted rent-control laws are hypocritical as far as local public control is concerned, but perfectly consistent with the New Federalism's support for landlords and developers. Republican Senators have also introduced legislation to remove from municipalities the legal right to regulate cable television companies, citing federal preemption. The Administration has loosened federal regulation of the environment and of worker health and safety while opposing the enactment of state and local toxic-disclosure laws. Local communities that have sought control over municipal airports regulated by the FAA have met with no sympathy from Reagan's appointees. The Reagan Administration's plan to dispose of federally owned property specifically favors selling to private owners, not to local public authorities.

Similarly, Reagan's urban policy focuses on deep cuts in funds for urban planning and economic development. The policy tells cities to go it on their own or contract out city services to private business, and turn over city planning functions to benevolent large corporations. Cities are supposed to seek financial support from corporations for major urban development projects under the catchall phrase "public/private partnership." Almost invariably, these partnerships are less than equal, with the corporations doing the planning while the city government facilitates corporate plans using municipal legal powers. Like the massive urban renewal schemes of the 1960s and 1970s, the interests of urban minorities, the poor, ethnic working-class neighborhoods, and local small businesses are sacrificed in the process.

A classic case of the public-private partnership in action occurred in Detroit in 1981–82. The city used its legal power of eminent domain to take over the white ethnic neighborhood called Poletown, to level all the buildings including churches and schools, and turn the land over to General Motors for a new auto plant.

There is other evidence of the Reagan Administration's real intentions in the New Federalism:

• Federally chartered saving and loan institutions got administration backing and won their case against states' preventing "due on sale" clauses to be inserted in mortgage-loan agreements when it came before the Supreme Court. The Administration also supported a Senate bill to allow *state-chartered* S & Ls to demand the signing of a new, higher interest mortgage when a home changes hands.

• Again in the Supreme Court, the Administration sided with the nuclear power industry against safety regulations, arguing that Washington, not the states, has the right to decide whether a nuclear power plant can be built even if adequate federal waste disposal plans have not been adopted.

It would be a mistake to read these examples as showing that the Reagan Administration supports strong central government over states' rights. That is not the issue. Washington intervenes when local public control acts contrary to the needs of business. The underlying theme of the New Federalism is therefore not local control but that corporations and rich individuals represent the public interest in their private economic decisions and should have their way. And whenever local public control and business conflict, pro-business national policy will predominate. The problem is not so much Washington's intervention, but rather the fact that Washington is intervening against the public in favor of the private, on the dubious assumption that business knows what is best for America.

Local Control: Democratic Planning from the Bottom Up

Our concept of local control is totally different: local interests are best represented by locally elected public officials when they are committed to the interests of the community at large, rather than to businesses or wealthier individuals in that community. By the very weight of their numbers, consumers, workers, renters, home-owners, and small businesses—acting through their elected officials and planning councils—should control local and state development.

In Chapter 7 we proposed national reforms that are designed to bring the economy under greater democratic control. Only the national government has the power to counteract and democratize the large corporations. Many of our reform proposals—such as requiring worker representatives on the boards of corporations and legislating in-plant health and safety committees—utilize the powers of the federal government not to centralize bureaucratic control but to give new democratic rights to citizens as workers and consumers, just as the New Deal reforms gave workers the legal right to bargain collectively. And only the national government can develop national guidelines for income assistance, affirmative action, nondiscriminatory wage policies, and health-care and education standards.

These reforms at the national level will affect millions of Americans in their workplaces and in their communities, but they are not sufficient themselves to revitalize American society. For that we need local and state government institutions that have enough economic clout and constituency backing to make municipalities and regions effective economic planners and investors in the public interest.

From a democratic point of view, the main appeal of local control is that local and state governments are more likely to be representative of local constituencies and, one hopes, responsive to their needs. The composition of city councils and state legislatures does, in fact, reflect the population in the communities and states better than does the Congress. Local consumers and workers are usually clearer in their own minds on community and state issues that affect them directly, whether it be the installation of a nuclear power plant or the building of transportation systems and housing.

Federal Financing and Decentralized Decision-Making. Reagan's New Federalism ostensibly turns control over social welfare programs back to state and local governments but does so as it severely cuts their funding. Local authorities are left either with the unpopular task of presiding over health-care, welfare, and public-education reductions or of raising local and state taxes.

This brings home a fundamental dilemma of democratic control: financial support for many locally controlled programs will have to come at least in part from the federal government. Indeed, for two reasons many programs *should be* partly financed from Washington under guidelines set centrally and administered locally. The first is that federal income taxes are more progressive than state income and sales taxes and local property taxes. The second is that only at the national level can the poor be protected against local majorities that try to keep them from local and state revenues.

For rich states, the question of money is less an issue than what the money is to be used for. For other states, state-employee pension funds and regional craft-union pension funds are already controlled at state and regional levels and can provide—through state development banks or directly—locally controlled financing for state and local investment projects. But in most states, even the existence of pension funds leaves a host of other needs, including welfare programs, Medicaid, community-run health-care programs, and compensatory programs in public education, still dependent on outside funding, unless they are cut severely. From the standpoint of national unity, the way in which these needs are filled should be subject to national guidelines and aided by federal funding when states and communities cannot achieve minimum standards for all their residents. Even *Fortune*—voice of corporate America—recognizes that

> *Federalist Papers* or not, in modern times the expressions of our highest values—our desire to stay free, to eliminate racism, to care for the elderly and the poor, to let ideas compete freely—have come from the national government and from national leadership. Those values cannot be fixed at the Office of Management and the Budget. Nor can their defense or enlargement be entrusted to 50 little republics with uneven resources, with limited control over their own prosperity, with borders that make no modern sense, and with environments that can narrow minds. (June 28, 1982, p. 42.)

Furthermore, income per capita is a measure of how much the federal government should contribute to such programs in the states. Yet this guideline is often misleading: for example, Texas, Wyoming, and Louisiana all have relatively low income per capita but vast mineral resources which produce high tax revenues. Even so, those states receive a greater per capita share of federal dollars because they are considered poorer than low-tax-base states like New York. A better measure of a state's need for federal dollars is its tax capacity. This would give more money to states like New York and Michigan than they now receive. The Northeast and Midwest should get more funds because they are less able to raise money locally and have a higher percentage of poor and unemployed. But, as *Fortune* notes, the measure of income per capita does not guarantee that Texas or Louisiana is going to allocate more state monies for welfare and education. That is why we need federally established minimum standards for welfare, health care, and education. Under those standards, states better able to pay would have to take up the slack between the amount of federal funding and their present levels of commitment to these programs.

In a national economy and society, therefore, local control has to be subject to national goals. Reagan's New Federalism has set its national goal as the expansion of private business control over resources and economic development. Our goal is the expansion of community and worker control. In some areas, such democratic control would be expressed nationally and would become part of national policy, particularly in issues of equalizing access to resources and equal treatment before the law. In other areas, such as local economic development, local, state, and regional control should determine processes and outcomes. Our version of the New Federalism would use federal funds to improve local publicly controlled programs, not to turn control over public programs and resources to private business.

Municipal Planning Commissions. The question for us, then, is how democratic control is going to function. Fortunately for the implementation of democratic planning, this huge urban nation with its federal system of state and local governments already has many mechanisms for local and regional participation. Too often, however, existing governmental mechanisms are underutilized, ignored, or controlled by a local business elite and/or powerful regional and national corporations. These mechanisms must be reformed and revised, and some new local and state agencies will have to be created to assure that citizens as residents of neighborhoods, cities, and states have the opportunity and the means to participate in planning their economic future in as democratic a way as possible.

One such existing local government body that can be reshaped, empowered, and revived is the municipal planning commission. Almost every city in the country has a planning board or commission that regulates land use through the legally recognized powers of the municipal corporation. These planning bodies consist of local citizens appointed by the mayor or city council and are served by professional staffs of varying size and quality.

In most cities, the planning commission does not plan in a positive or active way. The commission reacts to plans proposed by the private sector, primarily by developers and large corporations, for projects. The commission also oversees more mundane matters such as side-yard encroachments and remodeling regulations in residential neighborhoods. The major tool of these planning bodies is zoning, which has less than egalitarian origins. The first major zoning efforts in the United States originated in San Francisco in the 1880s to prevent Chinese laundries from expanding into the better white neighborhoods, and later in New York City to keep the garment factories from encroaching on the stately mansions in mid-Manhattan. New York's zoning law of 1916 went on to be the model for most other cities across the nation.[1]

Zoning has been used primarily to protect white, upper-middle-class residential communities, both in cities and in suburbs, from unwanted industrial commercial development and from multifamily residential developments that might house minorities or lower-class ethnic families. It is perhaps ironic that some of the staunchest supporters of Reagan and his antigovernment message —Republicans in the suburbs—have no qualms about using the governmental power of zoning to protect their communities and exclusive life-styles.

In the post–World War II boom, zoning laws that restricted large developers in downtown areas were ignored or overruled by variances, so that urban renewal projects could proceed. In many cities, separate development agencies were created that ran the urban renewal process behind closed doors and with little or no citizen participation in the planning process.

Most planning commissions are dominated by local business interests, particularly the real-estate/development industry. The members of these commissions are usually interested in facilitating private business plans rather than planning in the public interest. They equate the public interest with the total of private development decisions.

We advocate a new, positive role for local planning commissions that includes a creative use of zoning, but goes beyond it. A new role for the local planning commission assumes an active, grassroots democratic movement that wins representation in local city government and breaks the hold of the downtown business/Chamber of Commerce/real-estate interest over the city planning process.

1. See Sam Bass Werner's excellent study, *The Urban Wilderness* (New York: Harper & Row, 1972), especially pp. 28–37.

A revitalized and democratized local planning commission would, first of all, systematically gather data about the local economy and local land use. Utilizing the yearly business license tax form or some other collection document, the commission staff would computerize data on employment by all local firms. Each parcel of land, its zoning, current and potential use would also be logged in the computer. Census statistics and metropolitan labor department data on unemployment would also be computerized, giving the commission an accurate and up-to-date statistical picture of the local community.

Each neighborhood, through community organizations such as PTAs, churches, fraternal organizations, and block clubs, would fill out neighborhood needs assessment forms which would include requests for new streetlights, road repairs, parks, and other capital improvements; new neighborhood services needs such as commercial stores (markets, drug stores, laundries, et cetera) or day-care centers and other local social services; and estimates of unemployment, especially among youth. The planning commission staff would assist in gathering this neighborhood-based data and computerizing it.

A variety of tools is needed to act on the data to generate balanced economic growth that both provides jobs and meets local needs; also the public-private partnership must be redefined, with the local government aggressively representing the public interest as it is defined through the neighborhood-based planning process.

One tool, already legally recognized in some states, is the development agreement (the local equivalent of the national planning agreements described in Chapter 7). In Santa Monica, California, for example, where a progressive coalition won control of the government in 1981, the city has entered into a development agreement with one firm that requires the company to provide a day-care center and a public park on the site of a large office-restaurant-shopping complex, and to build one hundred units of middle-income rental housing off-site, in return for the right to develop the private office complex.

Underlying the development-agreement approach is the concept of mixed-use zoning, where residential and commercial uses co-exist in or near the same buildings. Mixed-use development embodies the vision of a city that is much less restricted and segregated by use and class than are most American cities.

Development agreements can also be used to direct hiring by private firms. In exchange for the right to develop or for loans provided by city-sponsored industrial development bonds or for the use of city land for an industrial park, firms would be required to hire and train a specified number of the locally unemployed.

These kinds of development agreements, in which the city extracts benefits through a contractual arrangement with private firms, are very different from the way most cities currently run economic development programs. Usually, the city gives away benefits through tax abatements or relaxed building restrictions or through city provision of roads and other city services.

It is not enough to rely on extracting jobs or public facilities from the private sector. The process works best in large-scale projects that are of sufficient economic magnitude to allow for trade-offs. Local governments must also have new public economic development mechanisms for providing jobs and services in small- and medium-scale enterprises. These enterprises need not be limited to the traditional privately-owned small business, but should include a variety of ownership forms such as minority and women-owned businesses, employee-owned businesses (worker co-ops), user-owned business (consumer co-ops), community-owned businesses (community development corporations), and nonprofit enterprises owned by churches, unions, and other locally-based organizations. The city should promote a genuine pluralism of ownership and enterprise opportunities and not rely on a single, ideologically-based approach to economic development.

In Santa Monica, the city has built senior housing using federal funds; has facilitated the construction of privately-owned, nonprofit senior housing by the Salvation Army; has funded a private, nonprofit community development corporation to build cooperative housing; and has signed development agreements with private developers that require them to build rental housing aimed at middle- and lower-income families. The city has also adopted an inclusionary (rather than exclusionary) zoning ordinance that requires private builders to include low- and middle-income units in at least 25 percent of all newly constructed projects. So the city government is using a variety of approaches to help alleviate the housing shortage and to allow different ownership forms to provide new housing opportunities.[2]

Housing is an area in which some American cities have been innovative. In California, Santa Barbara and Berkeley assist in the construction of cooperative housing projects. Most large cities have housing departments or agencies with technically competent staffs. Some cities sell municipal bonds and use the proceeds to make below-market mortgage loans to low- and middle-income residents. However, most city-sponsored housing programs have suffered from the Reagan cutbacks in funds for assisted housing.

Cities fall short in economic development planning mechanisms. In order to plan in a positive manner for meeting community economic needs, city government must have its own financing agencies. This means that every large- and middle-sized city should have its own municipal development bank and/or a public development corporation to engage in entrepreneurial activities.

There are many existing models from which American local government can learn. In West Germany, most cities have municipally-owned banks that finance both public and private development ventures. In the Basque region of Spain, a cooperatively-owned bank loans money to local workers to start employee-owned businesses, and finances the expansion of existing cooperatives. In addition to providing loan funds, the technical staff of this co-op bank works closely with the applicants to refine their business plans and to increase chances of business success before they grant the loan. In the predominantly black south shore of Chicago, the private South Shore Bank, owned by a consortium

2. For a discussion of the planning policies of Santa Monica, see Derek Shearer, "Urban Populism: The Case of Santa Monica," *Journal of Planning Education,* University of Cincinnati, Summer 1982.

of foundations, engages in community-development banking by working closely with local black businessmen and community organizations to revitalize neighborhood commercial areas and to finance affordable housing opportunities. Ron Grzywinski, chairman of the bank, believes that it is a model for a system of municipally-owned development banks in major cities across the country.

In addition to finance, cities need to include the business planning function as an ongoing part of the local government's activities. Cities need public entrepreneurs who put their talents at the service of the community. One way to accomplish this is for cities to establish development corporations with a small professional staff that looks for business opportunities for the city to help plan and to invest in. This would involve providing venture capital to local entrepreneurs with the city taking an equity interest—again, a new version of public-private partnership.

The city of Madison, Wisconsin, during the administration of liberal mayor Paul Soglin in the mid-1970s, created the Madison Development Corporation, whose board is elected by voters in each ward. Funded originally with revenue-sharing and community-development block-grant monies, the development corporation works with enterprising citizens and neighborhood organizations to start new business ventures that reflect the needs of the city's varied neighborhoods. The Madison Development Corporation has helped to fund a cooperatively-owned taxi company, renovate buildings to house small businesses, and refurbish warehouses for both residential and industrial uses.

In England, some municipal governments such as Sheffield have established local Enterprise Boards similar to the American Development Corporation model. The Enterprise Boards share ownership in mixed public-private ventures and, in some cases, the boards promote worker ownership of business.

Many American cities have Redevelopment Agencies with considerable legal and financial powers. These agencies, with some staff redirection, can be utilized to revitalize downtown business districts through mixed-use development. To assure that revitalization is not simply a gentrification—where businesses serving poor, minority, or middle-class families are replaced with stores and restaurants geared to the "upscale" quiche and Perrier market—the public should have an ownership interest in such projects. Waterfront redevelopments in Baltimore, Boston, and San Francisco are examples of supposedly enlightened public-private partnership developments. But while those particular developments are pleasantly designed, have a pedestrian orientation, and a human-scale sense to them, they do little to create a livable city for the majority of urban residents, since they are aimed at tourism and the upscale market. The shops and malls are not integrated into the life of the town in an organic way.

Many cities also issue industrial development bonds (IDBs) as a subsidy to lure business. McDonald's fast-food chain, which hardly needs subsidies, has been one of the largest users of IDB funds, and the firm of Richard Viguerie, the conservative direct-mail expert, has accepted an IDB loan to expand its facilities in Arlington, Virginia.[3] Instead of using industrial development bonds as a sweetener to attract private firms to locate in a city, IDBs could help finance *publicly planned* projects where the city would play a large role in determining both their content—including what firms to lease space to and what products might be built or sold —and their form (urban design).

Again, American cities could learn from the Europeans. In Bologna, Italy, for example, the city government financed an in-town shopping-center project for Co-op Bologna, the city-wide, consumer-owned supermarkets. The shopping center consists of a host of cooperatively-run businesses oriented toward serving all income levels in the city. City ownership and development of shopping facilities could be aimed both at providing jobs for residents and at bringing an economic and social mix back into U.S. cities.

Cities might also consider directly providing consumer services such as homeowner fire insurance, energy audits and solar installation, curbside recycling, and burglar systems through a municipal-

3. Such varied uses of industrial development bonds are described in Harold Bergen, "Industry's Bondage Fetish," *The Washington Monthly*, January 1981.

ly-owned or -regulated cable television system. These and other services can be priced on an at-cost basis. With financial help from the federal government, cities could also sponsor consumer-controlled, community-based health maintenance organizations that would keep health costs under control and practice preventive medicine.

State Government as Entrepreneur and Planner

The Reagan Administration's proposal for a New Federalism, as outlined in the President's 1982 State of the Union address, called for the federal government to assume the full funding of one program—Medicaid—while transfering welfare, food stamps, and more than forty other programs to the states. The effects of such a policy, if actually implemented, are not hard to imagine. As Richard Wade, professor of urban history at City University of New York, noted in the *New York Times Magazine*, decentralization of transfer programs to the states would mean fifty different policies, fifty different standards, fifty different levels of benefits, and fifty new bureaucracies. Wade argued:

> The new federalism would place the poor and the handicapped, who lack clout, at the mercy of the state legislators. Suburban legislators, often with a vested animosity toward cities, would determine the priorities of state action. Municipal governments, already saddled with inordinate financial problems, would be required to raise new revenues or see traditional services curtailed. In the process, ethnic and racial tension would inevitably heighten, and restless, unemployed youth would turn to crime in even greater numbers. (August 1, 1982, p. 46.)

As we argued in Chapter 7 and at the beginning of this chapter, we believe that there must be a national standard for social spending and revenue-sharing coupled with national economic policies that provide for full employment. To decentralize the national safety net, to use Reagan's phrase, is to assure that in most states it will be full of holes.

What, then, is the role of state governments in our alternative economic policies?

Similar to the democratization of economic planning at the local level—outlined in the previous section—we propose a more direct role for state governments in the economic development process itself.

What passes for economic development policies in almost all states is a highly sophisticated form of Beggar-Thy-Neighbor. Practically every issue of *Business Week* is filled with fancy color ads seeking to lure business to Texas, Louisiana, Washington, and elsewhere. The most aggressive states promise not only a "good business climate" (which translates into weak or no unions and low taxes) but numerous tax subsidies, outright gifts of public funds, state-supported employee training programs, and the lifting of environmental restrictions and planning requirements. A few states such as California have tried to develop more long-range state industrial policies. However, these "plans" have until now been little more than an uncritical touting of high-tech industries and a call for more science and computer courses in secondary schools. Governor Jerry Brown, for example, appointed a state commission on industrial innovation that called for state assistance to these sunrise industries. This sort of action is like the policies proposed by neoliberals at the federal level. In 1982, a group of California investors announced that they would be willing to construct and operate a high-speed rail train from San Diego to Los Angeles, if the state government would issue bonds to pay for the project and relieve them of any environmental-impact reports then required under state law. The project was hailed by most Democratic state legislators as a model of private-public cooperation!

Rather than allowing private firms to set economic priorities, state governments can lay down priorities and then support economic development projects that meet the overall and targeted needs of the state's residents. There is no lack of technical information and policies for state governments to follow, were they willing to act as entrepreneurs and active planners. The Council of State Governments, for example, has issued a highly detailed, ten-book series on state economic development, and the Conference on Alternative State and Local Policies, a progressive research organization founded by activists in city and state governments, has published a briefing book on issues for state legislators. It discusses a variety of new programs for state governments to adopt.

Basic elements of an alternative democratic set of economic policies for state governments include:

Public Enterprise. States should establish their own public enterprises that provide vital services and generate revenues. One key area is transit, particularly inter-city passenger service and freight hauling by railroad. A few states in the Midwest currently operate their own rail lines. California is a state that should have its own publicly operated high-speed rail system. It should be state-run and -managed, but the federal government should assist in financing, as it has in the past with the construction of state highways.

States should also have their own public banks and insurance companies, particularly for auto insurance; they would be required to invest primarily in the state, and they would invest in a mix of public and private ventures, and in public-private joint ventures. One state, North Dakota, has had its own efficiently run public bank since the 1920s, and across the border in Canada three provinces have public auto insurance firms which offer lower rates than private firms and cut down on litigation in minor accidents. Some states might also create public firms to develop natural resources, as a number of Canadian provinces have done.[4]

State Capital Budget. State governments should have capital improvement budgets that detail the regional and local infrastructural needs of the state and give priority to projects that are linked to economic development. As with rail transit, the federal government might provide some of the financing, but the state government would plan and carry out the projects. Local and regional planning commissions in the state would develop lists of capital improvement projects needed in their areas and present them to the state body.[5]

4. For a more detailed discussion of public enterprises at the state level, see John Case, Leonard Goldberg, and Derek Shearer, "State Business," *Working Papers for a New Society,* Spring 1976.

5. An examination of how a state capital budget should operate is found in Book 9 in the State Development Series of the Council of State Governments, titled *The Capital Budget,* by Robert Devoy and Harold Wise (Washington, D.C.:1979).

State Economic Planning Agency. State governments must have the technical capacity to engage in economic development planning. This means that each state should have an economic planning agency or state council of economic advisers which, using input-output tables, develops a detailed model of the state's economy.

Enterprise Assistance. State governments should have departments or agencies whose mission it is to provide technical and start-up assistance to new businesses. The Canadian province of Saskatchewan, for example, has a Cooperative Development Department that provides technical and financial assistance to a variety of community-based cooperative ventures. A state department or agency for economic development could carry out feasibility studies for workers interested in employee ownership of their firms and assist community organizations interested in starting cooperative or community-owned businesses. Business schools at state-supported universities could be encouraged to develop new courses of study in democratic management, worker ownership, and cooperative enterprise.

Land-Use Regulation and New Town Developments. A few states such as California, Rhode Island, and Vermont have pioneered in state regulation of land use to ensure balanced development that does not destroy the state's environment. The California Coastal Commission and its set of regional commissions—created by voters through statewide initiative in 1972—has saved whole areas of the coast from overdevelopment, preserved access to beach areas for all income classes, and tried to include affordable housing in new coastal developments.

State land-use regulation must go beyond environmental concerns to link state land developments to housing and jobs. State governments should plan for mixed-income new towns as some European countries do, by linking locational assistance to industry and permits for subdivisions to a strategy of developing balanced urban centers rather than haphazardly subdivided suburbs, usually designed for a segmented income group. The development of high-speed rail systems in states would obviously allow for better land-use planning that would involve a series of smaller towns linked by efficient rail service. The interest of many American families in living in small and medium-sized towns has increased, and development of communications and the computer makes decentralization of industry more feasible than in the past. Left to private firms, this decentralization will only re-create the suburbanization process of the post–World War II period and create more income- and race-segregated communities.

Plan and Market

The point of this chapter is that greater public involvement in the economy, begun by reforms at the national level, does fit into the American federal system and can be linked to democratic government at the local and state levels. What is needed is a mix of plan and market. Rather than letting large, unaccountable private corporations do the planning for the society, democratic institutions at all levels of the society should plan priorities and guidelines in key areas, particularly finance, transit, land use, and energy. The planning framework should be arrived at through the kind of democratic process we have outlined, and then market relationships can be carried on *within* that framework and *within* a set of publicly agreed upon rules that protect consumers, workers, and communities and assures that economic growth is balanced, not cancerous. Flea markets, farmers' markets, and the thousands of small businesses that advertise in any city's Yellow Pages are all the proper province of the market. Other human relationships and needs require nonmarket solutions, arrived at through democratic participation and planning.

"Government" and "political participation" would have different meanings than they do now. First, the separation between economy and politics would no longer exist, even in theory. Economic planning, whether at the plant, community, state, or national level, would no longer be the activity solely of managers or mystically created by the "invisible hand" of "market forces." Investment policy, wage structures, local and state development policy, plant closures, and Federal Reserve policy would all be influenced directly by workers and consumers as part of their political activity. Large corporations located in communities and states would be much more closely integrated into the communities and states themselves, in the sense that workers or consumers sitting on the boards of those corporations would not be owners but simultaneously wage earners or consumers and representatives of the community. They would formally, not altruistically—like the old-time entrepreneurs—have double responsibility, as would members of the community and state planning councils. Similarly, with national full employment and retraining-for-displaced-workers policies, union participants on the boards of national corporations or the Federal Reserve would tend to operate not just as workers but with the public interest in mind. If labor is guaranteed work at reasonable wages, and wage differences between workers of similar skills are reduced, shifts in investments from one industry to another—particularly in the same state or community—will be supported by both worker and community representatives.

Second, the present adversary relationship between government and the public would necessarily change. This does not mean that there would no longer be conflicts between the two. But its nature would be different. The recently resurrected ideology of government as necessary but *inherently* evil because it restricts individual freedom, would be replaced by another ideology: government—when it is participative, just, and extended to people's economic activities—not only makes society possible but increases the quality of life. The idea is not to get government off people's backs; rather, it is to put government in people's hands.

9 Achieving a New Social Contract

The American people must decide in the post-Reagan years which road to take in trying to build a secure, equitable economic future. One road is profoundly undemocratic and antipluralist. It is a more authoritarian version of Reaganomics, embodying a survival-of-the-fittest mentality and excluding women, minorities, and labor from first-class citizenship and from full participation in American society. Economist Bertram Gross labels this future "Friendly Fascism."[1] Given the deeply ingrained democratic values in American society, such an authoritarian attempt to make the economy work would be highly unstable politically.

Another road is reconstruction of the economy and society by benevolent elites—technocrats and business leaders like Felix Rohatyn, designer of the New York City bail-out in 1977—a neo-liberal program in which labor is made a junior partner, and token women and minorities are included, but grass-root, democratic participation by citizens is avoided. In that model, citizens remain passive and participate primarily as consumers of video games and other high-tech products. Cable television offers a hundred channels in every home, while a handful of media conglomerates decide what people should see and read. Economic decision-making is left to leaders in Washington and corporate boards in downtown high-rises. This type of model may work to produce an economic

1. Bertram Gross, *Friendly Fascism—The New Face of Power in America* (Boston: South End Press, 1982).

boom in the 1990s, but it would paper over questions of unequal economic development, structural unemployment, and, above all, would ultimately debase the content of American culture.

The third choice—the democratic alternative—builds economic recovery on increased participation by workers, consumers, and citizens in the economic decision-making required to produce the goods and services Americans need for their own lives and the goods and services needed for a more productive, well-fed, well-housed, secure world. We believe that it best embodies American values and would best tap the tremendous reservoir of human resources available in our society. It is a road toward a mixed economy, but a democratic one. It is based on both planning and market relationships, but the planning is democratic and public, not corporate and private. Women, minorities, and organized labor are afforded full-employment citizenship and general participation in economic decision-making. It will lead to a more democratic and pluralistic society.

Reaganomics in Decline

The midterm elections in November 1982 all but destroyed Republican hopes of building a new majority based on laissez-faire economics and a revival of militarism.

Instead of a Republican-dominated Congress, the Democrats picked up twenty-six seats in the House. While the Republicans retained control of the Senate, a number of Republican incumbents narrowly avoided defeat; and those who did survive were forced to back away from Reaganomics in order to keep their seats. At the state level, the Democrats won seven new governorships and captured eleven more state legislative houses. At the end of 1982, the Democrats controlled thirty-four of the fifty Governors' offices and both houses of the legislature in thirty-four states. The state results wiped out gains that Republicans had made in rebuilding their grass-roots base. Republican losses would have been even greater if it were not for the Party's tremendous advantage in fund raising from corporate political action committees (PACs) and the voter appeal of Reagan's television personality.

The nuclear-freeze resolution, on the ballot in nine states, was approved nationwide by a margin of three to two. It was the largest citizen referendum on a single issue in the country's history. The freeze's success was a testimony both to grass-roots organizing and to citizens' fears generated by the Reagan Administration's constant saber-rattling and talk of winning nuclear exchanges.

What lesson do these midterm results hold?

Voters showed that the issue of economic security—notably unemployment and social security—was a deep-seated concern, and the nuclear-freeze vote indicated support for at least slowing the Reagan increase in military spending. Most important was the fact that liberal Democrats scored decisive victories in those states where the candidates were supported by grass-roots coalitions of labor and citizen organizations.

Although heavily outspent by millionaire supply-sider Lewis Lehrman, Democrat Mario Cuomo won his New York Governor's race because of the strong electoral organization that he had built with labor unions, minority groups, and consumer groups. The women's vote also played a crucial role in his election. In Texas, the Democratic state ticket won by running a tough anti-Reaganomics campaign, aided by a well-organized labor and minority get-out-the-vote effort. In numerous House races, liberal Democrats relied heavily on labor/citizen coalitions. Marcy Kaptor in Ohio, Lane Evans in Illinois, Barney Frank in Massachusetts, Peter Kostmayer in Pennsylvania, and Alan Wheat in Missouri all won their Congressional races with the assistance of grass-roots organizations and labor unions. Successful Democratic gubernatorial candidates—Richard Celeste in Ohio, Toney Anaya in New Mexico, and Anthony Earl in Wisconsin—ran hard against Reaganomics and reached out to labor, environmental, pro-freeze, women's, and minority organizations for crucial campaign support. In states such as Rhode Island, Missouri, Minnesota, and Connecticut, where Democratic candidates almost defeated incumbent Republican Senators, strong labor/citizen organizations were essential to the challengers.

And in the South, a number of Democrats won by appeals to black voters. Former segregationists George Wallace and John Stennis found it politic to run as nonracist populists—a sign that race-baiting politics in the South may finally be over.

In California, Jerry Brown and Tom Bradley lost their races for higher office because they failed to reach out to grass-roots Democrats. Each candidate was defeated because he ran as an individual, not as part of an organized Democratic campaign effort. Both relied almost entirely on TV and radio messages to voters. Neither attempted in the slightest way to build a grass-roots organization of labor, environmentalists, women's groups, pro-freeze groups, and minorities. As a consequence, Brown was rejected by voters for his personality and style, and Bradley, unfortunately, for his skin color.

The truth is that either candidate could have built a winning liberal coalition. In other hotly contested races in California—for example, Philip Burton's Congressional campaign, environmentalist Gary Hart's state Senate race, and 1960s activist Tom Hayden's state assembly battle—these liberal Democrats won by combining a technically competent media campaign with a grass-roots, community-based organization that went door-to-door to voters with a strong anti-Reaganomics message.

In preparing for 1984—an election that could be a watershed in postwar politics—Democrats have the opportunity to expand the labor/citizen organizational base and go beyond anti-Reaganomics to develop a positive program for national economic recovery.

The odds are certainly good that the Democrats can retake the Senate and win the Presidency in 1984. Economic conditions alone should favor a Democratic victory. The unemployment rate at the end of 1982 was 11 percent. Bankruptcies in 1982 were at the highest level since the Depression. For the first time since World War II, it appeared that American business would reduce its capital spending for the second consecutive year. In spite of a flurry of stock trading and profit-taking on Wall Street, business analysts predicted that a possible business upturn in 1983 would be weak and short-lived. Business investment would not lead the recovery, and hopes for a consumer-led recovery—even as the Federal Reserve tried to bring down the interest rates—seemed destined to be undercut by the growing ranks of the jobless.

Above all, President Reagan vowed to "stay the course" and hold firm to his economic and military policies.

The question for Democrats is: what will replace Reaganomics?

The most likely, though from our point of view not the most desirable, political scenario is the election of a candidate in 1984 or 1988 who emulates Jimmy Carter (the first neoliberal President —liberal on social issues, but conservative on economic ones) but fails to deal adequately with the economic crisis. Such an administration might practice a sophisticated form of state capitalism, in which the government would use tax monies to bail out declining firms while making workers in those firms "cooperate" in the bail-out by accepting lower wages. It would not restructure or reform the economy, but attempt to make it more efficient with a form of managerial capitalism run by technocrats in Washington, D.C. A neoliberal administration would not *mobilize* public support among women and in unions and community and minority organizations, and would not involve them in decision-making. Above all, it would not exert democratic control over investment, which is the key to economic recovery at home. Experts would try to make the economy work and hope that the public would accept their policies and results.

In response to the challenge of the Reagan Administration's assault on the New Deal and the attack by conservative PACs on liberal Democratic office holders in 1980, the Democratic Party's new leader, California lawyer Charles Manatt, has modernized the Party's national operation by adopting the campaign technology successfully used by the Republicans and the Radical Right: computer-targeted fund-raising mailings, national party TV spots, and technical workshops and campaign assistance to Democratic candidates. Manatt has also formed the Lexington Group—to bring together wealthy Democratic donors—and has spoken in favor of maintaining the Reagan tax breaks for corporate America to stimulate investment (and presumably business contributions to Democrats).

Like the national party officials, most Congressional Democrats propose technocratic and uninspiring alternative economic packages. For example, the report of the Democratic Congressional Caucus Task Force on Long-term Economic Policy, released by Representative Tim Wirth in September 1982, is a neoliberal white paper that highlights the goal of creating "a favorable climate for investment," while totally ignoring the role of large corporations in declining and shifting investment. The document uncritically calls for reliance on high-tech industry as the engine of future growth and recommends formation of a national commission on capital formation to explore ways to raise funds for these firms. No mention is made of the role played by existing banks, insurance companies, and pension funds in the current or future investment picture. Finally, the House Democrats advocate a "new partnership" between capital and labor to be embodied in a national Economic Cooperation Council in order to clarify "complex economic choices." The council is not to be a national planning agency, simply a forum for corporate leaders and a few labor leaders to talk about economic issues. There is no talk in the report of empowering labor to make the unions equal partners with corporations in economic decision-making.

This approach is not only technocratic, it is also uninspiring and asks little of American citizens other than to trust in government experts and corporate leaders to lead them out of the economic crisis. It lacks the emotional, evocative appeal of conservative social Darwinism—at least Reagan and the Moral Majority stir the blood—and ignores the realities of corporate capitalism and where both have already led us. It also implicitly relies on export-led growth with continued declines in real wages of American workers to support American competitiveness abroad. It seeks salvation outside the dynamic of our own work force's wage and productivity increases.

An alternative is a Left/liberal populist movement for economic democracy that grows in strength in the 1980s and plays an influential if not a leading role in the next Democratic administration.

While the building of a grass-roots citizens' movement for economic reform will most likely not be led by the existing Democratic Party leadership, one of the Presidential contenders—perhaps Senator Alan Cranston or former Vice President Walter Mondale—could emerge as the champion of a revived labor and liberal reform effort. That effort, however, to be successful, will have to rely on an activist, grass-roots base among unions, community organizations, and environmental and nuclear-freeze groups.

This activist base—what might be called an indigenous American populist base—grew out of the movements centering on issues of the 1960s: civil rights, anti–Vietnam War, women's rights, consumer and environmental protection. As 1960s activists have grown older and become more experienced, their influence has begun to be felt in trade unions, in universities, in newspapers and magazines, and in communities. These activists, now in their thirties and forties, will play a key role in determining the shape of the country's response to the economic crisis. They are economic democrats. They believe in the extension of democracy to economic decision-making from the plant to the national level.

Pieces of this movement already exist. It is an updated New Deal coalition waiting to be brought together as a cohesive national political force. The components include: the more liberal trade unions such as the UAW, the Machinists, and public employees; women's organizations such as NOW; the grass-roots nuclear-freeze groups; tenants' organizations in a number of states; the environmentalist and Nader consumer protection groups; minority organizations such as Jesse Jackson's populist neighborhood movements and community organizations such as ACORN, Massachusetts Fair Share, and the Ohio Public Interest Campaign; liberal professionals; New Left activists and liberal politicians; gay-rights organizations; and (potentially) small-business people and family farmers. Together, these organizations and the constituencies they represent constitute a majority of Americans.

What Role for Labor?

A key component of any such reformist political force is the American labor movement. Even if unions now appear weakened under the Reagan Administration's assault—such as that on the air-traffic controllers—they still represent 20 percent of American workers and continue to be politically potent in pushing for economic and social change.

Other advanced industrial countries have developed a social consensus on economic policies, particularly economic growth combined with economic security. Japan has one model—paternalistic and corporatist—which certainly works there but is not suitable for the United States, given our diversity and commitment to democratic values. Austria also has a model, called a "social partnership" among business, labor, and government. It produced the lowest rates of inflation and unemployment of any advanced industrial country in the 1970s. The Swedish economy, with 90 percent of its work force unionized, for many years operated under a framework of industrial cooperation and achieved high rates of economic growth and rising social welfare.

As a response to the present crisis, some business journals and corporate leaders in America have called for a similar social consensus to lift the United States out of its economic difficulties. *Business Week* editorialized May 11, 1981, "Clearly, a changed social and economic environment in the U.S. demands that labor and management create a new relationship . . . a participative stage" (p. 98). A poll taken by the same magazine a year later found that while all chief executives of major American firms were in favor of extracting concessions from labor in the current economic recession, the managers of unionized firms were willing to offer unions more of a say in how the companies are run in return for gearing compensation to how well the company does. Executives in nonunionized industries were much less interested in such trade-offs. The existence of a relatively strong union is a necessary component of better labor-management cooperation.[2] So, for example, the "social partnership" arrangements in Austria and Sweden, relatively successful in promoting economic growth with full employment and lower inflation than other European countries, are predicated on a strong, cohesive union movement and a government—usually social democratic—that defends the interests of working people.

The problem in the United States is that the positions of the potential partners in a new social consensus are not equal. Most large corporations, as shown by their contribution to the Reagan onslaught against the standard of living of working Americans, regularly attack both labor and government programs that benefit labor. We noted in earlier chapters that the Reagan Administration has consistently enlisted the federal government on behalf of corporate capital against unions and other working men and women, both white and minority.

There can be no New Social Contract until labor and government can act from positions of strength, freed from constant attacks by big business. This will inevitably involve struggle in the political arena. The corporate offensive of the 1970s, the economic recession, and Reagan's election put the labor movement on the defensive. With a few notable exceptions, most leaders of national unions accepted the situation and retreated, at least temporarily, before the conservative attack. This may well be a tactical maneuver. It is true that at the national level the AFL-CIO and its leader Lane Kirkland are developing a closer relationship with the Democratic Party, and they intend to play a more direct role in the Presidential selection process. But the overall thrust of the unions' response to Reaganomics has been politically timid. The labor movement still seems locked into its postwar mold of cooperating with corporate management, even as big business is trying to drive labor back into the 1920s.

2. Studies by Harvard economics professors Richard Freeman and James Medoff, and others, found that the existence of unions raises productivity in American industry. See *Fortune,* December 1, 1980, pp. 149–152.

A few leaders have urged resistance to worker givebacks on wages, benefits, and work rules. A campaign to fight concessions was begun in mid-1982 by Anthony Mazzocchi, former vice-president of the Oil, Atomic, and Chemical Workers. Mazzocchi called for a moratorium on American corporate investment overseas and for collective-bargaining agreements that provide workers a say in corporate decision-making. He also criticized corporate mergers and unproductive speculation.[3]

Labor will have to ask more of the next President than a sympathetic Secretary of Labor. It should align itself with grass-roots organizing groups around the country, forming with such groups local chapters of a Progressive Alliance, as the UAW once proposed, began to organize, but failed to sustain, and should organize its membership to support a program of economic reform such as we have outlined.

Pressure for such political steps will have to come from within the labor movement's rank-and-file, from locally based efforts such as Mazzocchi's, and from leaders like the Machinists' William Winpisinger who are not afraid to criticize corporate power.[4] Whether American labor is up to the challenge is an open question; the answer will certainly affect the chances for developing a successful national economic reform movement.

The Rainbow Coalition

It would be a crucial error to lead a grass-roots, popular movement into third-party electoral efforts. The American political system may have weak parties with deliberately vague ideologies, but the two-party system itself is still relatively enduring. Winner-take-all Congressional and state legislative districts and strong directly elected executives help to keep the two-party system firmly em-

3. The Institute for Labor Education and Research in New York, headed by economist David Gordon, provides economic research to support Mazzocchi's organizing efforts. But this is just a beginning.
4. The Machinists' Union has developed a Rebuilding America Act which includes many economic reforms that we favor. An outline of the Act was released by the IAM at its 1981 legislative conference.

bedded. A vote for a third-party candidate is viewed by most voters as a vote for the opposition to American institutions. Even the campaign for a maverick independent like John Anderson lost steam because it operated outside the two-party system.

Unlike Europe, American political parties do not play much of a political or social role between elections. They do not provide organizational homes for the mobilization of party members, nor do they have social or cultural functions. As social scientist Everett Carll Ladd notes, "The [American] party system defines itself around contests for elective office."[5]

Ladd argues that a stable national governing coalition is almost impossible to achieve because of the decline of the party system and the influence of both the media and special-interest political action committees. But it was not the party system which brought on the New Deal reforms. FDR's program was formulated and implemented in spite of, not because of, the party system. Most of the key reforms of the period were a result of and an interaction between grass-roots populist pressure and a flexible, nonideological President. The Democratic Party, as a party, did not formulate the policies of the New Deal, although later it came to stand for them, and the Party and its elected leaders became New Dealers, as it were, after the fact.

It was primarily the *extra-party* movements—Huey Long's Share the Wealth clubs, Father Coughlin's National Social Justice organization, Dr. Townsend's pension plan, Reno Milo's Farmer Holiday Association, John L. Lewis' militant CIO, the Unemployed Councils, Upton Sinclair's EPIC movement in California, Olson's Farmers Labor Party in Minnesota, and other grass-roots uprisings—which provided the popular pressure for structural reforms in the economic system.[6] These militants made the New Deal happen.

In similar fashion today, it has been the nationwide grass-roots,

5. *Where Have All the Voters Gone* (New York: W. W. Norton, 1978), p. 75.
6. For an excellent analysis of two such movements, see Alan Brinkley, *Voices of Protest—Huey Long, Father Coughlin, and the Great Depression* (New York: Alfred A. Knopf, 1982).

extra-party nuclear-freeze movements which motivated some Democratic Party leaders in 1982 to introduce a nuclear-freeze measure into the Congress. Like FDR, they have had the good sense to move along with such a popular movement.

In the 1970s, elements of this new populist base began to engage in electoral politics, mainly at the state and local levels. In some cities and states, new political alliances have supported candidates or issues and have won electoral victories. In Texas, consumer activist Jim Hightower was elected to the statewide post of Agricultural Commissioner, running on a populist platform. The Ohio Public Interest Campaign supported liberal Democrat Richard Celeste in the gubernatorial race; OPIC's research director worked as head of issues for the Celeste campaign. The New Jersey Tenants' Union has provided key support in the electoral victories of progressive Bergen County executive Peter Shapiro. Similarly, the Boston Tenants' Union backed pro-renter candidates in city council elections. The California cities of Santa Monica, Santa Cruz, Davis, and Berkeley have all had majority governments made up of Left/liberal political coalitions. In San Francisco, Cleveland, New York, Detroit, and other major cities, 1960s activists have been elected to city council seats. In Burlington, Vermont—the state's largest city—a community activist and self-declared socialist, Bernie Sanders, won election to the Mayor's office as an independent in 1981 and was reelected in 1983.[7]

Of course, a few political victories in these cities and states do not constitute a majoritarian movement or herald new political realignments. All they suggest, as did similar state and local populist victories in the early 1930s, is the *potential* for a new nationwide majority.

Historically, New Deal legislative reform ground to a halt because the tide of grass-roots-pushed reform played itself out in the early 1940s. Mobilization for world war rather than social

7. For a more detailed discussion of the political changes in the 1970s, see our *Economic Democracy: The Challenge of the 1980s* (Armonk, N.Y.: M. E. Sharpe, 1980), Chapter 9. For an updated report on municipal politics in Santa Monica, Santa Cruz, and Burlington, see the series of articles by David Moberg in *In These Times*, January 12–18, January 26–February 1, and March 23–29, 1983.

reform came to dominate the political scene. After 1945, the Cold War and McCarthyism sapped the strength of progressive reform movements. It is also true that reform groups made some critical strategic errors. One was seeking to form a third party, as Henry Wallace did in 1948, leaving control of the Democratic Party to Harry Truman, big-city bosses, and conservative southerners.

The task of economic democrats is to function within the Democratic Party in times of elections without forfeiting grass-roots organization and mass mobilization of citizens. This does not mean spending time and energy fighting over the selection of party chairmen or the wording of resolutions at party platform hearings, but it does mean running candidates directly in Democratic primaries and in local nonpartisan races. These should not be "education" efforts, but running to win—to mobilize the *potential* majority into an actual majority. As these offices are won, they should be used to put forward the ideas of economic democracy. With this strategy, the candidates are not ambitious lawyers making a career out of politics; instead, they are selected from among proven leaders in constituency organizations such as local labor unions, consumer groups, women's groups, and neighborhood-based organizations.

Carrying out this strategy effectively requires a national organization which would be a "rainbow coalition" of all those with a stake in a progressive role for government.

If such a national, mass-based coalition effort were undertaken in major cities and states and were able to raise sufficient funds, then it could have real influence on the policies of the next Democratic administration. Using direct-mail techniques, the organization would build up its own PAC. It would offer training workshops to local and Congressional candidates. And it would establish a national Shadow Cabinet of progressive experts to issue position papers and to criticize current national policies, much like opposition parties in Britain do when they are attempting to build alternatives to the party in power. Even in 1984, the Democratic nominee would need the help of such an organization to win. In exchange for support, the organization would expect to see at least some of its programs enacted, and some of its Shadow Cabinet become actual Cabinet members.

In addition, what is needed is a national debate on the economy and an organizing tool like the bilateral nuclear-weapons-freeze initiative to anchor the discussion.

An Economic Bill of Rights resolution could serve this purpose.

The underlying principle of an Economic Bill of Rights is that citizens in an industrialized, urban nation both want and need an adequate level of economic security and they have a *right* as citizens to a decent job, health care, housing, education, old-age security, and a clean, safe environment. It is at the opposite end of the philosophical spectrum from the Reagan Administration's social Darwinist view of life—survival of the fittest. Reagan and his backers believe that economic insecurity is good for people, that fear stimulates workers to work harder, while greed should drive the rich to invest.

The concept of an Economic Bill of Rights resolution has an honorable liberal history. The idea was proposed by President Franklin Roosevelt in his 1944 State of the Union message in which he told Congress:

> We have come to a clear realization of the fact that true individual freedom cannot exist without economic security. . . .
>
> We have accepted, so to speak, a second bill of rights under which a new basis of security and prosperity can be established for all, regardless of station, race, or creed. Among these are:
>
> The right to a useful and remunerative job in the industries or shops or farms or mines of the nation.
>
> The right of every farmer to raise and sell his products that will give him and his family a decent living.
>
> The right of every businessman, large or small, to trade in an atmosphere of freedom from unfair competition and domination by monopolies at home and abroad.
>
> The right of every family to a decent home.
>
> The right to adequate medical care and the opportunity to achieve and enjoy good health.

The right to adequate protection from the economic fears of old age, sickness, accident and unemployment.

The right to a good education.

FDR's speech was based on economic work done by his National Resources Planning Board, headed by economist Gardiner Means.[8] In 1943, the NRPB had issued a report on postwar America that called on the federal government to guarantee full employment and "guarantee and where necessary underwrite equal access to security, equal access to education for all, equal access to health and nutrition for all, and wholesome housing conditions for all."

As we have described, FDR's government never guaranteed economic security for *all*—but it did provide for some entitlement programs. These are the programs that the Reagan Administration has fiercely attacked. Reagan and his big-business allies have torn up the New Deal social contract between labor and capital and the social contract between citizens and government—particularly those citizens who happen to be women and minorities. The reconstitution of a New Social Contract for American society should not be left to the corporate community, nor to the Atari Democrats in Congress. It should be a popular democratic undertaking with the widest possible participation by citizens in their roles as workers, community residents, and consumers.

An Economic Bill of Rights, drafted in the form of a resolution, could be the centerpiece of a citizens' debate on the economy, organized around teach-ins and community meetings and followed by city and state votes on an Economic Bill of Rights initiative. The debate would focus not only on the desirability of such a bill but also on the means to achieve it.[9]

8. The experience of the NRPB is discussed in Martin Clawson, *New Deal Planning—The National Resources Planning Board* (Baltimore: The Johns Hopkins University Press, 1981).

9. There is an increasing number of books that outline alternative economic strategies. Some of the most thoughtful include: Barry Bluestone and Bennett Harrison, *The Deindustrialization of America* (New York: Basic Books, 1982); Ira

A variety of policy ideas such as greater economic control of investment through public development banks and other vehicles; public spending for such public goods as an urban infrastructure and mass transit; job creation through environmental protection; democratizing the corporations through federal chartering and/or worker representatives on boards; and promotion of community- and employee-owned enterprises could be put forward and discussed in the context of guaranteeing the Economic Bill of Rights.

It is important to translate policy proposals into more accessible forms—pamphlets, flyers, videotapes, articles, and films—as background material to fuel the national debate. A small national coordinating office similar to the nuclear freeze headquarters in St. Louis could aid local groups in organizing the discussions of economics and in introducing the Economic Bill of Rights resolution onto city and state ballots.

Some will say, as they did with the nuclear freeze, that an Economic Bill of Rights is simplistic. In fact, it is basic. The Reagan Administration and their business allies reject the idea of citizens' rights and the government's responsibility to guarantee them in the economic sphere. It is time that progressives and liberals offer a different economic philosophy to the people of America.

Economic Bill of Rights Resolution

The United States is an industrialized, highly urbanized nation possessing great wealth and natural resources. All

---

C. Magaziner and Robert Reich, *Minding America's Business* (New York: Harcourt Brace Jovanovich, 1982); Sam Bowles, David Gordon, and Thomas Weisskopf, *The Waste Economy* (New York: Doubleday, 1983); Gar Alperovitz and Jeff Faux, *Rebuilding America* (New York: Pantheon, 1983); and Seymour Melman, *Profits Without Production* (New York: Alfred A. Knopf, 1983). All of these—and other new works—provide plenty of ideas for a citizens' debate. And organizations and think-tanks brimming with bright, articulate economists also abound: the National Center for Economic Alternatives; the National Center for Employee Ownership; the research departments of the AFL-CIO and other unions such as the UAW, IAM, and AFSCME; the Institute for Policy Studies; the Full Employment Action Council; the Urban Institute; the Brookings Institution; and so on.

inhabitants of the United States should have the right as citizens to a decent life, free from fear of economic insecurity. Citizens of all races, creeds, sexes, and cultural backgrounds should have the opportunity to develop their unique potential as human beings through meaningful work, a decent family life, and fulfilling leisure. It is the duty of government to provide for these opportunities.

Therefore, the Congress of the United States, as representatives of its citizens, shall pass the necessary laws and adequately fund programs to ensure the following economic rights:

1. The right to a decent job for all those willing to work.

2. The right to adequate health care for all regardless of income.

3. The right to a good education.

4. The right to decent, affordable housing.

5. The right to protection from the fears of old age through a secure social security system.

6. The right to nutritious food at a reasonable price.

7. The right to provision of the basic utilities of light, heat, telecommunications, and transportation at a fair price.

8. The right to a clean, healthy urban and rural environment in which to live.

9. The right to a secure and stable community.

10. The right to participate democratically in places of work and the affairs of local and national government.

The challenge for the coming decade is aptly summarized by Stephen Marglin, a professor of economics at Harvard. Writing in the *Harvard Magazine* (January-February, 1980), Marglin noted:

> The real issue of the 1980s is not planning, but what kind of planning. If planning is to be democratic in process and end product, the entire structure of the capitalist economy must be overhauled to become significantly more participatory, from the shop floor to the corporate board room (pp. 23–24).

Democratic planning is the key element of A New Social Contract. The contract itself is a social consensus around equality and democracy for *all* Americans. This new contract, however, will not be written by experts or leaders. It will be forged—as democratic gains have been won in the past—by Americans themselves, as they struggle in the coming years to be equal partners in the economy. It is this struggle that will define the new relations between citizens and their government, and citizens and their daily lives as consumers and producers.

Out of this struggle can come a fairer, more productive and more democratic economy.

Resources on
Economic Policy

In addition to the sources cited in the text, the authors have, over the years, made use of the following sources of reporting and analysis on economic matters.

- **Working Papers**
  Published for the past ten years, this bi-monthly journal of public policy is an indispensible source of articles on alternative politics and policies. Particularly relevant to this book, is the special November/December, 1980 issue, "Reviving Industry: On Whose Terms?" which featured a debate between economists Lester Thurow, Barry Bluestone, and Bennett Harrison.

  Back copies of *Working Papers* can be obtained from: 186 Hampshire Street, Cambridge, MA 02139.

- **Business Week**
  This McGraw-Hill publication provides thoughtful and objective coverage of news about the business community. The editors regularly prepare special reports on national economic issues such as "The Reindustrialization of America" (June 30, 1980) and "America's Restructured Economy" (June 1, 1981).

  Information on reprints of the special issues and on subscriptions can be obtained from: P.O. Box 430, Hightstown, N.J. 08520

- **U. S. Joint Economic Committee**
  Created by Congress in 1946, the JEC is an invaluable source of reports and hearings on economic matters. For example, in

preparing this book we consulted such JEC studies as "The Role of Small Business Enterprise in Economic Development" (May 14, 1981), "Environmental and Health/Safety Regulations, Productivity, Growth and Economic Performance" (August 1980), "Business Management Practices and the Productivity of the American Economy" (Hearings May 1, 11 and June 1, 5, 1981), and "Monetary Policy, Selective Credit Policy, and Industrial Policy in France, Britain, West Germany, and Sweden" (June 26, 1981).

A publications list can be obtained from: U.S. Joint Economic Committee, G 133, DSOB, Washington, D.C. 20510.

● *Ways and Means*

The monthly newsletter of the Conference on Alternative State and Local Policies reports on innovative approaches to city and state government. The Conference also publishes in-depth studies on such topics as tax reform, investment of public pension funds, and employee ownership. Particularly useful is the study, "The Issues of 1982: A Briefing Book."

Subscriptions to *Ways and Means* are $10 a year. A complete publications list is available from: Conference on Alternative State and Local Policies, 2000 Florida Ave. N.W., Washington, D.C. 20009.

● *The Council of State Planning Agencies*

Under the editorship of Michael Barker, the Council has prepared a series of policy papers and working papers on such topics as "Industrial Policy," "Social Security," "State Regulation and Economic Development," and special studies such as "America in Ruins," on the decay of public infrastructure in the nation's cities. The Council has also published a ten-volume series on state development policy that should be required reading for all state legislators.

For a publications brochure, write: Council of State Planning Agencies, Hall of the States, 400 North Capitol Street, Washington, D.C. 20001.

● *Institute for Policy Studies*

In 1978, this liberal 'think tank' published *The Federal Budget and Social Reconstruction*—a study requested by forty members of Congress. A new Federal budget study for the 1980s will be published in 1983. In addition, IPS publishes a number of studies on the international economy and on national defense policy.

For a publications catalog, write: Publications Department, Institute for Policy Studies, 1901 Q. Street, N.W. Washington, D.C. 20009.

● *Union Research Departments*

The research and public relations departments of major industrial and public employee unions frequently publish useful studies on the economy. For example, the Industrial Union Department of the AFL-CIO publishes a regular newsletter on pension fund investment titled *Labor and Investments,* and the International Association of Machinists has published a booklet called "Rebuilding America" that describes IAM's program for economic recovery.

For further information, write: Industrial Union Department, AFL-CIO, 815 16th Street, N.W., Washington, D.C. 20006; International Association of Machinists, 1300 Connecticut Ave. N.W., Washington, D.C. 20036; the United Auto Workers, Solidarity House, 8000 E. Jefferson Ave., Detroit, MI. 48214.

● *Economic Democracy: The Challenge of the 1980s*

This work, written by Martin Carnoy and Derek Shearer, contains an extensive bibliography of additional research organizations and reference works related to economic democracy. The book is distributed to bookstores by Pantheon and can be ordered directly by mail for $15 hardcover, $9.95 paperback (postpaid) from: M. E. Sharpe, 80 Business Park Drive, Armonk, N.Y. 10504.

Index